Farewell

To

Islam

BY

SAIID RABIIPOUR

1st Edition

2009

This book is the result of my own experiences, as well as research done by reading and listening to many resources available on line, along with books, as a support to my own knowledge and teachings. The contents of this book are all true. However, I have changed the names of those who had any part in my rescue for their safety.

No part of this book is meant to disrespect any person or religion. It has been an eye opening experience for me, as I hope it to be for you. If you are a Christian reading this book, I hope that you receive more encouragement and knowledge, and that this book would strengthen your faith even more. If you are a Muslim, or of any other faith reading this book, I pray that this might encourage you to seek for yourself what it takes for a person to spend an eternity with his creator, knowing that good works alone will not get you there. Muhammad never gave any promise or assurance of heaven to anyone by just performing good deeds.

If you wish to write me, my email address is:
SaiidR@bellsouth.net

www.xulonpress.com

INDEX

God's Unending Love 7

Chapter 1 My Childhood 17

Chapter 2 Iranian Navy 31

Chapter 3 A NewPage in my Life 43

Chapter 4 The Citadel 55

Chapter 5 A New Passage! 73

Chapter 6 Turmoil in Iran 85

Chapter 7 Growing in Faith 93

Chapter 8 My Career with Radio Shack 107

Chapter 9 30 Years Later - Iran Under Islamic Republic 117

Chapter 10 Touring Historical Cities of Persia 129

Chapter 11 The Trap 149

Chapter 12 Hamid's Departure and My Delay! 173

Chapter 13 First Attempt to Leave! 185

Chapter 14 The End of My Rope! 199

Chapter 15 Another Lie 213

Chapter 16 Strange Phone Call! 221

Chapter 17 The Rescue 231

Chapter 18 A View from the Mountaintop 241

Chapter 19 Border Town 249

Chapter 20 Another Challenge 267

Chapter 21 Victory 287

Chapter 22 Conclusion 297

Over the years that I have known him, I have come to realize that Saiid is a remarkable man. His enthusiasm for life is both amazing and contagious. His curiosity is endless. His ability to adapt to a culture totally different from the one in which he grew up is extraordinary.

What really sets Saiid apart from most is his hunger for GOD. He is one of those all too rare individuals who has found God and yet seeks Him still, for he knows there is more to know of God than he has yet discovered.

In the pages that follow, you will read about part of his journey with God. I can tell you firsthand that the experiences he describes have changed him and his family and friends. May God use these pages to help change you as well.

May you understand more fully through real problems and real faith THE GOD who is faithful and true.

Rev. Joe Pressley

Dedication and thanksgiving:

I would like to dedicate this book, as a way of giving thanks, to my dear wife Ursa, who has been by my side all the years of our life together. She has not only been my wife by God's approving hand, she has been a great mother of our three daughters: Crystal, Alyson, and Elizabeth. And now she is enjoying being a grandmother. She has stood by me as my best friend through thick and thin, sickness and in health and the difficulties that life has to offer. She has a meek spirit that makes people around her easily love her. Her humble attitude promotes peace by allowing others to be first. She has not learned these qualities from others, or by reading books, but from God as her spiritual gifts. Though she will tell you that she is far from perfect, she always desires the perfection that our Lord has hidden in her heart. She always thinks of others before her own needs. I am blessed to have her as my wife and helpmate.

I would like to take this opportunity to thank family and friends from all over who were there for us during this challenging time. The support that we received was overwhelming! It came in the form of prayers, phone calls, visits, emails, cards, and financial help. Our church family, and especially our Sunday school class, showered us with love and support! I want to especially thank my daughters and their families for being there for my wife when I could not be. I am truly blessed to have three loving and beautiful daughters who love the Lord!

This book is the story of my life up until now. God saw me long before I realized who I was and He planned my future without me knowing where I was headed. Now I look back and see the hand of God all over my life, and I want to give Him all the praise and glory that is due to Him. All of the things that have happened, and the people I have come to know while on this journey, were not by accident. They were all part of God's divine plan.

Saiid

Dear reader,

I want to thank God for granting me the privilege of sharing with you the story of my life. I am grateful to be alive and to be able to share my testimony. This is the story of a young man born into a Muslim family in Iran, as it was destined by the will of God.

It's a story of an ordinary person just like you, but with different circumstances, environment and influences. In fact, my story goes forward as one of many examples of how Jesus can transform a life of uncertainty to one of real hope and assurance.

Can anyone plan the journey of their life from birth to death? Our lives can change in a moment, but there is One who never changes!

Looking back, I never dreamed where my journey would take me, but it is so wonderful to see the changes God has made in my life and how He brought me to where I am today. Frankly, I do not know why God has chosen to be with me the way He has, but I know now more than ever that His hand has always been on my life.

I must confess that I am not perfect by any means, and many times I chose the wrong road in my walk. Yet, God's faithfulness never changed.

Our Creator, who chose to make us in His own image, has a great deal of interest in every one of us. Furthermore, He has sacrificed so much for us. Whether you are Jew or gentile, black or white, Muslim or Christian, or from any other country, ethnic or religious background, God loves you, and that is a fact that neither you nor I can change!

After graduating from college in 1977, I had the desire to write a book concerning my experiences and challenges I faced during the time I was going to school here in the United States. But time went by, and my desire slowly faded. Then in the year 2005, after another challenging ordeal in Iran, God gave me the desire one more time to write my story. This time the theme and purpose changed. It became all about God and how He transformed my life. I now recognize Him as my True Guide!

The events that you are about to read are a small portion of what God has done in my life since childhood. I am neither a scholar nor a teacher, but this testimony is written with much prayer and meditation. Through these last few years that I have been working on this book, my goal has been simply to share with you some of what God has done in my life so that you too, will know that He would do the same for you!

Because of His great compassion, God has shown me His great mercy and love every step of the way! As far back as I can remember, I have always felt His presence and often talked with Him, but I never knew how He would answer me. I now know that God's ways are amazing and beyond our comprehension!

The Bible tells us that when Jesus came to this dark world as a Light, the world did not receive Him. Even His own people, the Jews, rejected Him. Still, the people within His inner-circle did not understand Him until after His resurrection. Although possible, it is not easy to understand God's love without experiencing, hearing or reading his love letters, which is the Word of God, the Holy Bible.

The Bible clearly speaks of Jesus of Nazareth, a man attested by God and by many miracles, wonders, and signs which God did through Him. Many responded to the message of His good-news, or 'gospel', and the way to salvation. His message has always been to testify to the Truth, and to save the lost, and for that very reason, He came to this world as a man, the only begotten Son of God. (Later I will talk more about the Son of God for those who may not be familiar with Him)

Here are some key scripture verses below:

The angel told Joseph, "And she will bring forth a Son, you shall call His name Jesus meaning 'Jehovah saves', for he will save His people from their sins." (Matthew 1:21)

Jesus said; "I have come that they may have life and that they may have it more abundantly." (John 10:10)

Jesus said "For the Son of Man did not come to destroy man's lives but to save them." (Luke 9:56)

The Prophet John the Baptist says this about Jesus: "Behold the Lamb of God who takes away the sin of the world!" (John 1:29)

Peter, an apostle of Christ, said this in the Book of Acts: "Nor is there salvation in any other name other than Jesus Christ, for there is no other name under heaven given among men by whom we must be saved." (Acts 4:12)

The only way to the Father is through Jesus Christ. Jesus said to the Apostle Thomas, "I am the way, the truth, and the life. No one comes to the Father except through Me. If you had known Me, you would have known My Father also; and from now on you know Him and have seen Him."(John 14:6-7)

As you see from these scriptures, the greatest miracle in anyone's life is to receive the Truth and His invitation to spend an eternity with the Creator of this world. Also, the most rejoicing of times in our lives are when we know that our names are written in the Lamb's Book of Life. (Luke 10:20 and Rev. 21:27)

"In addition, the Father judges no one. Instead, he has given the Son absolute authority to judge so that everyone will honor the Son, just as they honor the Father. Anyone who does not honor the Son is certainly not honoring the Father who sent him. Jesus said, "I tell you the truth; those who listen to my message and believe in God who sent me have eternal life. They will never be condemned for their sins, but they have already passed from death into life." (John 5:22-24)

Please read this book with this question in mind; are we here on this earth by accident or for a purpose? Our perception to what the answer is will determine our life long attitude toward our goal while we go through this journey of life.

Saiid

Introduction

What you are about to read are three separate excerpts from this book:

It was Tuesday, May 31, 2005, three days after my return from my incredible journey. I felt like I had escaped from the land of no return! *"**The land of Ayatollahs**"*

I definitely did not intend for it to end like this. I wanted to be able to visit Iran again one day. But, it is one thing to lose a loved one to eternity, and another thing when you cannot be with the ones you love here on this earth, <u>ever again</u>. To have never been able to see my family again was more than I could bear.

It was in the afternoon and I was home alone. I was exhausted, so I decided to lay down on the couch in my living room for a nap. I quickly fell into a deep sleep and began to dream.

My dream took me back to my journey as I traveled over the mountain ranges of Iran and Turkey; my link to my wife and children back in the U.S.A.

The two men that accompanied me were like two angels of God and were in charge of delivering me out of harm's way to safety.

The path was narrow and rocky, but the horses were surefooted and knew their way. It was still daylight when we began the trip and there was not a single cloud in the sky.

A gentle and cool breeze was touching my face as if it was the hand of God. It was very pleasant!

As the sky turned to darkness, the moon appeared with her beautiful smile. She was complete and bright, and her reflection lit our path; another reminder that God was with me. Everything was peaceful as we waited on top of the mountain in the cold night to cross the border. At times I wanted to give up my fight, but then I would feel God's presence and incredible strength, helping me to overcome my weakness.

Suddenly I woke up. As I opened my eyes, they were focused on some photographs which happened to be pictures of my family back in Iran. I slowly raised my head, and a fear like I've never known before overcame me! My body started to shake as I uttered these words to myself:

"Oh no, this can't be happening! I'm back in Iran. I didn't make it through!"

Then I asked myself, "Who brought me to this house?

Whose house is this and what will they do to me now?

Will they torture me or put me in prison?"

Confused and terrified, I got up slowly, my heart beating rapidly. I began to look around wanting to know where I was and how I got there.

As I was trying to get my bearings, I slowly walked from the living room to the kitchen. It was then I realized that I was safe in my own home and this was just a dream. Then, all the events of my dream flashed through my mind like a filmstrip. My entire being was filled with such an emotion, mixed with praise and thanksgiving. I realized at that moment that more than ever, we serve a God who loves and cares for us no matter who we are or where we are! I was so thankful to be home.

****

As our airplane approached the Mehrabud airport in Tehran, a big commotion took place within. Almost everyone in the plane started talking and it sounded like a swarm of bees; very hard to understand. People started to move around and change their clothes, especially the women. The dress code had to be Islamic for all who lived in or visited Iran, whether you were Muslim or not. You were required to change your attire to match the expectation of the country and its ruling.

Everything felt frightening. The plane landed, and silence and stillness took over the atmosphere. You could hear a pin drop. The air was so tense and stressful, and my stomach was curled up in a knot!

We were then taken to the terminal where we had to have our passports checked. Hamid, my brother, was in line ahead of me. As we went through a small gate, one by one, an officer with a stern face checked us in. He entered my Iranian passport number into a computer and stamped my entry.

Then suddenly, I spotted a man with his upper body stuck out of a window on the second floor, calling with a loud voice, "Saiid!" His voice was echoing all over the terminal and it did not sound pleasant at all.

The security man who was on the floor signaled the guy who was calling aloud through the open window, using his two-way radio, and asking, "Is it number one or number two?"

The voice responded that it was "two".

1) Meaning serious   2) Not so serious

I wondered what they wanted from me. I had no dealings with this Islamic government. Then why are they calling out my name? Why was I being singled out? Was I in trouble?

All kinds of strange things were going through my mind. I was surprised by what was happening. I was not sure if it was a dream, an illusion or what!

As soon as I got home to my parents house, I called my wife. She was very concerned and so was I.

"As soon as I heard his voice on the phone, I knew something was wrong. My heart sank as he told me what had happened at the airport. Everything had gone so well on his first trip, but this time was different and I heard the concern in his voice."

(*My wife, Ursa*)

****

The thought of being locked up and away from my family and grandchildren was my worst nightmare and brought many tears to my eyes.

The day came when I had to make a very important decision, the decision to escape from Iran. I knew there would be no one to blame no matter what happened. I did not even tell my wife since she was sensitive to this option. She made it clear to me from the beginning not to do anything that would jeopardize my life. Deep within my heart, I knew that she would not approve of what I was about to do. But I felt I had no other option if I wanted to see my wife and children anytime soon, if ever.

Besides, God was giving me the peace I needed about this decision, and was providing the means. He was with me all the way through this dangerous escape. All I had was my faith in Jesus Christ to carry me through these mountains. <u>I was giving up my logic for faith</u>.

I did not want to stay in Iran anymore with its unexpected surprises. I knew that if I died, I would go to heaven to be with the Father, and if not, God would use me for His glory.

Honestly, I was not sure how I would have responded if I had been caught. Would I be bold enough to confess my new faith, which could result in severe punishment or even death, just like the early Christians? Or would I lie just to save my neck? Then I would be lying to myself and my God by denying Him. This is something no Christian ever hopes to be confronted with and I was not ready to be tested.

When a soldier is tested, he has had much training before going to war. They prepare themselves mentally and physically to face those tough challenges, even death as war sometimes demands. But I had never been in that type of situation before and I was not sure how I would have reacted. I pray that I would have made the right choice with the help and strength of God above!

****

These are three short excerpt of my story. Now I am going to take you back to the time when I was born and raised as a Muslim boy. I want to show you how God the Father called for the transformation of my soul to the Truth of His Son, Jesus Christ, and for my **"Farewell to Islam".**

I hope that you enjoy it and are blessed by it.

Saiid

Chapter 1

My childhood

My name is Saiid Rabiipour, and I was born in Tehran, Iran, on November 26, 1953 and this is a brief story of my childhood.

When my Dad was twenty-five years old, he married my Mom, who was only fourteen years of age at the time. According to the customs and traditions of that time, this age difference was allowed.

In those days you didn't fall in love in order to get married. All marriages were arranged by the parents, and that's the way it was for my mom as well. She was only thirteen years old when a woman knocked on the door of her home. My mom and dad lived in the same community, but didn't really know each other. They just knew of each other through other families in the community. The lady asked if she could come in, and proceeded to ask my mom's parents, my grandparents, if her son could have their daughter's hand in marriage.

Oh, what an exciting moment! Someone was asking for their daughter! (*I presume that those were the first few words that entered my grandmother's mind*) What a blessing from God who has shown favor toward our family!

In those days, most people thought that girls were born for others while the sons were meant for the family. Sooner or later, they needed to marry off their daughters, so the sooner was the better for the family! In the Islamic history, Prophet Mohammad was offered a six year old Aisha, daughter of Abu Bakr, when he was about 50 years of age. Three years later Mohammad married her. Abu Bakr was one of the closest companions and advisers to Mohammad. He became the first caliphate or ruler after Muhammad's death. So marrying young was not only okay it was considered a blessing.

This was how it began. One day my dad, Hosein, was walking on the street where my mom's house was and he saw this beautiful young girl standing at the door. She captured his attention and his heart; love at first sight! That's all it took, just one look!

He ran home that day and told his mom that he had seen the woman he wanted to marry and would she go ask for her. They didn't even know her name. What is her name?

Her name is Pari (meaning angel)

Pari's father was a butcher and her mother, of course, was a housewife. In those days women did not work outside of their homes. The husband was in charge and the bread winner of the family.

Pari's parents, of course, said yes. So about a year later, Pari and Hossain were married! At first, they lived in a room set aside for them in his parent's home. They were surrounded by his sister and brothers as well as his Mom and Dad. This was a good thing at first for my Mom since she was so young. She learned many things by living among them, but living so close with the family soon became a hardship on her, and in time, my mom and dad were able to afford to move out and into their own place.

Their first child was a boy. They called him Mohsen. Everyone was happy since they considered it a blessing to have a boy. It was a sign of good measure from our God. So they continued and behold the second child was also a son. The family really believed that God was showering them with more blessings and favors. His name was called Parviz.

You see, having a son in those days translated to having social security at the older age for the parents. It wasn't that the girls were bad; they just belonged to others in their eyes. But the sons always belonged to the family no matter where they were.

Well, guess what? The third child was also a son. They called him Saiid, your humble servant. And the family continued to rejoice among the families and friends and in the community.

So the family grew larger and ended up with four sons and four daughters. Years later my mom lost one child on purpose. She first lied about it, telling me that she lost it accidently. I took and buried him under some dirt right outside of our home. She later told me that if she knew he was going to be another boy she sure would have kept him. But at the time she was not willing to risk of having another girl, especially when she already ended up with four daughters. He was about the size of the palm of my hand, and you could see everything. He was a life.

I was very young and did not understand everything about life or death. Whatever anyone would tell me, I believed. My mom said that she lost the baby by picking up a bag of cement, heavy enough to cause her to lose the baby. But some years later she told me the truth. Don't mistake about it, I love my mom no matter what. She is and has always been our 'Angel'.

Everything was going good until a turn of the tide, which caused a change in our destiny and caused some turmoil within our family.

Years later I lost my two older brothers at a young age. Parviz, who was hit by a truck, lost his life while performing a good deed. He stopped to remove a bag of wheat from a curvy highway to prevent an accident for other travelers when a truck who could not see him in a timely manner killed him and his friend; and a few years later a knife stabbing, claimed the life of Mohsen, my oldest brother when three men attempted to steal his car after they were given a ride to their destination. I was away and did not have a clue of what was going on and was not there to wipe away the tears from the gentile faces of my mom Pari (our angel) and my dad. They were so gracious to me that they did not want me to feel their pain or hear the disappointed voices of their loss. They wanted me to focus on my school and dream without any distractions.

Then it was my oldest sister's family. Her husband got involved with illegal drugs. He ended up doing a few wrong things at the bank he was working at and ended up loosing his job and eventually early death due to excessive drug use.

Though I was far away from the challenges my family was facing back home, I was facing my own with some unexpected events while going through my college years as I will discuss them at later chapters.

Then in the year 1980 the eight year war between Iran and Iraq began which crippled the economy of Iran, caused many things to go up in prices, and put more pressure on people. My youngest brother, Hamid had to serve his two year service in the military during those dreaded unwelcomed war. Fortunately and by the grace of God he finished his service without any bad consequences.

So, those beautiful memories and joyous times of having four sons which was the pride and joy of every family turned to an explosion by the turn of events in our world. Was it a blessing or cursing from the lord? That I can not answer. But I do know that what my parents were dreaming from the beginning was just a dream! And if God was up to something greater, that we could not tell or understand at that time.

My youngest brother, Hamid, lives in the USA now. He has a wonderful wife, Tina and two very fine children, Nicholas and Maggie. My four married sisters live in Iran with their respective husbands and families.

My parents loved all of us very much and saw to it that we had what we needed. We were not wealthy by any means but I do not remember lacking anything either. I went to a public school and participated in sports such as soccer and volleyball. These sports are very popular in most of the schools there.

Front row (left to right): me, cousin, Parviz, Mohsen holding my cousin
Back row (left to right) aunt holding cousin, mom holding sister, dad
(Center) grandmother, aunt and uncle in his army uniform

Education was very important to me, therefore I spent a good amount of my time studying and doing homework. My father had a sixth grade education and my mother had none; As a result they always encouraged us to seek a better education. I had to choose a major course of study by the time I reached the ninth grade. With the help of my good teachers and their recommendations, I chose mathematics.

These teachers were excellent in helping us and even though math was one of the toughest subjects, they helped me to understand and do well. As a result, math became my friend and numbers turned out to be my game! Now, though it may sound strange, when I look back at my math note book that I kept from those days, they look like Greek to me!

The electricity was not very reliable in our home. At least twice a week we lost our power, but we were always prepared with oil lamps to light our home in order to continue our normal life. There were many nights when I had to study, and do my homework using an oil lamp as my only light. But, I was always happy and content even under those circumstances. Early on my mother used a kerosene stove to do all of her cooking, but later she graduated to a higher standard and used a propane gas stove when we were able to afford to buy one. She has always been a simple and loving mother!

My father worked as a photography lab technician where he would develop film. Everyone at his work loved him for his dedication and commitment to his work. Some of the key personnel that he worked with were Armenian Christians who were very kind to him. My father's boss gave him a piece of land as a bonus for being with his business for such a long time, and for his loyalty to his job. He later had a house built on that land. We moved into that house with much excitement since we were living in a multi-family and crowded house that we were renting. Our new community which was called "Tehran-Noe" was far away from the busy part of Tehran at that time.

At first, we had no city water in our new community; therefore, we had to purchase a tank of water to pour into our underground storage. We then used a hand pump to get the water we needed, which mostly was used for washing and cleaning. It was my responsibility to get two buckets of fresh water from a public well every other day, which was about a quarter of a mile away from our home. This water was mainly used for cooking and drinking.

My father had many friends whom we grew up and spent lots of time with. During the summer we would go on picnics in the mountains, north of Tehran or by the rivers near Karaj. Sometimes we would travel by a chartered bus to as far away as the Caspian Sea for a whole week. We would sing songs; dance, play, walk, and mountain climb or put on a play for everyone. We would visit different friends or families at their homes during the winter seasons.

Since my dad had worked most of his life in the field of photography, he initially owned his own 8mm camera (without sound) and later advanced to a super-8mm movie projector and camera (with sound). In every outing, he would film the events and would later show them at our house on one of four huge white walls as a screen. We always had the largest group of friends in our house when it came to his turn to host a get together. I have many great and fond memories of my childhood growing up in Iran. Our family would orchestrate the biggest show as entertainment for the evening.

Radio was our only source of entertainment up until I was in high school. My brother, Parviz, quit school after finishing the ninth grade and got a job. I do not know why he chose to quit. Perhaps he felt the need to help my Dad since we were such a large family! Then at the first chance, when he had saved enough money, he was able to purchase our first black and white television set!

My life was very simple, yet our family led a content and happy life. We did not have any debts except for the house payment. We traveled by bus to many places we needed to go when they were not close enough to walk to. My high school was within the walking distance of less than two miles, which I did not mind to walk.

The state religion was Islam and most Iranians considered themselves as Muslims, but not by choice as Christians do. Christians choose their religion when they get to the age of accountability. But Muslims are born into it since parents are considered Muslims. We were taught religion studies in our school system and were expected to act accordingly in public.

We had little knowledge about other faiths and what we did know was distorted. Nevertheless I loved God and often talked with Him. Sometimes, I felt that He would answer my prayers, especially during school exams. Yet again, there were many things about God which were beyond my comprehension, and I did not dare question Him or the Quran! Later I will show you the Straight Path in the Quran as recorded in the Bible. It is fascinating!

My grandmother (from my mother's side) was an extremely religious woman. She was illiterate, yet she could recite the Quran as if she had her master's degree. She was a loving, caring and giving woman as well as kind and thoughtful. I never heard any negative words from my grandmother's mouth. We all loved and treasured her very much.

Growing up, it was my uncle (my mom's brother), who used to talk to me about God and the importance of following the five pillars of Islam with emphasis on the daily prayers.

Five pillars of Islam are:

1. Faith in the Oneness of God and the finality of the Prophet Muhammad;
2. Establishment of the daily prayers;
3. Almsgiving to the needy;
4. Self-purification through fasting;
5. The pilgrimage to Mecca for those who are able;

On the contrary, when I would ask my uncle about heaven, and how sure he was that we would get there by following these five pillars, he could not answer this question to my satisfaction. He would normally respond by saying that it would be better to be safe by obeying the five pillars of Islam just in case they were required for entry to paradise. If not, then you have not lost anything by performing them. He would talk with sincerity, but his actions toward his wife did not demonstrate charity or compassion. Instead, he would misuse his authority toward his wife by beating her when there were disagreements between them. It was hard for me to understand how he could be a Godly person on one hand and abusive to his own wife on the other. I did not have enough knowledge of the Quran to argue or question him, so I would only listen and remain polite as expected.

Five times a day you will hear the sound of the call to prayer from a nearby mosque or Radio. The sound of the call to prayer had a special effect on many souls, including me. Our home was only a few doors away from a mosque in our neighborhood. The voice of the Muezzin (a mosque official), who calls Muslims to prayer from a minaret five times a day, rightfully asks for us to come together, and pray to the Almighty God. His appeal was with such a confidence and sincerity that makes one stop and think about nothing but God. It touches your soul and pulls you like a magnet to face Mecca to pray.

But the reality outside of those emotions is much different. My religious teachers at our school often told us not to get into any kind of religious discussions with Armenian Christians who were also there as students. They also drilled into our heads that Jews, Christians and those of the Baha'i faith were not "clean" at all, and encouraged us to keep our distance from them. The sad part of those teachings was that they were included in the holy Quran! I found out that the Quran confirms all of what my religious teachers at school and my uncle were saying or doing, and considered them the words of Allah! (1, 2)

Those strange and out of the ordinary teachings were being taught by our religious teachers, and Mullahs alike caused many, including myself, to remain ignorant from the real Truth of the Scriptures, which I will talk about as we go forward. However, because of my limited knowledge, I participated often in the mosques, praying and worshipping Allah as part of our obligatory duties and traditions, especially during the holy months of Ramadan and Muharram. Allah was a god I never questioned, who seemed distant and unknowable.

But now, as I look back, I cannot help to notice that God the Father saw me in a place where I could not see myself.

27

Notes:

*1) **Concerning women**: As for the women the book of Allah is emphatic that they are inferior to men and if they disobey their husbands they have the right to beat them.*

Quran: "Sura 4:34 Men are the protectors and maintainers of women, because Allah has given the one more (strength) than the other, and because they support them from their means. Therefore, the righteous women are devoutly obedient, and guard in (the husband's) absence what Allah would have them guard.

As to those women on whose part ye fear disloyalty and ill-conduct, admonish them (first), (next), refuse to share their beds, (and last) beat (lightly); but if they return to obedience, seek not against them means (of annoyance)"

2) Concerning Friendship with non-Muslims

Quran: Sura 3:28 "Let not the believers take for friends or helpers Unbelievers rather than believers: if any do that, in nothing will there be help from Allah: except by way of precaution, that ye may Guard yourselves from them. But Allah cautions you (To remember) Himself; for the final goal is to Allah."

Chapter 2

Iranian Navy

In 1972, I had just graduated from Vesal High School in Tehran, Iran in a community called "Tehran-Noe". My major course of study was in Mathematics. In Iran, you must study and do well in all the courses you signed up for that year. Failing one course would result in having to take all the courses over again the following year. Education and achieving good grades was very important to me since I intended to advance my education by going to college after graduating from high school. I would study long hours at home and with friends in a library while researching extra materials needed to pass the entrance exam to one of the universities when the time came. However, due to the shortage of universities in Iran and because of the very difficult entrance exams, I was not successful in achieving entrance to any of the universities there.

I took advantage of my summer sessions and acquired some courses in English and Typing, while at the same time I worked alongside my older brother, Parviz, in a photo shop. He worked as a lab-technician in a photo shop called "Photo Rima". His boss was an outstanding Armenian individual that I met. Though we did not get into any type of religious discussion, he treated us like his own sons! This was my first encounter with a Christian.

After finishing my high school, I somehow ended up joining the Iranian Navy. When I say somehow, it is because, I never asked nor applied for it. It fell in my lap as part of God's plan in my life!

While searching for other universities, I saw and responded to an advertisement in one of Tehran's local newspapers about working on a commercial cruise liner, which they were accepting applications.

The Iranian Navy had provided the facilities and the space needed for 300 students to take their exam. Two groups were chosen based on the results of the exams. The first group consisted of twenty people, which later I learned were chosen for the commercial cruise liner. The second group consisted of only twelve students, whom the Navy chose to train internally. I was included in the latter group.

Though it was flattering to be chosen as part of the Iranian Navy, they never gave us the option of whether we wanted to serve in the Iranian Navy or not. I never applied or asked for that job. They just took us, proceeded to give us haircuts, and measured us for a military uniform!

I had never had any dealings with the government and was very inexperienced, not knowing what questions to ask.

As a result I went home very confused that day and discussed the matter with my Dad. Luckily, the following day my Dad met a Commander from the Navy in one of the social gatherings and told him briefly about me and what had taken place at the Navy base. He told my Dad that if I had any questions to please come by his office and that he would be glad to answer any questions that I might have.

So, the following day I went to the Commander's office in order to consult with him and ask him some questions concerning how we were handled. The Commander was not in his office at the time, but there was a young officer sitting there on one of the chairs in his office, also waiting to speak with the Commander.   He inquired about my business and I told him about the questions I had regarding the Navy. He then proceeded to tell me that he recently came back from overseas after finishing his four years of schooling there.

(*I thought to myself that maybe he is the one that I should listen to since he just finished going through what I was about to.*)

He continued by telling me that after a few years of education they would bring you back and treat you like a "football" by kicking you from the North (Caspian Sea) to the South (Persian Gulf) and vice versa.   He then told me that he had been back in Iran and on active duty for several months, yet to this day he had not received a station or job assignment. He then advised me to choose the civilian life instead, where I could be my own boss and be in charge of my own destiny.

(That day, I left the Commander's office feeling more confused than ever. I knew though, that the military might draft me someday anyway for a two-year service. But, if I chose this route, I at least would have the opportunity to go overseas with the Navy and further my education. The thought of becoming an officer made me feel proud as well, not to mention that the uniform was very appealing to me. So I decided to stay.)

Anyhow, the Navy sent us to an area north of Tehran where the rest of the cadets were already going through their basic training. It appeared that they were twelve cadets short of completing their quota in this previous group of recruits and that is why only a small group of us were being selected at this time. To make matters more confusing, when we got there, the four months of training had just finished, and as a result, we were all sent home the following day!

The next step was for us to report to an English class where we studied English for approximately three months. Then the Navy would choose specific schools in the United States for specific courses of study for all of us. Later in chapter four, I will talk more about the challenges I faced in my designated school. In the mean time while we were taking our English training, we participated in some military ceremonial events.

One of the things that caught my eye was this: During speeches or military ceremonials, the commanders would salute to just a picture of the Shah (the former King of Iran) and expressed to us that we all should be committing our loyalty to him, rather than to the country!

At any rate, during my first year in the Navy, I had numerous good experiences. We made several field trips to the south, including "Khark Island" and other locations in the Persian Gulf region. We visited many Naval Bases as well as the famous Abadan oil refinery, one of the largest in the world. Their goal was to teach us to protect the country and the places of importance from the aggressors, as the whole world was after what we had in abundance-"**the oil**!" But it was already too late, because most of the oil profits were going outside of the country! I began taking notes mentally since I was not familiar with of those military implementations.

Eventually on January 16, 1979, Shah Mohammad Reza Pahlavi and his wife, Empress Farah, left Tehran and flew to Aswan in Egypt to go into exile. Many of his high-ranking officers either left with him or were killed by this new Islamic regime. A good example of that, (according to the people of Iran), was what happened to the Prime Minister, Amir Abbas Hoveyda. He was being charged for wrong doings done by the Shah and his government against the people of Iran.

He was supposed to go before the courts to answer questions as to why he or the Shah held, killed, or tortured so many political prisoners. While they were transporting him, one of the religious hardliners who acted as the judge, jury, and the executioner pulled his gun and killed the Prime

Minister in cold blood before he could have a chance to defend himself in a court of law.

That Judge, (according to some Iranians that I have spoken with), was one of the ruthless religious hardliners of that time and brought much fear among the people of Iran, making them subservient to this new regime.

Under Islamic regime many things changed. Women lost their freedom and were forced to cover their whole body including their hair. Men were not allowed to wear shorts. The Iranian education curriculum, though it used to have some religious study, became more Islamic at all levels, including universities. Many faced harsh punishments and imprisonment by questioning the motives of this new regime or opposing the Islamic government by suggesting that religion should not be involved in the politics of Iran.

Among those opposing were some of their own clergies like Ayatollah Boroujerdi and Ayatollah Montazari, both with huge followers. They initially were in favor of the change and reformation of Iran under Ayatollah Khomeini, but later disagreed with the harsh treatment of the citizens and pulled away from him. Ayatollah Khomeini issued an order to the Judicial Officials to judge every Iranian political prisoner and kill those who would not repent of anti-regime activities. According to the report by "Telegraph.co.uk", more than 30,000 political prisoners were executed in the 1988 massacre. Prisoners were loaded onto forklift trucks in groups of six and hanged from cranes in half-hour intervals.

Many have asked me from my perspective whether the Shah was loved or hated. Neither my family nor I were interested in politics. I never knew any other person except the Shah of Iran as our king. He was a good king based on my limited knowledge. I have always loved and respected him, pleased of his accomplishments. I also was proud of my country as well. I watched one of his early interviews with Barbara Walters of ABC news on American television, where he was expressing that his people loved him and he felt the same toward his people. I could not agree any less with that statement. This pride especially increased when I noticed leaders of many countries around the world were in harmony and agreement with the Shah and his leadership. An example of that was Iran's legendary 2500 years of continuous statehood when the Shah declared his political leadership on the international stage, which Mohammad Reza Shah and his dynasty appeared secure.

This 2500 year celebration of Iran's monarchy consisted of an elaborate set of festivities that took place in October of 1971. It was the occasion of the 2500th anniversary of the founding of the Iranian monarchy by "Cyrus the Great". During this ceremony, the leaders of the whole world were in my country.

What a proud moment that was for us Iranians! Shah Reza Pahlavi, who called himself "the King of kings", stood proudly by the tomb of Cyrus the great, the king of Persia, dressed in full kingship uniform. With a loud voice, which was echoed all over Persepolis, Shiraz (Fars Province, South of Iran) saying: "Cyrus, rest in peace thus we are awake...rest in peace..." as the whole country was glued to the television, including me, listening and watching the whole ceremony. I must say that I was proud of what I was seeing and hearing regarding my country and its accomplishments.

Tomb of Cyrus the great

Frankly, I was in shock when I learned that the Shah of Iran left the country in 1979 after a few shots were fired! Little did I know that his military had already fired many shots into a crowd of demonstrators, and would have killed more if the Shah would have permitted it!

The Shah on the other hand did not want too much bloodshed and chose to leave the country instead with the hope of coming back to rescue his military generals and other high ranking officers. However, the one who called himself "Shah-han-shah" meaning the King of kings never returned back to Iran!

I was young and very naïve, and was not involved in my country's politics. My first impression was that God was in control and I did not think twice about what would happen next. History had already proven that the Shah of Iran had been a "Good Leader" compared to what we have now in his place (the Islamic Republic), though I did not agree with what "SAVAK" or the Shah's secret police was doing during his reign. Incidentally when the Shah came to power in 1953 with the aid of the United States, "SAVAK" was also formed and trained by the CIA to control and crackdown the oppositions.

Great Britain had returned the Shah in 1931. The Shah signed a deal selling Iranian oil to the Anglo Persian Oil Company, which today is called British Petroleum (BP). When the first democratically elected parliament and prime minister in Iran took power in 1950 they planned to nationalize Iran's oil assets, violating the still running oil contract with British Petroleum. The British Government followed that disagreement by a complaint against Iran in Belgium's International Court but lost the case against Iran's new government. Great Britain reacted by blockading the Persian Gulf, the Strait of Hormuz, halting Iran's trade and economy. The new prime minister, Mohammad Mossadegh ordered the British embassy in Iran to be closed. However, British determination and willingness concerning the control of Iran's oil, with the help of the USA and CIA, arranged a coup in Tehran, overthrew Prime Minister Mossadegh and restored the pro-western Shah to power.   After more than twenty years of the Shah's rule, there was a bloody revolution in 1979 after which Iran became the Islamic Republic it is today. (*Wikipedia, the free Encyclopedia*)

Anyhow, our classes ended after three months, and now the time was quickly approaching for our group, which consisted of fifty cadets, to depart for our assigned school in the USA. It was the beginning of the spring and close to our traditional Iranian New Year. Happiness was in the air as the aroma of flower blossoms signified the change in the season from winter to spring. It was an exciting time in my life. It seemed that everyone was buying new clothes, cleaning up and getting ready for "Norooz", which means New Year. There were many gatherings and farewell parties, especially in our home.

Shortly after the New Year, we finally headed for the airport. Many of our families and friends were there to see us off. All of my family was there also. They were proud of their son and his accomplishments. I had never flown in an airplane before; as a result I was very excited and nervous at the same time, eager to experience something for the first time in my life. I knew that I was going to a college in the USA for a few years. Going to a college, especially outside of the country, and flying in an airplane for the first time made my head swell up a bit. I wasn't even thinking of missing my family, or the time of my return. I was "walking on a cloud" within the frame of my mind, not realizing that only God was in control of my destiny and future!

My youngest sister, who was only seven years old, cried for me as we were saying our goodbyes to each other. I gently kissed her face to let her know that I will see her again very soon. Little did I know what lay ahead in my life's journey!

Though not very aggressive, I somehow managed to move forward. It seemed as though someone was guiding me! But I couldn't see nor was I able to comprehend who that was. I really did not have a mentor to look up to. Neither my parents nor I were very religious. I loved and respected my Mom and Dad, but they lacked many things I needed as mentors.

We finally said our farewells with kisses and tears and I began my journey for a destiny that only God could know!

Chapter 3

A new page in my life

Lackland Air Force Base

In the spring of 1973, our group left Iran for the United States of America. We had a lengthy layover in London, England. When we first arrived in London, the weather was very foggy and hard to see things. But as the time passed it became much clearer to see this beautiful city. Couple of my friends and I took a short sightseeing trip through the city. It sure felt strange seeing all the cars driving on the wrong side of the road but the city was so neat and clean as you were in a cute, but giant 'doll house'.

Soon we boarded another plane and continued our journey to the U.S. We had brought along lots of dried fruit and nuts to munch on, and we did not mind to show our hospitality to other passengers and flight attendants by sharing them. Everyone seemed to enjoy the pistachios the most. The trip was long, but we kept ourselves busy playing cards or watching movies.

Our first stop in the U.S. was New York JFK airport. We were all very excited about our journey and proud of our country and who we were. Everywhere we went we were well received by everyone. Iran was one of the closest allies to the United States at that time, and as a result, we would go through every checkpoint without anyone questioning or searching us or our luggage. (*Good old days!*)

Our next stop was Lackland Air Force Base in San Antonio Texas, where we stayed and continued our English education for fifteen weeks. We were the first large group of midshipmen who were entering a U.S. air force base for this transitional training. There were many activities already prepared for other Iranian airmen, but not for us. We stayed there for the duration of schooling, and focused our time and energy on preparing for our university education. We passed our "Test of English as a Foreign Language" (TOEFL) and entrance exams for our assigned university.

I was part of the group of twenty-five cadets that were chosen to attend the Citadel, a military college in Charleston, South Carolina. Our group was selected by the Iranian Navy to study Business Administration. Once more, I had very little military experience up to this point, and did not know what lay ahead. No one told me about the expectations of the Citadel, a tough and highly respected school. As far as I knew and was concerned about, I was going to a university to earn a degree and that was all. Boy was I in for a surprise! (I'll elaborate more on this, in chapter four.)

There were many nationalities at Lackland AFB that were there for various training, but our group was there for English comprehension and passage of the entrance exams to the university. For the short time that we were there, we had a great time meeting people who came to the base for different reasons, such as shopping, swimming, playing sports, and even going to church. It was there that I met some families who were nice to us and invited us into their homes and churches. They made us feel like as we were a part of them. I remember one occasion when a group of us were invited to someone's home for lunch after a church service. We played cards, chess, and did many other activities already planned for us. It was at this house that one of the guys in our group walked right through a glass door! The door was large and so clean that you could not tell if there was a door there at all. It made us all feel bad, but the owner was so nice, understanding, and compassionate toward the guy who did it, and the rest of us as well.

A friend of mine in Iran, who had already been to Lackland AFB, had told me about a group of people who came to the base every Sunday morning. They would invite foreign exchange students to their church for worship and fellowship. He also told me that I should go with them when they came to our barracks if I wanted to meet some good people. This would also help with my English and communication skills as well. That was another reason why I chose to go places to meet people without hesitation.

I recall on one particular Sunday morning when someone came with their church-van to our barracks, and invited as many students as he could to their church. I went along as well as some other students. When we arrived at their

45

church, we were taken to a class where they taught us about God and Christianity. The classroom was full to capacity with mostly foreign exchange students. We understood and agreed with most of his teachings concerning God and His messengers, until he spoke about us being "sinners" and in need of Jesus Christ who was also being called "The Son of God"! Suddenly, many hands would go up with objections and questions.

"Why do you call Jesus Christ, who is a man, the Son of God?" We asked.

Referring to us as "sinners" and to Jesus Christ as "the Son of God", was unfamiliar in our religious teachings, growing up as Muslims. We associated the word "sin" to those who may have done something terrible such as killing someone or having done something immoral which has great punishment and consequences. But since I had never killed anyone or done anything as terrible as that, I never thought of myself as a sinner!

I knew that we had made mistakes, made bad judgments and simply made bad decisions in our daily lives, but at the same time we believed that God would forgive us. This is why we recited these words from the holy Quran that "Allah, being the most beneficial and the most merciful" in our daily prayers.

Second, in the phrase "The Son of God" we understood that the word "son" was as a result of a physical intimacy between two persons and in this case, God and Mary. Since Mary was known as the "Virgin Mary", to the Muslims, therefore the idea of using the phrase "the Son of God" to us was false and wrong. In our eyes this phrase was also degrading God, and brought Him down to the level of a human being.

Anyway, we could neither understand nor accept what the teacher was trying to convey to us, so naturally the teacher had a hard time communicating this portion of the Bible to us. When we finally left the church, we were a bit confused.

Growing up under the influence of Islamic religion in Iran, no one ever tried to teach anything like this to me. Nevertheless, the people were very nice and good to us, never making us feel bad about not understanding what they were trying to teach.

On another occasion while walking around the base, I heard loud music and excitement coming out of a building nearby. It made me curious, so I approached the building and observed a large group of people playing music. Some were playing their guitars and drums, while others were singing and clapping their hands. They appeared to be very happy about what they were singing. But, when I learned that the singing and loud music was coming from inside a religious chapel, I was really surprised and could not grasp the meaning of the celebration!

As I was analyzing this situation in my head, thinking and questioning the reason for such excitement, I thought perhaps there was a wedding about to take place, or perhaps this was not really a church. You see, in the mosque that I used to go to in Iran, I was accustomed to hearing the sound of mourning, crying and reverence for those who died for the cause of Islam, as the Mullahs (teachers of Islam) articulated to us concerning Muhammad and his disciples.

These challenges intrigued my curiosity and I wanted to learn more about those issues in question and was not satisfied until I discovered them on my own.

Later on I did learn that Christian church services were more like a celebration where those who wished to worship, gathered together to celebrate the risen savior Jesus Christ, who took away their sins once and for all. Their worship was not out of obligation or duty, but out of gratitude and love for Jesus Christ.

Also, when I learned more about "sin" and Jesus as "the Son of God", it became much more clear to me about the real truth of God. In fact the truth about us being sinners and Jesus as the Son of God is recorded in the Quran! Here is a Sura 20:121which talks about man's first sin:

*"Then they (Adam and his wife) both ate of it, so their shame became apparent unto them, and they began to hide by heaping on themselves some of the leaves of the garden, and Adam disobeyed his Lord and **his nature became evil**."*

"Most certainly, all of us are children of Adam except one – his name is Jesus Masih (Messiah). Apple trees produce only apples! Can an apple tree produce oranges? All humans born in Adam's family inherit Adam's nature. The curse of sin in Adam is being passed down among his decedents. Jesus is the only man who never sinned. He did not sin because he was not born in the bloodline of Adam. He did not inherit Adam's sin nature.

Sura 3:45 (And remember) when the angels said: "O Maryam! Verily, Allah gives you the glad tidings of a Word from Him, whose name Jesus Masih (Jesus Messiah), the

son of Maryam, held in honor in this world and in the Hereafter, and one of those brought near to Allah."

Ayah 45 is the announcement to Mary that she had been chosen to give birth to the Prophet Jesus. Muslims around the world have two names for Jesus. They call him "'Jesus or Isa Kalumullah" (Word of God) and "'Jesus or Isa Ruhullah" (Spirit of God). Why do they call Jesus or Isa by these two names?

The answers are in Sura Al-Imran 3:45 and Sura Ambiyaa 21:91. God said that He would put his Word into Mary. What or who is God's "Word?" To better understand this, read Sura Ambiyaa 21:91 "...and she (Maryam) guarded her chastity, therefore We breathed into her of our Spirit and made her and her son a sign for all people."

Why do they refer to Jesus as "'Isa Kalumullah" and "'Isa Ruhullah"? The Quran makes it clear; Jesus is the Word (Kalum) and Spirit (Ruh) of Allah. No other person or Prophet carries these titles.

God's "Word" and "Spirit" that was placed inside Mary became flesh in the form of a baby. He told Mary to name the baby Jesus Masih. Masih or Messiah means "the anointed or promised one." 758 years before the birth of Jesus, the Prophet Isaiah wrote, "...a virgin will conceive and his name will be called, 'Immanuel' (Isaiah 7:14). "Immanuel" is a Hebrew word meaning, "God with us."

Jesus would be honored by all people in this world and forever in heaven and he would be one of those nearest to God Himself. The Quran paints a picture of Jesus for us. He is God's Kalum, Ruh, promised anointed one, and "a sign for (all) the nations" (Ambiyaa 21:91). When we want to go

49

somewhere that we have never gone before, we look for a sign to guide us. Where will we go if we follow Jesus?

3:46 *"He will speak to the people in the cradle and in manhood, and he will be one of the righteous."*

Jesus' birth was to be a message to the entire world and he was to be one of the righteous. How righteous was Jesus? God told Mary, in Sura Maryam 19:19, that Jesus would be "a faultless son."

The Bible teaches us that Jesus never killed anyone; he did not have a love for money; he never married; he spoke out against corruption among the religious leaders; he prayed every day; he fasted for 40 days and nights in which he did not eat anything at all; and he taught us to love our enemies. If Jesus ever committed a sin, then he would have ceased to be God's Kalumullah or Ruhullah and he could not have gone to heaven to be with God. Through Jesus, God showed the world how "complete" Muslims should live their lives. This would be a wonderful world if we all lived our lives like Jesus. Now I hope that the title Jesus as the "Son of God" is much clearer for my Muslim friends."

(A complete Muslim by Kevin Greeson and Quran)

During our stay at Lackland AFB, which is close to San Antonio, Texas, I had some good and bad experiences. I met many nice people who would make us feel welcome. An example of this was a retired Air Force Colonel who would come to the base on a regular basis to meet and invite a few foreign exchange students from the same country to his home. His wife would attempt to cook the traditional food based on the culture of the invited guests. We would eat and fellowship with each other while they made every effort to make us feel welcome. I think it was an attempt to keep us from feeling homesick.

I remember that in the Colonel's home there was a small round table filled with miniature flags of the whole world. He would take the flag of the United States and the flag of the invited guest's home country and put them in the middle of the table in order to make us feel special, with the other flags of the world surrounding them.   The food was great, the fellowship was awesome, and we surely felt the love and unselfish generosity this family, as well as many others like them showed us.

On another occasion, the Colonel took us to the historic Alamo, where we dressed up like cowboys. He supplied the clothes and fake guns for us and took a few photo shots. Everyone had brought their own cameras and the Colonel took pictures of us Iranian 'cowboys' so we could send the photos to our families back home. That was so thoughtful of him. Giving up his time and money for the people he did not know or may not see again! I wish I knew his name.

I also met another family, Mel and June Curtis, also an Air Force family, who treated me like their own son, welcoming me into their home. I spent much of my time with them. They treated me like part of their family, and when I got married June was there at my wedding representing my side of the family! To this day, we still communicate with each other.

The city of San Antonio was a lively city with lots of lights at night, fireworks and carnivals. I enjoyed the music on the river walk while being among people who seemed to be happy all the time. It was during one of those happy occasions when I ran into one of my English teachers from Lackland AFB. She invited me to a dinner at a nearby restaurant. We were sitting at a table to be served. After we ordered our food, the waitress asked us the kind of dressing we would like to have?

I waited for my teacher to say something.

She replied "French" would be fine.

Then the waitress turned to me and asked the same question. Our dining table was small, and I was perplexed by the same question as to how she was going to 'dress-up' our table! I really did not understand the question, and at the same time did not want to act dumb in front of my English teacher. All I knew of the word 'dressing' referred to "a dressing table". So, I was amazed by the question and responded, 'Make it Persian!'

I was anxious to see how she was going to 'dress-up' the dining table to our taste! She immediately responded that they did not have "Persian". I said okay then make it "French" since I heard the teacher asking for the same.

I had my eyes glued to the waitress with the expectation of seeing what type of "table-cloth" or "flowers" she was going to decorate our table with. I waited and waited and waited; the food came; we ate but I was still waiting to see what the waitress was going to do with our table. Finally we left the restaurant, but nothing was ever done to our table. I was really confused! Of course, later I learned the meaning of "salad dressing" for she failed to mention the word "salad" in front of "dressing". Lesson learned.

My only negative experience in San Antonio was that we heard gunfire and fights almost every week and there were always clashes between the Mexicans and Blacks in the city especially late at night, which made it uneasy for us when we stayed there late at night.

Well, our time had come and gone at Lackland AFB, and we had to move on. A prestigious and well known college was waiting for us, but little did we know what we had coming! Thus we passed all of our exams and prepared ourselves for departure to a military school that would surely change our lives. That school which you about to read in the next chapter is called "**The Citadel**".

Chapter 4

The Citadel

Another pivotal change

W ell, the party
was over and
along with that, my fifteen
weeks of English classes
ended. We passed all of
our exams and prepared
ourselves for departure to
our designated colleges.
My group, which consisted
of twenty-five students,
left Lackland AFB for a
military school called "The
Citadel" in Charleston,
South Carolina.

We arrived at the
Charleston airport around 2:00 am that day in early August
of 1974. There was a big tour-bus right outside of the airport
waiting for us along with a cadet officer, who was there to

greet and escort us to our assigned battalion and company at the Citadel.

As we were traveling toward our school, I noticed the city and its beautiful surroundings, with many waterways, bridges, and well-lit roads. I also saw many signs saying "The Citadel" along our way, making me proud to be part of that city and school. The school was well known not only in the city of Charleston, but also in the state of South Carolina and United States of America; for many students came from all over the USA to attend. We represented an international contingent, invited by the USA. A few of the other countries represented were Germany and Thailand.

We arrived at the college around 4:00 am. The bus went through a tall iron gate and a guard who was standing by the gate motioned his hand for our bus to go in after he recognized the cadet officer who was on board. The bus headed towards our battalions, which also had huge columns on all four corners with high walls. I couldn't help but to notice that all of the buildings there seemed to be gigantic as we circled a sizeable grassy area which mostly was used for military parades and exercise.

There were four battalions at the Citadel; and each battalion had four companies except the second one, which included the "Band Company". The bus would stop at each battalion for each of us to get off and proceed to the assigned room.

I got off the bus at the second battalion, retrieved my suitcases, and went inside through another iron gate where a cadet guard unlocked and opened the door for me to go in. He was nice enough to help me carry my suitcases to the fourth floor in company "F" where I was assigned. I was surprised and shocked when I noticed the gate being shut behind us using a padlock.

(Oh my God I said to myself!   That felt a bit awkward and scary to me.   The very first thing that came to my mind was how this place looked and felt like a prison!)

The cadet directed me to my room and offered help if needed. I went inside the room; the size of the room was about ten by fourteen feet with a bunk bed on one side and cabinets and desks on the opposite side. There was a window that opened up for fresh air but it was wired with mesh wire along with iron bars to prevent escape or suicide by cadets. **It truly was like being in a prison!**

I was too tired to think about anything else at that time.   All I wanted to do was to complete my studies and go back home to Iran.   I was not interested in wasting my time with anything else.   I decided to wait and see what would happen next.

I fell asleep on one of the beds without any sheets or pillows, granted I was not prepared with those things since no one had advised us what to bring. I must admit that we were given a book or catalog with the list of things to bring but we were too busy to read it. Even if we had read it we probably would have thought the Iranian navy had taken care of it for us. Nevertheless, I slept with my clothes on since it was cool that early in the morning. The next day I went to the school's supply store and obtained what I needed for the rest of the semester including my study books. The room was double occupancy but my roommate had not arrived yet.

At 5:30 am, the sound of the bugler playing 'Reveille' woke me up. The sound was very pleasant to my ear and I was eager to know what it meant. Five minutes later, it sounded again. I got up, looked outside, but nothing was going on. By the fourth or fifth time, that pleasant noise was not so pleasant anymore! I was not able to rest after that, so I decided to go downstairs to see what was going on. Then suddenly I heard the sound of cadets marching, with someone calling cadence,

"Left, Right, Left, Right"

"Where did everyone go?" I asked the guard at the front gate.

"They are gone to the mess hall for breakfast" he answered.

It was still dark outside, so I slowly walked toward the mess hall. When I spotted the building, I went in and joined the rest of my friends there who were gathered around one long table eating breakfast with much enjoyment.

As we were eating our last breakfast, with a great deal of freedom and ease of mind, I noticed that some of the cadets were eating their food by "squaring their hand" and then bringing it towards their mouth. It came across as very strange to me and I could not understand why they were eating like that! After breakfast was over, we stepped outside of the mess hall and again I spotted some cadets who were walking in the form of a square. Turning my head to the right and left, I tried to figure out why these cadets were walking so awkward. Needless to say, I was a bit confused at everything I was observing. No one had drilled us concerning this military school and the expectations of what lay ahead. Every event was a surprise for me.

A building labeled <u>Infirmary</u> got my attention. The first thing that came to my mind was that perhaps they had some "<u>mentally</u> <u>challenged</u>" students in the same school, who were there for observation. I couldn't help to think that since I had seen so many strange things such as iron gates, wired-mesh windows, or could it be that we would have to do the same "dance" as they were? **God forbid!**

I really didn't know what to think. Not having military background and training on one hand and facing a school like this with unfamiliar activities on the other hand, allowed numerous surprises to come to my friends and me. At any rate, at 7:00 am, I was instructed to introduce myself to the cadet Corporal in my assigned company, where he drilled me with a <u>loud voice</u> on how to communicate!

My first response was; "Sir, I am not deaf; you do not have to yell at me!" Not realizing that it was part of their system. He yelled again even louder telling me not to look at him, and to repeat after him these words: "Sir, my name is cadet recruit so and so" and some other stuff. It appeared as if everyone was angry at each other, with all the yelling and facial expressions.

A QUOTE FROM ONE OF THE YEARBOOKS EXPLAINS IT WELL:

"Wow- this place looks crazy. Go to that desk and do what? Get your toe on the line, Mister, and keep your eyes straight ahead." Those were the first wonderful words of welcome from my cadet cadre Corporal. I really was not expecting a tea party, but this guy was ridiculous. All this parading around with an "idiot bag", gym shirt and shorts, and black shoes and socks! What kind of dress code is that? (This "idiot bag" was nothing but a laundry bag we were made to carry on our shoulders while going all around the campus, from one station to the other to collect the material or uniforms we needed to use later on. Then they made us dress in gym shorts and shirts with our dress shoes and

referred to us as 'knobs' or 'zeros' which was military slangs!)

Two days later, the system came in to effect. Little did we know what horror lurked behind those pillars! About 10 o'clock in the morning, they rushed us onto the quad in neat little rows, leaving us without supervision. What is going on? The silence was killing me and then ...

I heard the front gate creak as it slowly closed to a metallic slam with background music of a jet engine. Sweat began to pour down my brow and then someone spoke over the loudspeaker. Gentlemen of the Class of 1977, your system is now in effect!"

All hell broke loose! They (cadet cadres) were coming to us and calling us names, right in our faces, telling us to run, to do push-ups and many physical activities that I did not mind to do, but they did not have to be nasty about it! For the next three weeks, everything was intense. I lost a lot of weight. No one was friendly toward us.

It was during one of those days when we were told to get ready for a picture taking event. I got excited and put on my white Iranian Navy uniform in order to make a good impression. Then, the next thing I knew, we were taken to the public bath and shower room. They cornered all the freshmen against the wall and we were packed like 'sardines'. One of the upper classmen was holding a stick in his hand, and pretending to hit us if we didn't pack ourselves in while the rest of them were making jokes and laughing at us. Boy I was angry and so humiliated especially being in my Iranian uniform. Sweats were running all over my head and face, while at the same time my blood was boiling inside me, fixing to explode. I hated what we were there for. If that was their military training, I sure did not want to be part of that. They were acting like a bunch of kids!

WAS I THE ONLY ONE THESE CADET CADRES HATED? *I felt I was being picked on a lot including, being called a 'camel jockey'. But that didn't bother me since I had never ridden a camel before. Nevertheless, I was determined to be the best and go along with their system; that is until the first inspection. That night I stayed up until 2:00 am cleaning up my room, shining my shoes, or anything else I thought needed to be done. I wanted to show everyone that I was the best.*

Saturday morning inspection came. We lined up outside while the officers in charge inspected our clothes, haircuts, shoes, and rifle. Then the cadet officer came to my room to inspect there too. I did well, passing my inspection. The cadet officer congratulated me for having a clean room and moved on to the others.

Well, I was happy about the result of the inspection and was looking forward to a relaxing weekend, especially since I was up so late the night before. In addition, I was looking forward to getting together with the rest of my countrymen to see how they were doing since we had not seen each other for the last two or three weeks. (*Wrong! Another surprise was waiting for me!*)

Saturday Morning Inspection

Once the inspection was over, we were instructed to line up outside of our rooms and the cadets in charge yelled, "Hit it and give us fifty push-ups, you zeros!"

Suddenly, every freshman went down to the ground <u>except me.</u>

"Why?" I asked!

"You have to, because I told you so." One of the cadet officers exclaimed.

All kinds of thoughts were running through my head as I was trying to analyze the situation, and trying to understand why we were being punished! I worked so hard, stayed up late, my room was clean, and I had passed my inspection. Why were they punishing me? I felt humiliated by this action and was getting angry. Blood was rushing through my head as every upper classmen in that hallway was in my face pressuring me to explode! At that moment, I

had no desire to be part of their "game" or that type of behavior.

"You'd better get down and do what we say or you will get demerits!" the officers yelled as they stormed toward me, getting in my face.

"Go ahead and give me demerits!" I responded to them, and pushed my way out and walked off the formation.

Well, that day was the beginning of my misunderstandding about the Citadel and the way the system worked. The following week, I found out about a frightening incident that happened to one of my countrymen. While he was fast asleep, several cadets stormed into his room in the middle of the night, bagged him into a laundry bag, and dragged him all the way down from the 4th floor of the barracks to the middle of the quad. They tied the bag in a knot and left him screaming! He was scared to death!

This experience about my friend put a great deal of fear in me, that they might do the same or something worse to me. As a result, I had to start thinking about how to protect myself against the unknown actions by other cadets.

The door to my room would not lock; therefore, anyone could come in at any time. However, after I heard what happened to my friend, I became more cautious and used my toothbrush to lock the door from the inside. I also slept with a rod by my side (the rod that I used to clean my rifle), just in case someone would try to attack me at night. The situation was so bad that I could not trust anyone anymore. Every night I would be shaken at the slightest noise or movement, opening my eyes to see what was going on. I also told my roommate that I had better not catch him being a part of any conspiracy against me and he never was.

Resigning From the Navy

Many complaints were passed on to the Iranian Naval attaché in Washington, DC and as a result, we had several visits from them to our school; but nothing was changed or done after their visits, even though we were promised otherwise.

However, it was during one of those visits by an Iranian Naval officer to the Citadel that my name came up by the school administrator, claiming that I was not happy with their system and was having a hard time adapting. Then, I was asked to pack up so the naval officer could escort me back with him to Washington and ultimately back to Iran to resign from the Navy. This was shocking and dreadful news for me since I was the only one whose name was mentioned. Actually I figured my friend who was bagged in the laundry bag would go before me. But it was too late and the decisions were made, so I went along with their plan.

On our flight back to Washington DC, the officer who was escorting me fed me a bunch of non-sense scare tactics to frighten me. He said that the consequences of my rebellion would be great for me and my family back home. I did not respond or question him since the verdict was already assumed for me to go home.

It wasn't my idea to go back home. I never minded to be part of the military training. What I had so much problem with, was the unnecessary hazing, name calling, and pressuring us to do something against our will. During my four years of schooling at the Citadel, we participated every summer in some kind of real military training. We went to Norfolk Virginia for Marine training and to Corpus Christi for Aviation training. Another summer I was on board the "USS Joseph-Hewes Destroyer" and I loved every minute of that. But the Citadel's training, to me was a game of "Mickey-mouse" stuff, and very humiliating!

The following day I discovered surprising announcement. Nine other Iranian students protested and were asked to leave the Citadel for the same reason as I was. They joined me in Washington, DC with the same expectation of returning home and to resign from the Iranian Navy. This was good news for me since I felt the Navy was looking down on me and my negative attitude toward the whole thing. But I was not the only one who was disappointed and displeased by the way we were handled by our own Iranian Navy and lack of information concerning the system at the Citadel.

At any rate, we stayed at a hotel in Washington, DC for ten days while they communicated our desire to the Iranian Government to arrange for our trip to go back home for resignation. But due to pride and embarrassment to the Iranian military under Shah Reza Pahlavi, they lied to us by telling us that if we went back home we would be punished. This is what we were told:

1) That they would send us into their prison when we get back to Iran,

66

2) That they would take our father's house for the expenses that they already spent on us, and

3) They would also send our fathers into prison as well.

I didn't mind their threats against me, but their intimidation against my father had a deeper affect on me. They were very shrewd in persuading us to go back to the Citadel by using manipulating words and fear tactics and by scaring us with threats against our families.

So, instead of going back home to Iran, all but two students turned back to the Citadel. These two expressed that they would prefer prison over the Citadel! One of the guys who chose to go back home was the one who was hazed by being bagged inside the laundry bag.

The eight of us came back to the Citadel with our heads hanging down like sheep, scared and embarrassed. As a result, there were rumors all over the campus that the Iranians were trapped here at the Citadel, because if they resigned from the Navy and went back to Iran, they would face prison.

Upon my return to school, I was transferred from "F" company to "H" company. I was trying my best to adapt to the military fraternity system. Everything was going ok for a while, until one morning at the breakfast table after I had served some upperclassmen, a cadet Corporal (who was a member of the "sword drill", who kept their heads shaved in order to intimidate others) was sitting right next to me. He started demanding different things and watching my reactions. When he noticed my frustration, he asked what I was going to do about it "you so and so". He called me names, but when he called my mother a nasty name, I lost my temper! That was the worst thing he could have said, and as a result I punched him in the mouth, almost causing a fight to erupt, but we were stopped by other cadets. That night I was not permitted to sleep in my own bed for my own safety. Instead an arrangement was made for me to spend the night in the infirmary with the other mentally challenged students, ha!

The rumor of that incident was all over the campus within less than an hour. Many congratulated me for standing up to an upper classman, but I was not happy about what happened. In fact, I was terrified for sure to be dismissed from school for having raised my hand to another cadet. Later, I was charged before the school's Court Martial to three hundred hours of confinement and walking tours; which I gladly accepted since I did not want to go back to Iran and their prison!

This Court Martial was conducted by the cadets of the school. Except for the size of the room, it was similar to a real life courtroom. I had to hire my own lawyer to speak on my behalf and there were also witnesses involved. Earlier that week, I had been summoned to meet with a Colonel who was a ranking member of the college staff. He told me that the consequences of what I had done might be severe and may also be cause for my dismissal from the corp. of cadets. It was then that I became terrified of being sent back to Iran to possibly face prison, not to mention the embarrassment this could cause my family. That was not the right way or my intention to be dismissed from a well known school and resign from the Iranian Navy.

Hence, at the court martial, I made it easy for everyone involved and told them how sorry I was for what I had done and that I would accept the responsibility and any punishment they decided to give me. After deliberation, they decided to give me 300 hours of walking tours. Every weekend, I had to walk back and forth on the barrack quadrangle with a rifle on my shoulder until all 300 hours were completed. I gladly accepted this punishment and was very grateful they were not going to send me back to Iran.

Five months later, we heard from the two guys who returned home. They had been able to resign from the Navy without any problems or consequences. There was no such punishment as going to prison or any financial burdens. At that time, we learned a big lesson and our eyes were opened to something new. Our own Iranian Navy lied to us. They kept us here by misrepresentation and deception. I felt so bad in my heart, as though someone whom I trusted the most stabbed me in the back.

Therefore, because of the pressures from the school system on one hand, and lies and deception from our own Navy on the other, we thought twice about what we had gotten ourselves in to and we could not ignore what had just happened to us. This news had caused much disappointment and became the subject of our conversation for many weeks and months to come.

The state of my faith was in question. I didn't know what to pray or who to blame. I felt like I had been hung in mid-air. At times, I felt like I had been thrown to the wolves and I was on my own to stay alive, or like a sheep without a shepherd, lost without purpose or direction. It took me three years to really understand the mission of the Citadel as a military college, and what was the meaning behind all the hazing and non-sense. I just wished we had been better informed before we stepped our foot into that military college.

Now, life outside of the citadel was great. One summer, two of my friends and I traveled to California for sightseeing. We flew to Los Angeles and there we rented a car and cruised the west coast from San Diego to San-Francisco. We went to the HMS Queen Mary, San Diego Zoo, Disney Land, Universal Studios and Hollywood and much more. It was very educational and in some cases weird concerning places and people we met or saw for the first time!

One Christmas holiday I also traveled to San Antonio, Texas by taking a Greyhound bus. This way you can start and stop any place you wish until you reach your destination. So, I stayed a night or two in Atlanta Georgia and toured the historical places there, which was very interesting. Then after visiting my friends Mel and June Curtis in San Antonio I flew to New York and spent a few days there sightseeing the Statue of Liberty, FBI building, United Nations building and much more before heading back to my school. Another Christmas holiday I went home to Iran for a visit which I will talk about in the next chapter.

I spent other summers and holidays around Charleston, Folly Beach and Myrtle Beach with my friends. We shared the expenses to rent an apartment during the summers since the school closed the barracks. I enjoyed learning to cook a few meals by trial and error, but for the most part it turned out good.

There were two other students from Iran at the Citadel before our group came. These two (Hoshi and Siya) failed their courses while they were in England for four years as students and were sent to the Citadel, being a more disciplined school, to finish their courses. So, I decided that I would stay here in the USA for as long as I could before going back home to serve in the dogma of the Iranian Navy, just like Hoshi and Siya.

As a result, I failed one of my courses on purpose. It was my economics course. I just didn't take the required four exams, only the last one during the semester. That did not give me a good enough grade and it brought my average low enough to fail in that course. But as the time passed a new event changed my perspective all together. I will discuss them in my next chapter titled "A New Passage" which encouraged me to finish my courses on time by participating in the summer school program. Thus, it took me four years and one summer session to graduate.

My major course of study was "Business Administration" and my minor was in "Math". I took math to keep my grade point average "GPA" up since it came easy to me. The last course of mathematics that was offered in my courses of study was "linear equations" and I made 100 on it. My worse subject was "American History", and since I was not planning to stay in America at that time, I showed little interest in that subject. But I didn't know what was ahead of me or what God had planned for my life!

Nevertheless, many of us, including myself, stayed here in the United States of America, and said good-bye to the people that we could not trust and work for any more. Later I realized that it was God's will and purpose for my life.

Chapter 5

A New Passage!

It was one of the toughest decisions in my life to stay in a country where I was still struggling with the language, culture, and many other aspects of America life. Here is how a new chapter emerged before my eyes. During my sophomore year at the Citadel, while on a weekend pass from school, I met a young lady by the name of Ursa Jackson. We met on the elevator of the <u>Francis Marion Hotel</u> in Charleston South Carolina, when we both were searching for the snack and drink machines!

My English was very poor, but we managed to talk for quite some time. She invited me to where all her friends were staying and we carried on our conversation for several hours. I believe this meeting was no accident, but ordained by God!

Ursa was from a small town in South Carolina called Bennettsville, which was about three hours away from Charleston. She played the piano at her local church and was encouraged to use her talent and entered a local county contest. She won first place in the contest and received an invitation to Charleston for the state competition.

It was there that I met my future wife, without realizing or expecting it at the time. We were not sure if we would ever see each other again after that early morning encounter. I was planning to go home to Iran soon for the upcoming holidays; but to be courteous to each other we exchanged our names and phone numbers. I told her that I would call her later when I came back from my trip.

The time soon came for me to leave for Iran. I would be there through Christmas and the New Year of 1975, as well as to participate in my sister's betrothal ceremony which took place around the same time.

Incidentally, while we are talking about marriage, let me say that marriage between a man and a woman under the Islamic law is nothing more than an agreement between the two persons. For the most part you don't even have to be in love in order to marry. It is a necessary step based on the natural desire of a man to be married to a woman or women (up to four). It is a very important social covenant and often it is arranged by the families involved.

But marriage between a man and a woman under the Christian doctrine is a picture of Christ and His Church. It is a love relationship. As Christ being the head of His Church and loves her sacrificially. The Church loves Christ as her Lord and follows Him with all her heart. That is why you are to marry only one. But since men or women sometimes lose their focus and get tempted, sin enters their mind and they act as the world does, which is not part of the Christian doctrine or teaching.

While I was there, my brother Parviz gave me his car to drive around as I wished. One morning while driving to the naval personnel office to give an account of my whereabouts, I had difficulty finding a parking space. I was on a one-way street with cars parked on the left and right sides of the road, leaving only enough space for one car to pass through. Suddenly, the driver of a Jeep belonging to the city of Tehran (being obvious by a logo on its side door), attempted to pass and squeeze by me. But due to the tightness of space, his tire guards hit the side of my car. The driver of the Jeep got out of his car, and instead of apologizing for hitting my car, he angrily raised his voice, wanting to blame me for not driving fast enough.   This experience, among many others similar to that, got my attention while at the same time made me feel like being in a "cage".

I was surrounded by people who seemed to always be angry! Perhaps the pressures of life and society had made them like that without them realizing it. These "negative" experiences made me reflect on how different it was in America.

When I first came to the United States, it was very exciting for me, but after a while, I became very apprehensive and uncomfortable because my mind could not digest the amount of freedom that was available here. However, after my trip to Iran in 1975, I realized how much there was to appreciate about this country. It is true that you will see excessive amounts of freedom in most western nations, and many find themselves having a hard time dealing with that, especially those who come from a closed society as mine.

In the USA, you may be faced with many good and bad challenges due to so much freedom but ultimately you decide how to respond to those challenges. As an example: Though I am free to drink alcoholic beverages, I choose not to do. I am free to gamble, but I do not like spend my money that way. I am free to express my thoughts but I refrain from hurting anyone by misuse of my language. I am free to exercise my religious freedom and worship however I want without being considered a second class citizen or being treated badly. I am free from many things but my freedom should not be a license to sin.

But in Iran under the Islamic Republic, you truly feel you are living your life in a "cage"! Government jobs will not be given to anyone except Muslims. Regular job interviews are more about your religious background than your education and talents. You are not allowed to talk negative about your government. If you are a woman, you are not free to uncover your hair in a public place. Television, radio and newspapers are censored. You are told what to do from the time you are born until the time you die! Your credit score depends on what your neighbors say about you. In other words there is not a system of credit check in Iran. Therefore they check your background by asking people who live around you. That is why gossiping and being nosey is very common and expected in Iran!

Today in Iran, dancing, singings, holding hands and other things similar to that have to be conducted within the four walls of your home. You have to get permission to have a wedding festival. No one is allowed to speak against Islam if you wish to live! Other than Islam there are only two other major and one minor religion that are allowed to be practiced there. They are Christianity and Jewish and Zoroastrianism. But they are not free to speak publicly or evangelize about their faith. That freedom belongs to Muslims alone. Most may have rights, but not freedom.

Soon my visit ended and I returned to the USA. As I got off the plane, I felt like kissing the ground and thanking God for the freedom that I could not comprehend until my visit to Iran. Part of the freedom that I am talking about is the freedom of inner man. It feels like a peaceful wind that brushes and touches one's spirit and heart. You feel complete!

I returned to the Citadel and caught up with my schoolwork. Then one evening, I called my new acquaintance, Ursa to ask her if we could see each other again. She was busy with work, school, and church, so we were not able to see each other right away; but, we continued our friendship and kept in touch by writing to each other through the mail. Sometime later she invited me to her home where I met her parents, sister, and brothers along with many other relatives. They were all very kind and welcomed me as their guest. Ursa and her family attended a small church called Calvary Baptist where she was the pianist and her sister, Patricia, was the organist. I attended there with them when I went to visit her. She was also working at a department store called "Kress" while taking secretarial courses at a technical college in a nearby city.

She loved horses and had a couple of them on their farm. She attempted to teach me how to ride one since I was not accustomed to riding or being near them. One day when Ursa was at work, I decided to go for a ride by myself. Big mistake! The horses decided to turn around and go back

77

home and was out of my control! She took off so fast causing me to yell for help! I was fortunate that I did not get hurt, but needless to say I never tried that again!

Since I was committed to the Iranian Navy and was to go back home to Iran after graduation, we did not want to give each other any false hope that we might marry one day. As a result we chose to consider each other as friends. As our relationship grew we became closer and learned more of what we had in common. By visiting Ursa and her family on a regular basis, I was given the opportunity to learn more about typical life in an American family, their customs and traditions, and how people thought about things.

When the Easter holiday came, Ursa and her family invited me to spend the holidays in their home. By the passing of the time Ursa and I became closer and her parents decided that it would be okay if we fixed up one of their spare rooms on the second floor as my bedroom for when I came to visit. When I was on a weekend pass from the Citadel, I would drive to Bennettsville to be with them. And in time, I fell in love with their culture, and the purity of Ursa's heart.

A year later, during my junior year, I made a very courageous and daring decision. I decided to stay in America. A series of events surfaced and even helped in my decision.

One of our Iranian classmates who also was facing the same challenges as the rest of us decided to "jump ship" and left the Citadel that year without finishing his four year term. Then there was another freshman who left the Citadel. He was part of a new group of Iranian freshmen and was having a hard time dealing with the school system as well as the Iranian Navy. As a result he decided to flee to Florida by taking a car belonging to one of his Iranian friends. By this time we were assigned a liaison officer by the Navy to deal with our "issues". The liaison officer soon discovered where he was through the Florida State Police since the car was reported as missing. The officer went to the police department there to pick him up, but on the way back to Charleston, he lost him while they stopped for a bathroom break.

Having a liaison officer was good thing at first but as the time passed it did not please most Iranian cadets. Though he was our line of communication between us and Washington, his actions became more and more intrusive toward most of us. But since I was among the first students to come to the Citadel, he left us alone for the most part, but to the rest of the midshipmen he became a control freak!

No one was allowed to withdraw any of their own money from their bank accounts unless they had a permission slip from him! He was controlling and had to cosign every transaction they made, which involved their salaries. Furthermore none of our concerns were being reported to Washington to our satisfaction.

There was another friend and classmate of mine, Ali, who graduated one semester earlier than the rest of us. He also decided not to go back to Iran. I ran into him during my last semester and got a chance to see his new life he had begun here in the United States. He had a job as an insurance agent and had married a lady he was dating a couple of years earlier. He was one of my roommates during our summer breaks, and a very good friend of mine, but never encouraged anyone to do what he did, including me. But needless to say, many of us were thinking the same, yet kept it secret to ourselves to the very end. It was a combination of many negative issues that caused many of us to turn our eyes to the USA. So I had made my decision to stay here for many reasons, but if I had any doubt all I had to think about was the young lady who had stolen my heart!

It was around my senior year when the news of Ayatollah Khomeini and rumors of uprising in Iran came to us through those new freshmen who came from Iran. This was the first time I was hearing the name of "Ayatollah Khomeini" which was not good news for any of us to hear. I did not think much about him since I felt that the Shah's throne was secure.

It was during my junior year that I went to Ursa's parents to ask for her hand in marriage. Later I wrote a letter to my parents to let them know about my engagement. In response, I was challenged with a long disappointing and rejecting letter. That letter was from my father considering me still as his little child; full of fatherly advice since in my culture, parents mostly arranged marriages and he informed me about several nice, beautiful ladies waiting for my return.

I followed that up with another letter, which contained an apology, informing them that I was joking about the engagement. It was obvious to me that this was not the right time to share this news with my parents, since they would not be able to understand my circumstances or conditions here. I had not discussed these matters completely with them either. I felt bad that I could not talk freely with them by phone or by letter. In addition, I was hoping that by some possibility, conditions would change and I could take Ursa back to my home country after graduation. (Incidentally... we were not allowed to marry any foreign person while working for the Iranian government.)

A few weeks before graduation, in the summer of 1977 an unspeakable feeling came over me. I knew that the time was near for me to make the biggest decision in my life, which was to stay here in the USA and forsake my country of Iran, my parents and the rest of my family. My heart was torn between my love for my family and my love for Ursa. I prayed every chance I had about my choices.

I remember lying down on my bed in my room at the Citadel, crying to God like a baby, asking Him to show me the way... wishing to be a robot, controlled by Him alone. However, after a while I realized that I still had to make a decision as to what to do. Time was coming to a "point of no return."

On one hand, I did not want to dishonor my parents; while on the other hand, I did not want to destroy Ursa's future and break her heart, since I had given her the promise of my love. Honor and loyalty meant a lot to me. The code of conduct instilled by the Iranian Navy did hurt me, and as a result, I lost all my interest in them. My parents, though, still kept their honor and loyalty toward me, which was why I was praying so hard and so desperately needing God's influence and guidance.

I was going through my last summer school and was getting ready for the final exams when I suddenly realized that within weeks I had to make my final decision. In the middle of the week, I rushed to the town of Bennettsville where Ursa lived. It was a three hour ride away from my school. She was glad but surprised when she saw me.

"What is wrong?" She asked. "I need to talk to you," I responded.

Then we drove off toward a farm road, a peaceful area where we could talk and I could share my heart freely. I wanted to know how she felt or would respond to my request to possibly go back home for a short while before marrying her. Then after seeing my parents I would return to the States and marry her.

She said that she understood how I felt about my parents, and that what I was doing by staying here and forsaking my parents she could not do to her family. At the same time, she would not tell me what to do, for the decision was mine to make. She also responded by telling me that she had already mailed the wedding invitations; but if she had to, she would cancel the wedding. She said that she felt in her heart that once I left the country, I would not return anytime soon if at all.

I knew what she was saying was true. To be frank, I could not guarantee my return to the States either, but I needed to hear it from her. So, after hours of heartfelt conversation, I went back to school realizing that I could never be happy working for the Iranian Navy. In addition, if I stayed in the Navy, I would be miles away from where my parents lived and except for a short break, I would not see them regularly either. Nevertheless, I still needed the blessing of my parents in my marriage. It would mean so much to me if my parents would approve of my decision to stay here in the USA so that I could follow my dreams.

After seeking God's will through prayer, talking with Him and expressing my need for the blessings and understanding of my parents, I wrote a long, detailed letter to them. In that letter, I explained the reasons why I chose to stay in the USA, and had a friend of mine who was going back home after graduation to mail it for me in Tehran to prevent anyone (other than my parents) in Iran from reading it.

Shortly after graduation in May, 1977, I flew to Washington D.C. in order to pick up my passport and return ticket to Iran. Even though I had no intentions to go back home, I wanted to have all my documentation with me when I applied for my permanent residency here in the USA.

I hailed a taxi at the airport in Washington D.C. and asked the driver to take me to the Iranian embassy. I asked the taxi driver to wait for me since I was not planning to be there long. I was sitting in the office, talking to one of the personnel hoping to get my passport and ticket right away when the taxi driver came up to where I was. He wanted to know how much longer he had to wait for me. That prompted me to ask the same question from the office personnel as to how much longer it would be. He then told me that the person in charge with the key to the safe was not there yet. The safe was where they kept all the passports and tickets and it would be better for me to pay off the taxi driver.

Finally, after waiting for one hour, I was given my passport and airline ticket. I left the embassy to catch another cab to the airport. I was a bit nervous while walking around the airport, and kept watching behind me to see if anyone was following me, but I noticed nothing out of the ordinary. I flew back to Charleston, SC and said hello to my new life here in the USA.

This was the beginning of a new life for me here in the U.S. and I was very happy in so many ways. But unfortunately about the same time in my home country, it was the beginning of turmoil. This of course, made me sad especially for my family who would have to endure what lay ahead.

Chapter 6

TURMOIL IN IRAN

The end of Shah Reza Pahlavi dynasty

The Shah of Iran visited Washington in November 1977 toward the end of Jimmy Carter's first year as president. I saw many people carrying placards, and demonstrating against the Shah while it was being broadcast on national television. Some of the demonstrators even had their heads covered with grocery bags to prevent being recognized by the Iranian "Savak", the secret police. The welcoming ceremony was held outside on the lawn of the White House. However, the opposition and demonstrations were held against the Shah on the opposite side of Pennsylvania Avenue. There were two groups. One was pro Shah and the other against him. Fights flared up between these two groups and as a result tear gas was used by the police to keep them under control.

The Shah's personal photographer, who was also a good friend of my Dad, came to the USA when the Shah came for this formal visit with President Jimmy Carter. While he was here, he telephoned me to let me know that things were getting bad in Iran. Without going into details he assured me that my decision to stay here was a good one. He also wanted to know if I was okay or if I needed him to tell my

Dad anything. He also assured me that he would tell my Dad not to worry about me. As the time passed, I learned that the state of affairs in Iran was worsening. People were being killed and shots fired almost daily. Demonstrations were occurring in different parts of the city of Tehran as well as other major cities in Iran. Finally since the bloodshed was not achieving any progress, the Shah ordered his military to stop. Consequently with relieve of the military, not retaliating against the people, a revolution escalated across the country.

Later, the Shah of Iran, who called himself "Shah-han-shah, meaning king of kings" and his wife Empress Farah, left Iran. It was indeed a sad day for many who loved him but at the same time many were glad to see him go. Many people in Iran began to celebrate and dance on every corner of the country without realizing that their dance and celebration was only temporary and soon would turn to tears. The Shah said in an interview that he left Iran in order to prevent further bloodshed since he loved his people and what took place after he left was also a shock to him. American television of course was broadcasting all the events as they unfolded before our eyes, including the return of Ayatollah Khomeini later in 1979.

My Dad's friends and coworkers who were familiar with the western cultures and often traveled to Europe on business trips, assured him not to worry about me. Then another call came from one of our relatives who was a technician in the Iranian Air Force and was stationed in England. He also wanted to know if I was okay, but did not discourage me about my plans. He too expressed his concern about the situation in Iran at that time. Those phone calls gave me more peace and comfort about my decision and I felt the presence of God within my mind and soul.

Not long after I graduated in the summer of 1977. Someone from the Iranian Navy's personnel office called my Dad to ask him to come by his office. He did just that.

They asked him about me and wanted to know where I was.

My Dad simply told them "I gave you my son; I am the one who should ask you what you have done to my son; for you are responsible for him, not me."

Suddenly his tone changed and he replied that perhaps, Saiid is sitting next to a blonde lady right now and having a good time.

Dad answered: "I have no knowledge as to where he is or what he is doing. All I know is that I gave him to you and you lost him."

My Dad left his office without any retaliation or pressure from them, but the Navy kept a watch on my Dad's home for two months before they realized that I was not coming home. My family was well respected in our community and everyone knew us well. One of the storekeepers in our community was the one who alerted my family about them watching our house. But, my Dad was not concerned about their spying activities.

Azadi Circle in Tehran, Iran

Meanwhile, in September of 1977, Ursa and I got married and we became "one flesh" according to the teachings of the Christian Holy Bible. I also accepted my new faith, called Christianity, and was baptized in the water by its symbolic tradition and declared it publicly.

Though I was assured of my decision to stay here, there were still some strange and uneasy feelings in the back of my mind. The reason was this; since Iran had been a close ally to the Unites States, I was afraid that the Shah may ask for his men back and the USA might honor his wishes and we would be sent back to Iran against our will. As a result, during our marriage ceremony and before the exchange of our vows, my mind and eyes were searching all through the congregation for a possible objection from an Iranian naval representative. Then when the pastor asked the usual "Does anyone have any objection to this marriage? Speak now or forever hold your peace." My stomach knotted up for a few moments, until I heard no response from the congregation and I breathed a sigh of relief! Then he continued with the rest of the ceremony.

"I whispered to myself, you didn't have to ask that question, but Thanks to God, no one was there to object and everything turned out all-right."

Although, I understood the very basic doctrine of Christianity, I still had a long way to go in my spiritual growth. I was like a baby in this new faith, yet eager to learn and understand everything about this religion.

Unfortunately, early on in my faith and before Ursa and I were married, the pastor of Calvary Baptist Church who baptized me did a very deceitful thing. He talked me into giving him $1000 to invest in a made-up investment firm, and told me that whenever I needed that money he would give it back to me with interest added to it. At that time, I had no reason not to trust him, but it turned out he was nothing more than a con-artist. When I asked for the money back to use for our honeymoon, he put me off and avoided me.

I ran into him by accident a few weeks before our wedding, as we passed each other on the road. I motioned him to stop and he did. He wrote me a check and asked me not to cash it until the next day since he was on his way to the bank to deposit a certified check. Well, that check bounced like a rubber ball and I never saw him again. We were not able to go on a honeymoon right after our wedding, but we were fine with that and went to our home we were going to rent to start our new life together.

I learned a very valuable lesson in my new faith. We may come in to contact with many good and bad individuals during our lifetime; but when it comes to our faith, always remember that the only perfect person who ever lived and now lives in Heaven is the Lord Jesus Christ. He is the best role model for those who are seeking the **Truth**.

The same year I applied for my permanent residency to the United States of America. I had made up my mind that I would pursue everything legally so I could be free from any obstacles here or when I travel outside of this country.

In the year 1978, a year after our marriage, my Mom and Dad informed me that they were planning to come to the USA. My older brother Parviz died in a car accident and left behind his wife with a six-month old baby. I was here far away and my parents felt as if they had lost me too. These two events back to back killed my Mom's spirit. She had never flown in an airplane before; in fact she was very uncomfortable, and would get migraine headaches very easily, but was willing to do whatever that was necessary to see me. They did not tell me anything about my brother's death because they did not want to upset me or make me feel guilty. They wanted to tell me in person. This had happened before I got married so they had hoped that when I returned to Iran I would take care of my brother's wife and child. But by this time they knew this was not possible and that God had other plans for me.

We met and welcomed them at the New York J.F.K. Airport. They met my wife and her Mom, Molly, who traveled with us, for the first time. Ursa, my wife was also expecting our first child, Crystal, when they arrived.

They stayed with us for a few months, and this gave us lots of time to catch up on everything that had happened in our lives. It also gave them an opportunity to get to know my wife and her family whom they approved of very much. They saw that I was safe and happy and when they left, they were satisfied I had made the right decision.

They came back several more times after that visit and it was during one of those visits several years later when they brought my younger brother, Hamid, for me to take care of here in the USA.

God indeed answered my prayers when I poured my heart out to Him the day that I was in my dormitory, asking Him to make me a robot, wishing to have the blessings of my parents in my marriage. God is faithful and true.

Chapter 7

Growing in Faith

Before my conversion to Christianity, I studied the Gospels and asked numerous questions while participating in a Sunday school class at my wife's church, Calvary Baptist. I was in agreement with most of what I was reading in the Bible regarding God and His power. Therefore, when it said that Jesus was able to perform miracles, it was not difficult for me to accept that statement, for I was taught by my religious teachers in Iran while going to high school that Prophets of God were all holy and able to do the same.

Muslims believe: "In Islam, Prophets are men selected by God or "Allah", to be his messengers. Muslims believe that Prophets are human and not divine, though some are **able to perform miracles** to prove their claim. Islamic Prophets are considered to be the closest to perfection of all humans, and are uniquely the recipients of divine revelation either directly from God or through angels. The Prophet of Islam was given a number of miracles, but the best and lasting miracle is – the Quran. The Quran is lasting and permanent. Its guidance and inspiration did not fade and always animated people in their journey towards perfection!

Islamic theology says that all of God's messengers since Adam, preached the message of Islam — submission to the will of the one God.

Islam is described in the Quran as "the innocent nature upon which God created mankind", and the Quran states that the proper name "Muslim" was given by <u>Abraham</u>." (Fundamentals of Islamic beliefs by Ayatollah Noori)

Now, to justify my old faith as a Muslim and while in search of my new Christian faith, I came up with this answer using verse 3:84 from the Quran as my example: <u>Allah theoretically saying this to Mohammad</u>

QURAN SURA 3:84 Say: "We believe in Allah, and in what has been revealed to us and what was revealed to Abraham, Isma'il, Isaac, Jacob, and the Tribes, and in (the Books) given to Moses, Jesus, and the Prophets, from their Lord. We make no distinction between one and another among them, and to Allah do we bow our will (in Islam)."

That is, Christians and Jews were considered as Muslims too, since they bowed down in submission to the same God. So when someone asks me if I am a Muslim, I immediately answer "yes" for I submit myself to the same God and trust Him as my Lord and Savior. But if you mean by the word "Muslim" as someone who follows in the footstep of Muhammad, the answer is "no", because just as the Muslims claim, he died. But the LORD lives forever!

Now, as I continued my search for the "truth", I was faced with the next verse which created more questions in my mind and ultimately sheds a different light.

QURAN SURA 3:85 "If anyone desires a religion other than Islam (submission to Allah), never will it be accepted of him; and in the hereafter He will be in the ranks of those who have lost (all spiritual good)."

This verse contradicts the previous one by rejecting other religions other than Islam. By that I mean that the Muslims understood and were taught this verse as meaning to follow in the footsteps of Muhammad. The answer to this assumption became clearer as I read other verses in the Quran, and the gap got wider between Islam and other religions and my questions turned to doubt.

Here is another example: As for the Christians and the Jews, the order is to subdue them and impose on them a penalty tax, after humiliating them and if they resist, kill them. (Sura 9:29)

This Sura got me disturbed. So, I decided to read other translations for more clarity. Sadly it did not get any better!

QURAN TRANSLATED BY YUSUF ALI SURA 9:29 "Fight those who believe not in Allah, nor the Last Day, nor hold that forbidden which hath been forbidden by Allah and His Apostle, nor acknowledge the religion of truth, (even if they are) of the People of Book, until they pay the tax with willing submission, and feel themselves subdued."

QURAN TRANSLATED BY SHAKIR SURA 9:29: "Fight those who do not believe in Allah, nor in the latter day, nor do they prohibit what Allah and His Messenger have prohibited, nor follow the religion of truth, out of those who have been given the Book, until they pay the tax in acknowledgment of superiority and they are in a state of subjection."

Many declarations from the Quran sounded good, but were they? As you see, this type of double talk does not match what is in the Bible, (Jewish Torah or Christian Injil "the gospel"). God does not suddenly change to new guidelines or laws in His holy book that are contrary to what He already sent down.

Quran says that the true Christians and Jews will go to paradise, then in another Sura expresses not to take them as friends! I suppose they call the true Christians and Jews by their new name, "Muslims"!

And, the statement (*Muslims believe that Prophets are human and not divine, though some are able to perform miracles to prove their claim*) could not be true as taught by Mullahs or Imams. As an example, Moses who is recognized as one of the great Prophets of God by Muslims, Jews, and Christians did not perform any miracles by his own power. He could not even speak well, much less perform miracles. Aaron his brother was his spokesman. Every miracle that happened was done precisely as God commanded Moses to say or do. In fact, in all cases, God is the One who causes miraculous events to happen.

Psalm 77:14 Says: "You are the God who does wonders; you have declared your strength among the people".

In other words God is the One who does wonders or miracles. He is the One who can make something out of nothing; He is the One who can part the Red Sea by a single command; and He is the One who can walk on this earth in the form and appearance of a man if He chooses to do so! We cannot underestimate the power of God, His sovereignty and will is beyond human mind and logic. He does not have to report to or convince anyone, and we certainly cannot put Him in a "box" to fit our logic and limited understanding.

But because of my limited knowledge, and lack of wisdom about Christianity, my mind was rejecting two very important statements at that time:

*The first was why they called Jesus the "**Son of God**"?*

How could God have a Son? Moreover, why, with all His power, could he not save Himself from being crucified on the cross? Yet, he made blind men see, cured the sick and diseased, raised the dead, fed five thousand with a small boy's lunch, walked on the water, calmed a storm on command, and much more.

*The second was why the preachers of the gospel call us "**sinners**".*

I could not grasp whom they were referring to when they said that we are sinners, for I did not consider myself a bad person!

As a Muslim, we were taught that if we do more good deeds than bad we could go to heaven. **(But who could decide and measure that besides God***?)*

Therefore, I considered myself a good person since so far in my life I had done more good deeds than bad. *(I measured it. Ha ha!)*

However later, I began to understand that even though I was not such a bad person in comparison to others, I was still a sinner compared to our Holy God. The Prophet Isaiah said:

"But we are all like an unclean thing, and all our righteousness are like filthy rags; We all fade as a leaf, and our iniquities, like the wind, have taken us away." (Isaiah 64:6)

While Paul the Apostle of Jesus Christ echoes the same statement by saying:

"For all have sinned and fall short of the glory of God," (Romans 3:23).

You see God is holy, pure, and sinless while I am not. Therefore, in order for me to go to where He is, there must be a mediator, and that person is none other than Jesus Christ who is also holy, pure and sinless.

Again we read in the Bible: "For He made Him who knew no sin to be sin for us, that we might become the righteousness of God in Him." (2Cor. 5:21)

It was then when I realized that I was a sinner, and needed a Savior in my life. You may ask "why was God answering your prayers before you accepted the faith of Christianity?"

Although I did not understand everything yet about Christianity, a couple of things became very clear to me:

1) We are all under the dispensation of grace, therefore the whole world benefits. "He makes His sun rise on the evil and the good, and sends rain on the just and on the unjust."(Matthew 5:45)
2) God knows us before we are even born! He knows our hearts, attitudes, and motives. He provides many opportunities for us to accept Him and the gift of His grace. We are the ones who reject God by refusing to obey or accept the gift of His grace.

My Conversion

Jesus said, "No one can come to me unless the Father who sent me draws him; and I will raise him up at the last day." (John 6:44)

Since the desire of finding the truth was in my heart, especially the truth about the Son of God, the Father was drawing me to Himself. I was so eager to know Him that I did not mind asking tough questions as they came to my mind. I must admit that sometimes the answers were neither clear nor satisfactory, yet I continued "searching" and "knocking".

There were doubts at times and I was already beginning to have some concerns and thoughts pertaining to my family back home and the state of their faith.   But, I needed to know for myself before I could even think of others. I knew Christianity had to be a good religion since they also were teaching about God and His laws. I agreed to a water baptism before our wedding but missed the meanings behind that ordinance.

2 Corinthians 5:17 says: "If anyone is in Christ, he is a new creation; old things have passed away; behold all things have become new".

As a result, the day after I was baptized I went to look for this new creation by looking into a mirror after my water baptism! Boy! I was wrong I just got wet, and failed to understand what really took place. But I did not let that to be an obstacle in my path and continued to search and pray to know Jesus as God.

Another day as I was praying, I asked God to please help me understand the meaning of the Scripture when it refers to Jesus as the "Son of God". I then asked Him that if Jesus was truly the "Son of God", to please place Him in my heart so I would accept Him by faith.

A short while later after Ursa and I were married, an opportunity came my way. We were invited to go to Atlanta, Georgia with a group of three families to participate in a five-day seminar. The subject was "Basic Youth Conflicts" with Bill Gothard as our speaker. We were there to listen and learn those principals as the instructor used the Bible and God's principles in the above subject. The auditorium was packed with thousands of men and women who loved the Lord Jesus so much, and who wanted to learn His principles and it's applications in their daily life. Many came from far away cities. Some came in campers and RV's and some flew in by plane. It was an awesome meeting! I loved every minute we spent there. At the end of the five days, Bill Gothard gave an invitation to anyone who wished to accept Christ as his or her Lord and Savior. I raised my hand and repeated the "sinner's prayer", asked Jesus to come into my heart. Suddenly my doubts about Jesus as the Son of God disappeared. Everything was clear to me, just as I could see the palm of my hand. As the scripture says:

"And it shall come to pass that whoever calls on the name of the LORD shall be saved". *(Acts 2:21)*

Jesus answered the prayer I had offered up several weeks earlier and erased any reservation or question I had about Him. My heart lit up with a clear understanding about who Jesus was, which the Holy Spirit revealed to me.

From that point on I pursued my new faith with much excitement and by participating in His church and reading His book, the Bible, the Word of God, and by daily prayers. I have included the "Plan of Salvation" at the end of this book for those who are seeking the **Truth**.

Back row: My wife (Ursa), my Mom, me (Saiid), my Dad
Front row: Alyson, Crystal, Elizabeth and Majid (Parviz's son)
Hamid is taking the picture

My parents made several trips to the USA to see me. On their third trip in august of 1985 they brought with them Hamid, my younger brother, to stay with me. This also proved their blessings and approval on my decision to stay here. But getting Hamid into the country was not easy. I made several phone calls and sent faxes to the late Senator Strom Thurman's office in South Carolina. After spending a week in Germany with some relatives and with the help of the Senator, Hamid arrived here in the U.S. He lived with us for about two years, learning English and going to school until he found his way around and became self-sufficient. During that time he met a young lady by the name of Tina Glinski and got married in 1988. We lived in Florence S.C. at the time, and a few years later, they moved to Charlotte N.C. right after we moved to Asheville, N.C. Being very interested in theology and spirituality, he also converted to Christianity in 1992. God has blessed them with two Godly children Nicholas and Maggie and to this day all are very active in their church. Most recently Nicholas made a decision to become a priest!

A few years later God impressed upon my heart to go back and study the Quran as well as other resources to make sure I did not overlook anything. Part of my heart was still thinking back, wishing to find a common ground concerning salvation in both religions. But, if that was not going to be the case, I wanted to share the gospel with my family back home as well as other Muslim brothers or sisters who were still caught up in a religion of **"salvation by works"**.

On one occasion when my parents were here in the USA, we made a trip to Washington D.C. While there, we visited a mosque and I purchased a copy of the Quran in Arabic and English, translated by Yusuf Ali. I read the Quran throughout several times. I also listened to the audio version of the Quran over the Internet.

I also listened and read the transcript of several sermons by Sheikh Ahmad Deedad, a well-known and outspoken Sheikh who spoke against Christianity as it exist today. But the more I read the Quran and other resources (Books from Ayatollah Noori, Ahmad Deedad and others) the more I became disappointed about what I was reading in comparison to what the Bible teaches. I also found several profound verses in the Quran that I will discuss here as well.

My initial reaction was that in many verses, the Quran claimed to know everything about the merciful Allah, yet at the same time it was putting down all other religions outside of Islam.

Second: If anyone pointed to the errors and the contradictions in the Quran (which, there are many), Mullahs or Ayatollahs alike quickly pointed to the lack of understanding of the Arabic language and its interpretations. Then why did they translate the Quran to other languages if they were going to question it?

Third: Muslim communities as a whole were still holding to the traditions of Muhammad. Everyone I met always used the 'hadith' or sayings of Muhammad as their motives. Their Islamic laws for the most part are drawn from the Quran and the life of Muhammad even though it does not agree with today's social system and standards.

One example is this, "If any of your women are guilty of lewdness, take the evidence of four reliable witnesses from amongst you against them; and if they testify, confine them to houses until death do claim them, or Allah ordain for them some other way such as 100 flogging. But if two men among you are guilty of lewdness, punish them both, but if they repent leave them alone; for Allah is Oft-returning, Most Merciful!" Sura 2:15-16 (two rules for the same crime!)

At the end of a movie called (The Message), which was about the life of Muhammad, the announcer in the movie said: "If anyone worshipped Muhammad, let it be known that he is dead, but whoever worshipped God, let it be known that He is alive forever." Unfortunately in my opinion, the Islamic community as a whole put more emphasis on Muhammad than God! That's why they get so upset when someone draws a picture and calls it the picture of Muhammad, knowing that is not a true picture since they have not seen him. The message of Islam should have been only one thing; **"God is One"**. Worship Him only with all your heart, mind and soul and the right path to Him is Jesus Christ as you see in the next verses. This is the same message that has been given to the early fathers. As the Quran confirms the same in these verses:

Sura 3:50 And I (Jesus) have come confirming that which was before me of the Taurat (Torah), and to make lawful some of that which was forbidden unto you. I come unto you with a sign from your Lord, so keep your duty to Allah and <u>obey me</u>.

3:51 Truly! Allah is my Lord and your Lord, so worship Him. This is the Straight Path.

Jesus said that His life verified or confirmed what the Prophets had spoken about Him in the previous scriptures. The old Prophets spoke much about Jesus Christ. There are over three hundred prophesies (foretelling) about Jesus.

Jesus told us that our duty to God is to obey him (Jesus)! To show your highest respect to God, you must obey Jesus. The only command of Jesus that we find in the Quran is here in 3:50.

The command is clear, "Obey me". Later you will see an amazing promise of a blessing given to those who obey Jesus. Where do we find the commands of Jesus? They are found in the Injil (Gospel of Jesus Christ). How can you do your duty to God and obey Jesus unless you know what he has commanded you to do? You must find out what the Injil says so that you can know how to obey Jesus? The same Injil that Mohammed used is available today. When you find an Injil, be sure to check to see if it was translated from the original language written from manuscripts from the 1st century.

A road or path always leads us to something or someone. The Straight Path mentioned in this ayah (verse) is the road that leads us to God. It is a straight and direct road to God. There are no bypasses or turns. It is a direct path, which means that it does not stop short of its intended goal, which is heaven. So, who can travel on this path to God?

The answer is those who obey Jesus!"

(*A complete Muslim by Kevin Greeson and Quran*)

Just as some of those Pharisees or teachers of the law missed the mission and purpose of Jesus, many Ayatollahs or the teachers of the Quran misinterpret the message of Jesus today. But, they do claim that it is the same message as the one in the hands of 'the people of the book' that is the Jews and Christians.

Fourth: they all sin so naturally yet they sweep it under the rug as though it never happened, claiming that Allah will forgive them since they were Muslims.

Fifth: Islam as I know it is not the religion of peace and tolerance as they claim it to be, though there are many good people among them. Islam will not produce salvation, only obligation!

Sixth: Getting anywhere, especially in government profession in Iran belong to those who claim Islam as their religion.   I was listening to an interview of a young

Christian lady who just graduated from a university in Iran, and wanted to continue her education. This is what she said in her interview: When she applied to a school of Law in Iran, she was rejected. She was told that we do not need you for two reasons: Number one, you are a woman and number two, you are a Christian. We do not need either one as a lawyer in Iran!

Again I saw another news clip when a group of Islamic radicals using threats and painting remarks to retaliate against Mrs. Shirin Ebadi, an Iranian Muslim lawyer, human rights activist and a Nobel Peace Prize winner. They wanted to shut down her law office in Iran while police stayed at a distance and watched, because she was an outspoken woman lawyer, defending Iran's minority.

In so many instances Muhammad taught that if you do good deeds as small as giving water to a thirsty dog, you could gain paradise, yet at the same time he claimed that no one is assured of the paradise. Only Allah will decide who will go to heaven or who will not "insha-allah" meaning, God willing! And he is right to say that. No one is going to heaven unless their sin is wiped away, because where God is there is no sin. And that's why and for that very reason, Jesus who is called the 'Christ' came to this world to redeem mankind. This is why that is so important for us to put our trust in Jesus, our Lord and King and Redeemer. **Because, Muhammad is not able to save anyone! He is a man just like the rest of us, in need of a savior.**

Chapter 8

My Career with Radio Shack

Almost eight months before my graduation from the Citadel, I stopped at a Radio Shack store in Laurinburg, NC to purchase a turntable. The store owner and his wife were from New York and were very friendly toward me. They spoke very highly of Radio Shack as a good place to work. Though I was not searching for a job, they offered me a store catalog and pointed out the "employment opportunity" section where I could inquire, if ever I were interested in a job with the company.

Later when I made my decision to stay here in the U.S. in August of 1977, I applied at Radio Shack as a full time manager trainee. Being new in the work force in this country, I was apprehensive and afraid at first and was not sure if people would respond positive to me especially with my heavy accent. But soon I learned that people were accepting me for who I was and at that time never encountered any problems. In less than a year, I became manager of my own store in Greenville, SC, became a very successful salesperson, awarded a gold ring and won several trips as incentives.

After two years with Radio Shack, I felt I should move on to other opportunities, so I applied for a position at Duke

Power. The person who interviewed me was very nice and the interview went well. Then he asked me if I had my citizenship or "green card" which is the permanent residency card since that was required and was considered necessary for employment with them. I had applied for my permanent residency some time back and had gone through all the necessary paper work, health check and interviews and was waiting to hear from them. I was afraid they had rejected it since it had been so long, but I told him I would pursue it that very day.

So, with much excitement and full of hope, yet scared of rejection, I left the Duke Power personnel office, and headed home, to call the Immigration and Naturalization Service. The telephone rang several times but no one was there to answer my call. I had to leave a message on their answering machine and told them who I was and the reason for my call. Within a week from the time I called, and to my surprise, my 'green card' came in the mail and was in my hand without me talking to anyone any further. Apparently, they were waiting for someone to call and claim it. I praised God for His intervention and was excited about the possibility of a new job. As soon as I could, I went back to Duke Power to inquire about the job, but they informed me that the position was no longer available.

The more I thought about that event, the more I realized that God had a hand in it. It wasn't meant for me to have that job, but it sure prompted me to make that phone call to the INS! This resulted in the peace and assurance I needed that He would take care of me (little miracles of God)!

108

Have you ever wondered how God answers our prayers without you hearing a single audible voice from His mouth? God, miraculously opens some doors while at the same time shuts some as a guide for his children. He is unpredictable yet faithful. He is undetectable by our five human senses, yet authentic and genuine and can be recognized by our spirit through faith. I gave Him the praise and glory for that miracle. I then immediately applied for my citizenship and received my Naturalization papers with no problems or difficulties. It was as if God had already paved the road for me. And yes, I am still working for the Radio Shack Company after thirty two years. WOW!
God blessed us in our marriage and with our three children, Crystal, Alyson, and Elizabeth.

We were blessed to be able to raise our children without the need for a regular babysitter or daycare since my wife was able to stay home. They are truly gifts from God that were added to what He already blessed us with, and have brought much joy to our lives.

After living in Greenville, SC for a few years we moved to Florence, SC in order to be closer to Ursa's parents and stayed there for approximately 11 years.

In the year 1985, something unexpected happened which caused me to be involved as a witness in a court of law. A customer came to my store and purchased a telephone recording control to record his personal calls. But instead, he used it to wiretap his wife's telephone conversations without her knowing about it. He did indeed catch her and this resulted in him getting custody of their children. This particular story hit the national media that year and later on my store became part of the 20/20 T.V. program. John Stossel, the consumer reporter, and his crew were in my store. My store was in the middle of some minor construction and not ready for any kind of publicity, so I suggested for them to go to the store across town not knowing what was going on. But they insisted on doing their story in my store. They did not disclose what they were doing except that they wanted to do a story around electronic stores in general. Luckily my supervisor, Terry Kipick, was there at the time, so I directed them to him. I saw their camera crew shooting at anything they possibly could. Then I noticed the cameraman was aiming his camera toward the telephone recording device. When we saw the 20/20 program that weekend, it all became clear that it was about wiretapping and my store was one of the stores among many others in the story. Later that year I had to sit as a witness for the case of the man who bought the recording device from me. It was an interesting experience for me and I got to see first hand how the justice system works in this country.

Although I had mixed emotions about what people's motives were when they sued each other.

In July of 1989, I put in a request to transfer to Asheville, NC with my job. My request was granted. Our home was sold right away, the buyer paying in cash! The buyer even purchased my entire entertainment system and satellite equipment, which turned out to be great for us since we were going to live in a camper for the next year and half.

Ursa and I wanted our children to be able to start at their new school at the beginning of the school year, so I moved them to Asheville while I stayed behind at my brother's house for a few more months until my transfer store became ready.

That fall, during the time I was staying with my brother, Hurricane Hugo hit our region and destroyed much of eastern South Carolina, including the city of Florence where we lived. We lost our electricity for days. There were food and ice shortages and generators were all sold out in several States. If we had not sold our home at the time we did, our move would have been delayed or cancelled for a long time. Fortunately, and by the grace of God, my wife and children were already in Asheville living in a 32 foot camper, which had three bunk beds for the children. They stayed at a KOA campground for several months while we attempted to find a piece of land to purchase and to build our house on.

Before school started, Ursa looked for a suitable school where she wanted the children to attend. Once she decided on a school, she began to look for a piece of land in the same community for our future home and where we could keep our horse as well. Finding a piece of land at a reasonable price was not easy since we wanted it to be close to schools and town. Most property for sale was on the side of a mountain covered with lots of trees, which would be very expensive to clear and grade to build a house on. But once again God was good to us. Ursa found three acres of flat land with a barn and a creek that bordered it, so the horses would be able to drink water and have shelter. We

111

considered ourselves fortunate to find this flat piece of property for sale at a reasonable price in the mountains of Western North Carolina. She secured it with a deposit, and later we moved our camper right on the property. But because we lived in such a small place, we had to rent a storage building for most of our belongings.

One day, not long after we had been there, the pastor of a local church stopped by to meet us and to see if we needed anything. I suppose he felt sorry for us since it appeared we were living like gypsies! We had been visiting churches in the area, but had not decided yet where we belonged, so of course he invited us to his church, Gashes Creek Baptist Church. We loved the church and the people there, and soon we knew it was where God wanted us to serve. Rev. Hilton Moore, his wife Dot and daughter, Stephanie, became very dear friends and were our neighbors as well. They lived only a few houses up from us, and among many other acts of kindness, allowed us to move our things we had in storage into their basement. This was such a blessing since it saved us so much money.

We lived in that camper for almost a year and half and were very happy, but as the winter approached, we faced some challenges. At night, the winter winds would blow, causing the camper to shake and making it difficult to sleep. Sometimes when it was really cold, the pipes would freeze and we would have no water. And many nights, we would run out of propane gas in the middle of the night which of course was our source of heat! The diesel car I had didn't do well in the winter months. Needless to say, we had our hands full! But our hope was elsewhere. Even though things were tough at times, we never let our circumstances get us

down.   Now when we think back on those days, we
remember them fondly. Living in such close quarters wasn't
always easy, but it taught us a lot about each other and what
was important. My dad even came to visit while we were
living there, but thank goodness he was able to go back and
forth between our family and Hamid and his family in
Charlotte!   But I will tell you it was a beautiful sight when
we were finally able to see our new home being built.   It
gave us hope and we couldn't wait until the day we could
move in!

*This experience often reminds me of the short time we
live here on this earth. Our house on this earth is temporary
like a tent, but our real home is in heaven, where it is not
built by human hands, but by God's. Our hope is to one day
to be there, see the glory of His Majesty, and be in His
presence forever.*

We enjoyed going to our new church and became
involved in the many activities that were offered.   The
children were happy and enjoyed their classes and activities
as well.   We were happy to be in a place where we felt
unconditional love and where our children were being taught
Godly principals.

As our children became older and became part of the
youth group, we began going on annual beach retreats with
them to a Christian retreat center in Garden City, S.C. We
did this for several years and enjoyed it very much.   One
year while we were gone, our house was broken in to. Many
things were taken, especially electronics, and the house left
in chaos!   The police came and took a report and did
fingerprinting, but could not give us much hope that they
would be able to find out who had done such a terrible thing.

At first, we were afraid, not knowing who had done this or if they would be back. We all slept together on the living room floor for several nights because we were so afraid. Right after it happened, I had informed all my neighbors about the incident in hopes that they may have seen something or somebody that looked suspicious, but they had seen nothing.

I won't say that it was easy, but we felt God telling us that we needed to pray for and forgive those who had broken into our home   What good would it do for us to be angry and resentful towards people who so apparently and desperately needed to know the love of Christ! Well, a few days later, one of our neighbors called and asked the specifics of the TV that we were missing. Her son lived in the basement of their home and she had noticed a TV and some other electronics that she did not recognize. Sure enough, it was ours and it turned out that her son and some other neighbor boys had been a part of the break-in. I went to see them and their parents and, showed them my love and forgiveness, but since we had already filed a police report, we had to let justice run it's course. We just hoped that the light punishment they received would be enough to deter them from future criminal activities.

Since things were more expensive in western North Carolina compared to where we used to live in South Carolina, we felt the need for extra income, so we prayed for a job for my wife. She had not worked outside of our home the past 12 years since our first child was born. Suddenly God's grace poured out on us again and He provided a job for her at Fairview Family Physicians, which was directly across from the elementary school where our children attended!

This is how it happened: One day after a doctor's visit I asked one of the ladies there if they were looking for someone to fill a secretarial position, which was the training my wife had.   I thought I had seen an advertisement for that position in the paper. They informed me that they were really in need of a phlebotomist and x-ray technician and were planning to ask my wife to fill the position. I told them that my wife's schooling was secretarial and that was all she knew, but two of them responded in unison that they were willing to teach her everything she needed to know on the job. WOW! Isn't God so good!

I was so excited about the news, and how God was providing a job so close to the school and our home. I came home and encouraged my wife to go back and speak with someone about that position. She applied for the position and got the job. She spent the following weeks being trained for the job, which she was able to easily grasp. She enjoyed what she did very much. She had actually wanted to be a nurse when she was much younger, but the technical school she attended did not have a nursing program. So she took the secretarial classes instead.

God provided this job for my wife, and to this day, she is still working for the same practice, although it has expanded and has moved to a new location, called Parkway Medical Group.

Chapter 9

30 YEARS LATER
MY FIRST TRIP TO IRAN UNDER ISLAMIC REPUBLIC

My Mom and Dad came to see us several times over the years. But as they aged, they were not able to travel as often, especially trips outside of Iran. In addition, I missed my sisters and had never even met their families. My youngest sister was only seven years old when I left. Now she was married and had had three children! The oldest one was the only one who was married when I left. Now they were all married with families of their own. I had been hearing that my dad's health was not very good. He was losing his eyesight, his legs were giving out, and with his heart attack a few years back, it made me realize the need to go back to Iran and see my family before his health deteriorated any further.

So, after thirty years I made plans to go back to Iran. My wife was concerned for my safety since there was still fear of what might happen to me when I re-entered the country subsequent to staying in the USA after graduation. I reassured her that I had not done anything wrong against this new government. The old government was gone and based on the advertisements that I had seen regarding this new government, Iranians who lived abroad, were being encouraged to come back to their homeland. They claimed that they were willing to forgive and give amnesty to all those who left the country during the Shah's reign or under the old government.

The early part of the revolution was very hard for many Iranians who lived abroad in the USA or Europe, and who commuted to Iran to see their family and relatives. They faced all sorts of hardships such as being kept beyond their vacation time or their passports purposefully being misplaced. However, as the time passed, Mr. Khatami, a reforming president, was elected, and those hardships began to calm down and pressures were eased on the commuters. Many of my friends informed me that things had improved and for me not to be concerned about facing any problems.

At first, my brother Hamid and I had made plans to travel together in the month of September of 2003, but due to some demonstrations in Tehran and the surrounding area I changed my plans. For more than a week, university students in Iran had been staging nightly protests. They were chanting for democratic reform. Some clashed with riot police. Some called for the death of Ayatollah Ali Khamenei, Iran's supreme religious leader. Still others denounced Iran's elected president, Mohammad Khatami. I did not want to have any delays in my return back to the United States so I decided to delay my trip, but Hamid continued with his plans and made his trip to Iran with a friend whose name is Muhammad and who lives also in Charlotte NC.

The following March, which also corresponds with the Iranian New Year, one of my dear friends, Mohsen (also a converted Christian) and I traveled to Iran together. Mohsen came to the United States the same time I did and we were classmates at the Citadel.   This was his first return trip to Iran as well.

"I was hesitant, concerned, but at the same time excited for my husband when he started talking about going back home to see his family It had been almost 30 years since he had been back to Iran, but from the first time he mentioned it, I knew I could not discourage him. Deep down I wanted to say "No, don't go" but in my heart I knew I couldn't. After all, he knew the risks as well or better than I did. He had made the decision to stay here and marry me all those years ago, knowing it could be a very long time before he could go back again to see his family. He had sacrificed for me which was something I know I could not have done; to leave my family indefinitely not knowing when I would see them again. So I could not take that away from him. He had intentionally waited until our girls had grown up and had a life of their own so that if something ever did happen, they were taken care of. Besides, one of the reasons he was so excited about his decision was that he felt strongly that the time was right to go and share Jesus Christ with his family. And believing that certainly helped me to accept and support his decision and to commit to pray for him."

Ursa

Mohsen and I were very excited about our trip, but uneasy as well. As the plane approached Mehrabud airport in Tehran, suddenly almost everyone in the plane started talking, moving around and changing clothes, especially the women. The dress code had to be Islamic for all who lived in or visited Iran, whether you were Muslim or not. You were required to change your attire to match the expectation of the country and its ruling.

When the plane landed, silence and stillness took over the atmosphere. You could hear a pin drop. The air was so tense and stressful. My stomach was curled up like a knot! Once the plane stopped, we exited the plane, moved down the steps and boarded the buses that were lined up close by. The bus took us toward the gates to customs. It was late and dark, but you could still spot the airport police who were standing at every corner, watching people as they came in. They guided us toward the booths where our visa or passports were being checked. As I was standing in line, I could see a man on the other side trying to get someone's attention waving his hands. I did not realize that it was me he was waving at until I got through customs, and then I learned that he was the husband of one of my nieces!

There were at least four booths there that we could approach to show our passport or visa for the entry stamp. Each booth had a door about four feet tall and was three feet away from a booth with an officer inside. They kept the doors locked except to let passengers through one at a time by pushing a button to open it. When my turn came, I went in and showed my Iranian and American passports, but the officer only reached for my Iranian passport, not even acknowledging my American one. He then checked for the originality of the passport, asked a couple of questions, and stamped my entry to Iran. The people who worked at the Mehrabud Airport in Tehran seemed to be nice and eager to welcome us, but at the same time, their demeanor appeared serious and questionable. I was praying to be able to answer their questions without any hesitation, and not to run in to any problems at all. I held my breath and waited patiently until we were outside of the terminal and on the streets of Tehran.

A couple of my relatives were there to greet and help me with my luggage before we left the restricted area. After I picked up my luggage and left the inspection area, we went outside of the terminal where all of my family had been waiting patiently. They showered me with kisses, hugs and flowers. I was so excited that I started dancing on the street as we walked toward our cars. I cannot describe my enthusiasm and feelings at that moment. To be in my homeland after all these years was awesome! I was very happy to be able to come back to my homeland and see the faces of my mom and dad, and my four sisters and their children. It did cross my mind that I may have missed many opportunities by not going home sooner since everything was going so well, but at the same time I was trusting God's timing more than my own.

My vacation lasted three weeks and I did not encounter any problems with anyone. I thanked God for the opportunity He gave me to go home and see my family. We had so much to talk about and so little time. We all listened to each other very carefully and with much excitement. I had never told my sisters firsthand exactly what happened to me so many years ago and why I made my decision to stay in the USA. As a result, we were up until one or two o'clock in the morning most nights trying to catch up with the past thirty years of our lives. Since it was during the Iranian New Year, schools and most offices were closed for the holidays and as a result they did not have to rush back to their homes so quickly.

I am sure all of my siblings wanted to know who I had become, what I thought of everything, and what I liked or disliked. It was interesting to them as well as for me to get to know each one of them after all these years. One of the major changes in my life was that I no longer embraced my old religion and faith in Islam as they did. God opened my eyes to a new horizon and to a new light, which we call "the way, the truth and the life" or Christianity, and it was the desire of my heart to share that truth with my family there.

Contrary to Muslim belief, that family members disowned each other for leaving their faith, I was loved and respected by all my family and extended family members alike. They agreed with most everything I shared with them even though they could not talk about it openly. They often reminded me to be careful when we were around strangers as to what I said about my faith.

I must admit that it was not as easy as it sounds to openly talk about another religion other than Islam in a country where the majority (95%) of the people "eat and breath" Islam. Most of the people have a hard time understanding "freedom of choice" in a closed society where people are being told what to do, how to think, what to eat, what to say or not to say all of their lives. We are so fortunate to live in the USA, a country where we can choose for ourselves without being told what to say or what not to

122

say, what to believe or what not to believe, praise be to God! Anyway, the following day my Dad purchased a lamb and sacrificed it in my honor. We all "walked over its blood", and thanked God for my safe and long awaited journey to my homeland.

It is customary to sacrifice or 'ghorbani' a lamb and give some of the meat to the poor and neighbors in the name of Allah for a few reasons:

1) Every parent is to sacrifice a lamb (other animals if the means is not there) after the example of Abraham when he was about to sacrifice his older son Ishmael, according to the Islamic tradition. (Note: There was not any covenant with Ishmael, only blessings. See Genesis 17:19-21)

2) They also sacrifice for prosperity and good health. When someone who just returned from making a long trip, had a baby or other similar occasions.

3) When someone who pilgrimages or travels to Mecca once in their lifetime, which is one of the five obligatory pillars of Islam.

After the sacrifice, the participants step over the shed blood of the animal and thank Allah for his blessings. Although I hated to see the act of the sacrifice with my eyes, it reminded me of the shed blood of my Savior Jesus Christ who paid for my sin and sins of the whole world, so we might be free from the penalty of sin through Him. For the scripture says: *"In Him we have redemption through His blood, the forgiveness of sins, according to the riches of His grace."* (Ephesians 1:7)

Now, "sacrifice" according to the Bible:

The holiest day in the year for Jewish people is called "Yom Kippur" (Day of Atonement). This is the day, when Jews ask the Lord to forgive them for their sins of the year gone by.

What does the Lord want from us for the forgiveness of sins according to the Old Testament?

"For on that day the priest *shall make atonement for you, to cleanse you,* that *you may be clean from all your sins before the LORD"* *(Leviticus 16:30)*

" And he shall wash his body with water in a holy place, put on his garments, come out and offer his burnt offering and the burnt offering of the people, and make atonement for himself and for the people." (Leviticus 16:24)

"For the life of the flesh is in the blood, and I have given it to you upon the altar to make atonement for your souls; for it is the blood that makes atonement for the soul." (Leviticus 17:11)

124

The veil in the Jewish temple concealed God. The high priest went in once a year to make reconciliation. No one else was allowed in the Holy of Holies. The way to God was barred. They could not be perfect through the blood of bulls and of goats. These were provisionary and figurative ordinances until God took up the real work itself, in order to accomplish it fully and forever.

JESUS THE MESSIAH IS THE 'LAMB' OF GOD AND HOW YOU CAN FOLLOW JESUS TO HEAVEN AS WRITTEN IN THE QURAN

"Allah or God loves you and wants you to join Him in heaven after you die. But to go to heaven, your sins must be totally removed from you. To fix this problem, God developed a way that we could be totally forgiven and the curse of sin removed from us.

Starting with Adam, man could be forgiven of his sins if he followed the sacrifice system called "Ghorbani." With his sins forgiven and removed, he could join God in heaven directly after death.

The Ghorbani is a picture of the punishment that we deserve for our sins. Think of a courtroom where you stand before the judge. The judge is fair and just. Because of your sin, the judge sentences you to be killed. Even though you are guilty, God allows another person, one who is innocent, to receive your punishment. For God to throw away your punishment would mean that he is not a just judge.

Every crime must be paid for, this is justice. You deserve to die for your guilt of sin.

Think about the practice of Ghorbani. First, we are to find a pure animal. A sick or low quality animal cannot be

125

used for the sacrifice. Immediately before the sacrifice, we are to pray to God saying, "God, I am guilty of committing sin against you. I deserve to have my blood poured out of me until I die. So Allah, please have mercy on me and instead of taking my blood, take the blood of this innocent animal."

From the time of Adam until the time of Jesus, Ghorbani was practiced. God did not always require the blood of animals to be used for the Ghorbani. Abraham was told to do the Ghorbani with his promised son. At the last moment, God stopped Abraham from sacrificing his son. God was only testing Abraham's love and devotion to Him.

Since the death of Christ, followers of Jesus have stopped practicing the Ghorbani. Why?

Complete Muslims or the followers of Jesus know that the Ghorbani (sacrifice) was only a shadow of the ultimate sacrifice that God would do for all the people of the world: past, present, and future. For God to do Ghorbani for all of mankind shows us how much He loves us and gives us confidence that we can be totally cleared of the curse of sin.

But what would God use for His sacrifice for all the people of the world?

The Quran says that the birth of 'Isa (Jesus) would be a sign for the world. In order for God to do sacrifice for all mankind, he needed the most pure, holy, and powerful sacrifice available.

We have seen from the Quran that the purest, holiest, and most powerful blood in the world was that of 'Isa (Jesus). God performed a sacrifice by using the blood of the innocent 'Isa (Jesus).

What God did not allow Abraham to do to his promised son, God did with 'Isa (Jesus). This was an <u>act of love</u> unlike any act we have ever seen, the innocent giving his blood for the guilty. 'Isa took the punishment that we deserve. Now you know why Complete Muslims and followers of Christ are such grateful people. They understand that God did not give us what we deserve. The Injil says in John 15:13, *"Greater love has no one than this that he lay down his life for his friends."*

Today, you can become a Complete Muslim. All you have to do is to believe that God did a great sacrifice for you. He used the blood of 'Isa (Jesus) instead of your blood! Stop now, hold your hands up before you, and humbly tell God that you receive His sacrifice and thank Him for placing the punishment of your guilt upon 'Isa (Jesus). In this way, God will forgive you of your sins and remove the curse of sin. When you are cleansed of your sins, then you can go to be with God after you die. You can now live your life in peace knowing that after death, you can go directly to be with God."

(A complete Muslim by Kevin Greeson and Quran)

Chapter 10

TOURING HISTORICAL CITIES OF PERSIA

I had already told my sisters in advance that I would like to take them sightseeing for a few days. I wanted to spend some quality time with them since we had not seen each other for such a long time. Therefore, we decided to make a trip by bus to Isfahan and Shiraz in Iran. We decided on a day, packed a few homemade sandwiches and departed early in the afternoon. The name of the bus we were traveling on was called "Seir-O-Safar". We found it to be very comfortable and nice. There was a small television and video tape player available on board to keep us entertained. I utilized this way of traveling since it was more economical while at the same time we could see more of the country. It also gave us more time to spend with each other to relax and to share our hearts.

Our bus zoomed through town and headed toward Shiraz, which was about sixteen hours away. The bus drivers seem to own the roads by going and coming so often. At one point, I became very concerned when I noticed that our bus driver was maneuvering in a scary manner. A car was driving in front of us and was going faster than the posted speed limit, yet our driver wanted to go faster. Our bus driver attempted to pass him a few times but due to oncoming traffic he could not. Finally, when he was able to pass the car, he turned the bus hard to the right knowing the car was there and forced him off the road! The driver of the car quickly used his brakes and got out of the way of our huge bus to prevent an accident. I felt so bad for the driver of that car and thanked God for protecting him and his family.

As we traveled, I took the opportunity to talk to each one of my sisters. I wanted to share my faith with them so badly. I wanted them to ask me any questions concerning my faith that they might have, but I wanted to make sure I was not disrespectful either. They were my sisters and I loved them dearly, so I was very sensitive as to what to say to them. I prayed silently, asking God to guide me as we shared our hearts with each other. I would recall some events from the Bible and the lessons from it, then apply them to our conversation. I was not shy about telling them what Jesus would do or say regarding the subject matter. This was one of the ways I shared Christ with them.

It was not an easy task though. They claimed that they understood what I was talking about, but instead of asking me more about Jesus, they would provide rebuttal by offering their own opinion from the standpoint of the Quran. It reminded me of this scripture: **Matthew 6:22-23**: *"The eye is the lamp of the body. If your eyes are good, your whole body will be full of light. But if your eyes are bad, your whole body will be full of darkness. If then the light within you is darkness, how great is that darkness*!" In other words they acted and responded as they knew everything I was sharing with them yet they knew nothing at all. They were nodding their heads in agreement, but their minds were elsewhere!

The bus stopped for dinner at a roadside restaurant and for those who wished to have their evening prayers. We had already traveled a few hours and stretching my legs sounded good to me. My sisters did not care for the food at those types of restaurants, and had already prepared some from home for all of us. We ate our dinner and after a short rest and walk around the premises, we boarded the bus and continued our trip.

The bus driver was replaced with a fresh and rested driver, which made me feel better knowing how long the trip was ahead of us. The temperature was getting cooler as we approached the evening, so we asked the driver to turn on the heater. We travelled all night toward our destination. We arrived in Shiraz (the province of Fars) at about eight in the morning. My cousin was there to greet us since he and his family lived there. We stayed at my cousin's house for a couple of days, and then traveled to Isfahan. Both cities are historical and beautiful places for tourists to visit.

SIGHTSEEING IN SHIRAZ

Shiraz is located in the southwest of Iran. It is the fifth most populated city in Iran and the capital of Fars Province. The province of Fars, with a population of four million, is 121,000 km wide, 7.5% of Iran. It neighbors in the north Isfahan and Yazd; Bandar Booshehr in the west; its southern neighbor is Bandar Abbas; and Kerman is the eastern neighbor. It has four seasons, the temperature varying from –7 to 2 degrees Celsius in cold days of the year, to 35 to 40 degrees Celsius in the warmest days of summer.

Shiraz was the capital of Persia during the Zand dynasty from 1750 until 1781, as well as briefly during the Saffarid period.

Shiraz is known as the "city of poets, wine and flowers." It is also considered by many Iranians to be the "city of gardens", due to the many gardens and fruit trees that can be seen in the city.

Shiraz has had major Jewish and Christian communities. The crafts of Shiraz consist of inlaid mosaic work of triangular design; silver-ware; and pile carpet-weaving in the villages and among the tribes. In Shiraz, industries such as cement production, sugar, fertilizers, textile products, wood products, metalwork and rugs dominate. Shiraz also has a major oil refinery and is also a major center for Iran's electronic industries. 53% of Iran's electronic investment has been centered in Shiraz.

The popular attractions of Shiraz include first and foremost the tombs of the poets Hafez, Saadi, and Khaju e Kermani. Kermani's tomb is inside the mountain above the city's old Quran Gate.

One of the most historical buildings is the Kian. This building was constructed around the time of Cyrus the Great, and has been a popular tourist attraction ever since.

There are over 200 sites of historical significance around Shiraz. Persepolis is located in the northwestern part of Fars, 40 km away from Shiraz.

Persepolis

132

Persepolis is an ensemble of ancient monuments and palaces. The palaces were built by Darius I (521 B.C.), but for more than 150 years, designers, stone worker, engineers and others worked hard to complete the whole palace. Later, Alexander the Great destroyed it. We also find Darius in the Bible. According to Daniel 5:31; Darius began ruling the Persian Empire when he was 62 years old. God's Word tells us that Darius decided to appoint 120 satraps over the kingdom. The word satrap means "protector of the kingdom" and referred to a governor over a province or district.

"Now Daniel so distinguished himself among the administrators and the satraps by his exceptional qualities that the king planned to set him over the whole kingdom." (Daniel 6:3)

Daniel was indeed trustworthy, devoid of any negligence or corruption and he had favor in the eyes of King Darius. Persians were under a good king and trustworthy people like Daniel for many years until I believe Satan in the person of Alexander the Great came and destroyed the country and weakened the will of the people.

There are many tombs and shrines in the province of Fars that are either valuable for their historic past or are sacred as places of pilgrimage for Muslims. One of the most loved and dignified of all the shrines is **Shah Cheragh,** the tomb of the son of the seventh Imam of the Shiites. The tomb is also known as a tomb of two brothers 'Amir Ahmad' and 'Mir Muhammad', both of who were brothers of Imam Reza, the 8th Shiite Imam who took refuge in Shiraz, Iran during the Abbasid persecution of the Shiite Muslims.

I went inside the shrine for a closer look. I took my shoes off, as was required. They used this shrine as a mosque and a place of prayer, and it must be kept clean at all times. The floors were covered wall-to-wall with beautiful hand-made Persian carpets and the tomb was covered by thousands of large and small beautiful glittery and shiny crystals. Many lights and chandeliers were used to beautify the inside while the outside dome was covered with gold plated roofing. For the Islamic faith, the splendor of this Mosque made it a marvelous place as a house of worship, and the people came with the expectation of having their prayers answered.

Inside, the Mosque was packed with many worshipers who were there to pray at every corner, or to request whatever they wished by touching the door-posts or walls of the tomb. Many would offer "alms" by throwing money toward the center of the tomb. All four sides of the tomb were covered by tall and decorative iron bars, fashioned with beautiful designs. You could see all kinds of coins and paper money inside the four iron walls and near the tomb. People would express their wish silently to the soul of the holy person who is buried there.

Tomb of Shah Cheragh

"Significant populations of Shiite Muslims can be found in Iran and Iraq, and large minority communities in Yemen, Bahrain, Syria, and Lebanon but Sunni Muslims make up the majority (85%) of Muslims all over the world. Shiite Muslims believe that the twelve Imams or (Disciples) of Mohammad and their close relatives are "sinless" by nature, and that their authority is infallible as it comes directly from Allah. Therefore, Shiite Muslims often hold the twelve Imams in the highest regard and as saints, and travel on pilgrimages to their tombs and shrines in the hope of divine intercession for their prayers. Sunni Muslims on the other hand counter that there is no basis in Islam for an inherited privileged class of spiritual leaders, and certainly no basis for the veneration or intercession of saints.

Sunni Muslims challenge that the leadership of the community is not a birthright but rather a trust that is earned, and may be given or taken away by the people themselves through election."

(From Wikipedia, the free encyclopedia)

Incidentally,since Sunni Muslims do not consider the leadership of an Imam as a birthright, they reject the twelve 'Imamat' of Shiites including 'Mehdi', the one who is expected to reappear, unless he comes through an election. But on the other hand fundamentally they do agree with the leadership of Iran, standing up to their rival, Israel, in favor of Palestinian rights!

My personal thoughts are a bit different from them in reference to the hidden Imam. I believe when Jesus Christ returns as expected by all three major religions, Muslims will call Him their hidden Imam, while the Jews recognize Him as their Redeemer. But the Christian acknowledges Him as the King of Kings, the Lion of the Tribe of Judah. This way the whole world would be united together under the direction of His Majesty, our Lord Jesus Christ. Every knee should bow of those in heaven, of those on earth, and of those under the earth, and that every tongue should confess that Jesus is Lord, to the glory of God the Father!

As it has been promised by God through the words of the Prophet Isaiah saying:

And the government will be upon His shoulder.
And His name will be called
Wonderful, Counselor, Mighty God,
Everlasting Father, Prince of Peace.
Of the increase of His government and peace
there will be no end,
upon the throne of David and over His kingdom,
to order it and establish it with judgment and justice
from that time forward, even forever.
The zeal of the Lord of hosts will perform this.

Isaiah 9:6-7

Saadi and Hafez also have their tombs in Shiraz. They are two very famous and well-known poets that have their books translated in many languages worldwide. "Fal-e-Hafez" is one of the famous books written and used by many in Iran as fortune telling based on Hafez poems. We had fun at my cousin's house fortune-telling by reading "Fal-e-Hafez" for each other. We did this by wishing first, then randomly opening its pages to read what it says concerning our wish. The writings are sort of similar to our "Proverbs" in the Bible, full of good advice. One of my sisters later on purchased "Fal-e- Hafez" in the Persian language and gave it to me as a souvenir.

Back in my cousin's house in Shiraz, we enjoyed several delicious Iranian dishes, which I will never get tired of!

One of my cousins opened up the conversation by wanting to know what I thought concerning the "soul and spirit" of mankind. She also wanted to know if I was a practicing "priest", since she had seen me in a picture dressed up similar to one of the disciple's attire (*I was dressed up for an Easter drama in our church*).

Tomb of Hafez

I shared with them what I had learned from the Bible as they eagerly listened. Then the subject shifted to Islam and I witnessed something unexpected. I asked a historical question about Muhammad and his disciples, which related to some disagreements they had with the Jewish tribes living in the same land nearby. This resulted in Muhammad and his companions killing the Jewish tribes, taking their wives and children as slaves, and stealing their belongings as booty (money or valuables seized or stolen, especially by soldiers in war).

Surprisingly this opened up a 'can of worms'! The next thing I knew, I was reclining in my chair, watching a heated discussion between one of my sisters and my cousin's mother-in-law, arguing back and forth with no end in sight! I realized that they did not agree with the motives behind those wars. I decided I had better change the subject and move on to another topic, to prevent further arguments.

Recently, as part of my continuing research, I came across Dr. Khalid Zaheer, a Muslim scholar from Pakistan who through a written public debate with Ali Sina, admitted many other conflicts or problems from the message of the Quran as he was sorting them out. Here is part of what he wrote:

"I will tell you why I am saying that my quest, when I was reading the Quran then, was by large an academic one. I divided the passages I came across in the Quran into three categories:

- *There were passages that immediately struck me as the most outstanding I had ever come across;*
- *There was information in it that I told myself I would never accept;*
- *Finally, there were passages that I had reservations about.*

While the first category of passages kept me going, the other two were a continuous source of challenge to the possibility that I would accept the book as 'divine'.

I ask everyone to go through the Quran with an unbiased approach and you are going to experience what I experienced.

If anyone is claiming that no part of the book, from cover to cover, is making any impact on him/her, he/she is talking nonsense and belying the experiences of millions of intelligent people. I have no hesitation in saying that the first category of the passages of the Quran – the one that struck me as simply brilliant – was the most dominant. It always tended to undermine the other two categories. However, I managed to keep my wits intact and did not give in until the problems created by the other two were properly sorted out.

There were three ideas attributed to the Quran about which I had decided that I would not accept.

One of them was the understanding that Muslims were destined to enter paradise while non-Muslims were destined to hell-fire forever. This sounded so ridiculous to me and I told myself that I just could not accept any such suggestion.[1]

The other idea attributed to the Quran was that it apparently seemed to be suggesting that whoever "becomes a non-Muslim" after having been a Muslim, ought to be killed.[2]

Note:(1)(2) Grand Ayatollah Yusuf Saanei who lives in Qom, Iran is now claiming and teaching the same thing as Dr Khalid Zaheer on the first two notes as he describes them in his own web site.

The third one was that the Quran apparently claims that only God knows what is in the womb of a woman when she is pregnant. I could not fool myself by believing that what apparently was mentioned was the truth given that, thanks to the recent advancement in ultrasound-based technology, the gender of the unborn baby could be identified unmistakably.

On later investigation, it transpired that what I had decided to be unacceptable claims in the Quran was never a part of the book. I later realized that what I had initially thought to be Quranic concepts were not in the Quran at all."

Incidentally, a "non-Muslim" in the language of Islam is considered a "non-believer." However, Dr. Khalid is correct when he says that some of the things that are being taught and are circulating among Muslims may not be part of the Quran. They came to surface either by the self-serving Mullahs or from other authoritative sources, such as the **Hadith of the Muhammad.**

Unfortunately, at the conclusion, this Muslim scholar (Dr. Khalid Zaheer) chose to ignore those passages that he rejected initially, considered them as holy, the infallible word of Allah!

I will talk more about why Dr. Khalid chose to remain status quo under "**Sharia**" or the Islamic Law at the conclusion of this book.

SIGHTSEEING IN ISFAHAN

We continued our trip to Isfahan after spending a couple of days of sightseeing in Shiraz and the surrounding areas. **Esfahan or Isfahan,** located about 340 km south of Tehran, is the capital of Esfahan Province and Iran's third largest city (after Tehran and Mash-had). Esfahan is located on the main north-south and east-west routes crossing Iran, and was once one of the largest cities in the world. It flourished from 1050 to1722, and particularly in the 16th century under the Safavid dynasty, when it became the capital of Persia for the second time in it's history. Even today, the city retains much of its past glory. It is famous for its Islamic architecture, with many beautiful boulevards, covered bridges, palaces, mosques, and minarets. A "minaret" is a narrow tower of a mosque, from which the faithful are summoned to prayer. The call to prayer occurs five times each day.

Famous Naghsh-E Jahan Square, Isfahan

Iran is full of history and has many beautiful cities. Tourists from all over the world travel there to see these historical places. I love and miss Iran, and I am very saddened by the manner in which this new government has created so much distance between themselves and the rest of the world, especially America. I only saw a few foreigners as tourists there. However, the streets were packed with travelers and commuters from other cities of Iran.

In Isfahan, we stayed at a hotel close to the famous "Naghsh-e Jahan Square". When we checked in at the hotel, we all had to show our identification such as birth certificates, passports or marriage certificates to prove that we were related as brother and sisters. Majid, my nephew, and his wife, were also with us and had to prove that they were husband and wife in order to be able to share a room.

According to the hotel attendant, police will occasionally check the books and identity of the people who stay there as guests to make sure that they follow the Islamic law, which states that no man and woman may stay in one

141

room unless they are married or blood related such as brother and sister.

I suppose that is why "temporary marriages" are even more popular now than ever before under this Islamic government. Strange as it is, as long as I can remember, Islam in Iran has always offered "temporary" or "convenience" marriage for men who may be away from their home or family. These types of marriages are common in Iran and the wives of the married men often understand it since the society has been dominated by men. But the same act by a married woman could bring harsh punishment. A mosque Imam can prepare these temporary papers or contracts which could last for a specific period of time and usually money is involved. Nevertheless, here is another report that puts a different twist in this despicable act.

TEHRAN, IRAN: "New talk from Iranian Interior Minister Mustafa Pour-Mohammadi, who is promoting "temporary marriages" to help curb the country's social problems. Temporary marriage, or "sigheh", is a practice unique to Shiite Islam and has been a disputed practice in Iran for many years because many consider it a license for prostitution. This may now be looked at as a solution to a societal problem as some are now advocating for this to be institutionalized to help fight illicit sex in a country where sexual relations outside of marriage are banned under Islamic law.(Paraphrased from televised news, June 2007)

Iran first started promoting temporary marriage as an alternative to living in sin, 15 years ago, but it quickly came under fire by the country's hard line clerics. The President at the time, Hashemi Rafsanjani, proposed that this should be a way for men and women to satisfy their sexual needs and that there should not even be a need for a cleric. A couple could read out an oath in private to each other to marry. In doing so, a couple could be married for any length of time from one hour up to 99 years. The opposition won out and this became a strong taboo in Iranian culture.

Temporary marriages are in direct conflict with "Sharia", or Islamic law that has been in force in Iran since 1979. In Islamic law, extramarital sex is prohibited and punishable by flogging or stoning. Prostitution was banned at that same time, however, it has increased in recent years. Attorney Nemat Ahmadi said in relation to temporary marriages, "It will damage the foundation of the family. This will only promote prostitution." Ahmadi further argues that "sigheh" gives wealthy men a religious cover to have affairs."

Note: Iran became an Islamic republic in 1979, the year Ayatollah Khomeini returned to Iran from exile. Before then prostitution was legal under the Shah's government.

VISITING A CHURCH IN ESFAHAN

There is a well-known church in Isfahan called "Armenian Vank Church" that includes a museum for tourists to visit. One of my sisters recalled the name of that church and asked if I would be interested in going there.

What an opportunity! God paved the way. I replied, "Yes, I would love to go!"

We hailed a taxi and were driven to that church, purchased tickets, and entered. The church was very old and was surrounded by tall walls like a citadel. Inside the four walls of the church grounds was a sizeable yard that divided the sanctuary from the museum. At the entrance of the sanctuary, we saw a small platform with some mannequins dressed up with costumes similar to the early first century Christians, displaying their heritage. They also had a museum there showing their ancient Bibles and handwritings.

As we entered the sanctuary, a guide greeted and welcomed us. Photography was not permitted unless you paid in advance for that privilege at the ticket counter. Guides were present to answer any questions, but spoke only when spoken to.

The walls inside of the sanctuary had paintings with events in the order of Genesis to Revelation. I took that opportunity to explain the pictures and the events drawn in these paintings to my sisters. The guide who greeted us gave me his approval and confirmation with a smile as I was explaining the events.

Suddenly, a voice that I did not recognize asked: "Sir, may I ask you a question?" I was not paying attention to other people in the church, as my focus was on the paintings on the walls, and the explanation of them I was giving to my family. Unexpectedly, I found myself surrounded with many people, men and women, who were listening to my explanations. These people were all Muslims who were there inside the church to learn more about Christianity.

Frankly, I was not prepared to meet that kind of challenge there, especially with the group of people that I did not even know! But the Holy Spirit enabled me to continue to talk about His truth!

My sisters stood there with their mouths wide open in surprise as the group continued to ask me questions. When we left the sanctuary and headed toward the museum, the same group of people followed me! Again, God gave me another opportunity to share the good news of Jesus Christ, with people whom God put in my path; Praise God!

A scene of the interior of the Cathedral

The whole time that I was talking about Jesus, I emphasized His purity and love for mankind and that this was the most important thing. Then at one point, I offered a statement with a little hesitation and suggested that we shouldn't bring it up for discussion. They should search and study on their own. Afterward I told them that if they could see Jesus as being the best based on the examples He left behind for us, why would they want to settle for anything less? (Of course, I was referring to Muhammad as a lesser

145

person than Jesus, the Son of God). Then one person whom I did not recognize as being part of the first group started to challenge me with an argument that Jews considered their religion to be the best too. One of the guides, who were listening to us, picked up on our conversation and immediately stopped his argumentative rebuttal. For a short few seconds I feared for a heated dispute, which I was not ready for!

My nephew had warned me to be careful especially when I was asked where I was from, especially being from America. So, on that note we left the building. On our way out, another visitor approached me with a smile on his face, saying; "We know all of what you were saying" yet they could not expose themselves for the fear of their lives.

I was so fortunate that no harm came to me. I learned later that if you wish to visit Iran, you must not attract people to yourself. Because if the authorities see you giving speeches and attracting people to yourself, they consider it a threat against their government and you could be prosecuted for a crime of insurrection. If you travel there as a journalist or any other type of fact finding mission, you must inform the government in advance about your intentions. They will more than likely assign someone to be with you as guide or chaperon. The tricky part is if you stay beyond your assignment time frame in order to visit family and friends, it would be to your best interest to close the doors to any large gathering or photography in order not to be accused of spying. We are fortunate to live in a country where we can express our thoughts about religion or politics in an open forum.

I remember that on one occasion a Christian was stabbed with a knife when a small group was demonstrating peacefully in one of the streets of Tehran. In Iran, Christians may have rights but not freedom! Within the last year several Iranian men and women were put in prison because they were accused of spying, but after a few months they were let go. This demonstrates their love and compassion under the Islamic Republic!

Many people in Iran thought that an Islamic state type government would be more compassionate toward them. They hoped for prosperity along with spiritual and economic growth. However, after over two decades of Islamic leadership in Iran, people were losing their trust in their government; not only due to problems economically or with the lack of prosperity, but in spiritual issues as well. These subjects were the main concern in every home. The reason was because most were fed up with the lies and misleading words of their leaders who put so much fear in the minds of their people. They were not able to speak freely in the public forum without being criticized or pushed out of the way, and for that reason, people were searching for another kind of leadership in religion and politics. People still remembered the false promise of the late Ayatollahs, who encouraged the nation for their support, to have an Islamic republic in exchange for the nationalization of the nation's resource of oil, and that everyone in the country would benefit monetarily.

Iranians love their hot tea, and they use sugar cubes to sweeten their tea. Due to the lack of sugar imports, the Islamic government announced that the consumption of sugar-cubes was 'harom' (sinful), and encouraged people to eat 'dates' instead. Later after the Iran-Iraq war ended, their relationship with neighboring countries was restored and sugar imports increased. Then the government announced that if you dip the sugar-cubes in the hot tea first before consumption, it would be 'hallal' (pure). These announcements became part of many jokes and much laughter among the people there.

As a result, when I was in the homes of different families, the subject almost always came up about their frustration with their religious leaders. They were eager to know about my belief and faith in God. They all listened carefully and with excitement and had many questions about Christianity.

My first trip to Iran was very promising, fruitful and without any problems. It gave me more encouragement and hope than ever before, and affected my decision to go back to Iran again the following year in 2005 and to continue my dialogue as before. But...

Chapter 11

"The Trap"

O n Tuesday March 22nd,2005, I had the privilege of going back to Iran with my brother Hamid. This date also happened to be in Farvardin, the first month in the Iranian calendar and the start of the New Year, or 'Nowruz'.

We had been planning this trip for six months prior to our departure. I was so excited that I had my suitcases packed and ready months ahead! I hoped that God was leading me to my homeland this second time to have the same success as the first, and that the door would then be open for future trips as a Christian missionary. I was very anxious and excited, wanting to know what God had in store.

The day finally came and I met my brother at the airport in Charlotte, NC at about 3:00pm. Hamid's wife Tina, my wife Ursa, my daughter Elizabeth, and my grandson Roman, were there to see us off. We prayed to God for our protection and safety, and for Him to bring us back home to our loved ones as soon as our visit was over. At 5:00pm, we left Charlotte and flew by way of Memphis, Tennessee (TN) to Amsterdam via Northwest Airlines (NWA) and from there by Royal Dutch Airline (KLM) to Tehran, Iran.

We arrived in Tehran on Thursday March 24, 2005 at about 12:10am. We had two hot meals while we traveled and made it there on time without any problems or delays. The flight was great!

But just like my first trip in 2004, the same feeling came over me as we were about to step off the plane. It was dark outside and felt creepy and frightening! Laughter disappearred and quietness took over, but as we stepped out of the plane and walked down the steps, I heard a man's voice calling "Hello Uncle Saiid!"

It was my niece's husband, who worked at the airport. It sounded so pleasant to my ears to hear my name being called. I was comforted and encouraged by that friendly voice, especially hearing my own name! It truly lifted my spirits after feeling the loss of freedom in such a restricted atmosphere while being among strangers. What an awesome welcome to my homeland! After hearing that salutation, I smiled and walked down the steps toward the transit buses with renewed confidence.

We were then taken to the terminal where we had to have our passports checked. Hamid was in line ahead of me as we went through one by one. An officer with a stern face checked me in. He entered my Iranian passport number into a computer and stamped my passport. As we left the checkpoint and headed toward the baggage claim, I heard a voice echoing through the hallway as though it was coming through loud speakers, calling someone's name; "Mr.

Rabifar". We soon learned that he meant my last name "Rabiipour", but was pronouncing it incorrectly.

So at first we ignored it and continued on. By this time, a couple of my relatives were there with us. They had obtained special passes to greet us there before we entered the general terminal.

We were on the steps, going up toward the baggage claim, when I spotted a man with the upper part of his body stuck out of a window on the second floor, calling with a loud voice "Saiid!", and echoing all over the terminal. It did not sound as pleasant as the first time and did not feel comforting either, but since "Saiid" is a common name, I ignored it as well.

Finally, the man stuck his head out of the window one more time, calling my name for the third time "Mr. Rabiipour". This time he correctly pronounced my last name.

One of my relatives whispered into my ear, "Saiid, I think they are calling for you" Then he told me "wait, let me see what is going on."

By then, I was already at the luggage pickup and was searching for my luggage. Hamid had already started going toward where the call came from, and soon came face to face with a man holding a two-way radio on the ground level. Nader, one of my relatives was right behind Hamid.

Hamid introduced himself by his last name and asked the man how he could help?

The security man who was on the floor signaled the guy who was calling aloud through the open window using his two-way radio, asking; "Is it number one or number two?"

The voice responded that it was "two".

1) Serious   2) Not so serious

The security personnel then asked for Hamid's passport. (*If it had been a serious matter, they would have handcuffed him immediately and taken him to jail. When this happens to people, it could be the last time they see daylight for a long time! Hamid really showed his bravery by going forward as he did!*)

Hamid handed him his passport, questioning the security personnel as to what seemed to be the problem, but the question was ignored. He took Hamid's passport, gave him a receipt, and instructed him to go to the passport office on Africa Street to pick up his passport in a few days. They would not volunteer any information as to why they had to keep his passport. And they failed to verify his first name to make sure he was who they wanted.

Hamid had a strong suspicion that they were after me and not him. He knew that he had not done anything wrong to cause any problems, besides, he had been to Iran several times before this trip and nothing had ever happened. But he went along and played their "game". This action by my brother, and the mistakes of the authorities, enabled me to have more time to ponder what was going on rather than being ambushed by the unknown. I am grateful to this day for Hamid and his courageous action.

Hamid returned to the baggage claim where I was picking up our luggage. Nader and Ali-Reza (two of my relatives) were there with us as events were unfolding. The rest of our families were outside the restricted area waiting for us. We gathered all of our bags and went out of the terminal to where our families were waiting patiently. Outside of the terminal, our parents, our sisters and nieces, and nephews, all greeted us and showered us with many kisses and flowers. However, as a result of the security incident, we lost our excitement somewhat. There was no dancing on the streets like my first trip. There was no lamb sacrifice either. We simply walked to our cars and headed toward Karaj, the city where my parents resided.

We all gathered at my parent's house where I explained the situation to everyone. I told them that I was sure that they were looking for me, not Hamid, and that it most likely had to do with when I was in the Iranian Navy. I explained that I would find the best way to deal with the situation, but for now, I just wanted to enjoy and celebrate our visit with each other.

So, we visited, enjoyed delicious Iranian delicacies, danced, and were happy as much as we could be. I did not want to think negative thoughts, but it weighed heavy on my mind. I needed time to think and pray for the right course of action. I was a bit embarrassed, but it was beyond my control. I called my wife that night to tell her the news and the desperate need for her prayers and the prayers of all my family and brothers and sisters in Christ.

Would God answer our prayers?

"As soon as I heard his voice on the phone, I knew something was wrong. My heart sank as he told me what happened at the airport. "This can't be happening" I thought. "Everything went so well on his first visit a year ago!" But this time was different and I heard the concern in his voice. We both knew that they meant to take his passport instead of Hamid's and that it most likely had to do with his decision to stay here instead of returning to Iran after college. We tried to be optimistic and think that once he talked to them, it would all be straightened out in a timely manner and he would be on his merry way, but little did we know what lay ahead.

Before we hung up, we agreed that we needed to try to keep our faith strong and to offer prayer and praise to God in this situation. I assured Saiid that I would call and email everyone we knew to pray as well. The uncertainty of it all was hard, and I have to admit I felt this incredible feeling of helplessness. He was in a country that had no U.S. Embassy that I could contact for help. I wasn't sure what the next step was; what to do or who to call. My mind was reeling as I tried to absorb what was happening. But I knew I had to do everything I could to help him."

(Ursa)

The first few nights in my parent's house, I tossed and turned almost all night thinking about my situation. I would pray to seek God's wisdom, but for some reason I felt distanced and could not get the needed comfort from Him.

On February 25, 1983, the day I became a citizen of the United States, I was given an opportunity to change my name, but, being proud of my heritage and my homeland and wanting to relate to my past, I saw no reason to change it.

The Judge in charge during my naturalization ceremony told us that this country was based on immigrants like us, and that diversity is good as long as there is unity and respect for each other.

I was not involved in anything illegal against Iran or anyone in that country. I did however, disagree with the way the Iranian Navy treated me and because of their lies I chose not to be part of their military force.

Many of my friends here in the USA respect me and my heritage and I have always promoted Iran and Iranian culture while living here. But the fact that they were planning on taking my Iranian passport away from me made me feel like a prisoner in my own birth country.

But for now I needed to rest. Everyone was sleeping but me. The change of location and jet lag didn't help matters, but I needed to stay quiet for the sake of the others. I had some ibuprofen and allergy medication with me to help me with my backache and sleeping, but they did not help. A few days later due to the stress I was under and the lack of sleep, and possibly taking too much medication, I became sick. I could not keep anything on my stomach and was taken to the local doctor's office. The doctor said that I was most likely suffering from food poisoning from something I ate. I was hooked up to an I.V. and was given some medication. I got better within a few hours and then I was allowed to go back to my parent's house.

The First Lie!

Early Saturday morning, Hamid, Ali, Nader and I got in Nader's car for Tehran to go to pick up Hamid's passport as they had told us to do at the airport. Nader had his own car and used it as a private Taxi cab. As a result, he was able to drive me around for the next two months. Ali also had a car of his own and was with us the whole time as well. Ali was a truck driver and owned his own truck, but since it was too much on his back he had hired someone to drive for him. That allowed him to stay at home and do the administrative part of the work. It was very generous of him to share his income between the two of them.

We located Africa Street and found the Passport Office. They told us that they did not have Hamid's passport, (this was a lie which we found out later.} They told us that we needed to go to the military courthouse to pick it up. So we then drove to the military courthouse located in Tehran at a place called "Ghasr".

Tehran is a very busy city and it is very difficult to find a parking place. We found ourselves driving around the block several times to find a spot to park our car. We finally had to park in an alley next to someone's house. I stayed in the car while Hamid, Nader and Ali went inside. At this time I was not involved since they kept Hamid's passport by mistake. We would later proceed to clear my name and try to solve my issues.

The military court was located in a six-story building with many small courtrooms on several of it's floors. After running around and asking questions as to where to go, we finally reported to an office where the clerk of court was familiar with our issue and in charge of our problem. He began by asking Hamid, "Did you have any problem with the military?"

Hamid answered, "No sir, I served and finished my two year service many years ago."

The clerk of court asked, "Do you have your discharge papers from the service with you?"

Hamid answered, "No sir, they are in America where I live."

The clerk went back and forth from one office to another, asking other questions of Hamid, and finally came back and said, "You are Hamid but we are looking for Saiid."

He then apologized to Hamid for the mix-up on the name and for his passport being confiscated at the airport. He said that the Iranian Navy had issued a complaint against Saiid. The clerk then told Hamid to go back to the passport office and that he would make a call to them to release his passport.

We both had two passports; an Iranian one and an American one. The Government of Iran would issue passports very easily to all Iranian born individuals who lived abroad. This way they could treat them as Iranians and according to their laws without violating another country's laws by harassing their citizens. That's why when I presented my passports to the officer in charge when we arrived to the airport, he did not even look at my American passport. It was also Hamid's Iranian passport that they confiscated.

157

Anyhow, this ordeal at the military court took at least two hours before we were finally able to leave. We then left the court house and back to the passport office to get Hamid's Iranian passport.

While we were in Tehran, we also did some sightseeing. We exchanged our money for Iranian Rials, and enjoyed the food in one of the restaurants there. The food in Iran is outstanding.

My parent's house is located in a city outside of Tehran called Karaj. There is a major six to eight lane highway that connects the two cities together. The distance is only about 45 miles from one city to the next, but because of the heavy traffic, it took us 2-3 hours each way. We had to travel on this road every time we needed to go to Tehran, which was almost every time the government offices were open.

By then we knew for sure that the Navy wanted to speak with me, so we started to look for the best possible means to approach the situation. So, Nader, Ali and I went to Tehran the following day. When we arrived at the Navy base, which is located in the northern part of Tehran, I stayed in the car while Nader and Ali went inside.

Nader and Ali spoke to Colonel Mirshekar, head of the personnel department, about my situation. He responded calmly and with confidence saying, "We usually work with people in this situation. He is not the first or the last person to go AWOL from the Navy. Other people in similar situations have had to pay a fine anywhere from 3,000-18,000 dollars, but Saiid himself has to come forward and introduce himself before we can touch any files".

With that information we went home and started making phone calls to the people we knew in the military for advice, searching for the best way to approach the Navy headquarters. As a result, it was suggested to us to speak with Mr. Ahmadi at the Information Department of the Navy, as he would guide us as to what steps we needed to follow. Therefore, we made an appointment to see him.

He received us well and directed us to a room. Nader, Ali and I went in. There was not anything in that room except a few old chairs with leather seats and a coffee table. It did not even have windows to the outside. After a very short interview, he requested that I write brief statement as to what happened thirty years ago. He wanted me to explain my reason for choosing to stay in the United States. After all, the Navy had sent me there for an education and expected me to come back and serve as an officer. I did as he requested. My Farsi was "rusty", so I asked Ali to write the letter as I dictated my story to him.

Mr. Ahmadi then asked us to give him a couple of days and then he would call us to come back for a continuance of our dialogue. We gave him a couple of phone numbers in order to communicate with us. He preferred a local number so they would not have to call long distance, so I gave them the number of one of my sisters, Farzaneh, who lived in Tehran.

As soon as we left the Navy base, I called Farzaneh to let her know we were there. She insisted for us to come there for lunch. We had a great time of fellowship at her home. The food, as usual, was great and we shared the events of the day with her.

159

My vacation was short and I did not have a lot of time to waste, so a few days later when I still had not heard from Mr. Ahmadi, we decided to head back toward the Navy Base to check on the status of my case. We got up early in the morning and left Karaj at 6:00am. Ironically on our way to Tehran, Ali's cellular phone rang. It was my sister Farzaneh, saying that someone from the Navy base had just called and wanted us to come. This time Hamid was also with us.

So the four of us went to the office of Mr. Ahmadi, but this time he did not come out to greet us. Instead, he sent someone else to inform us that we must go to the personnel office and speak with Colonel Ansari who was the assistant to Colonel Mirshekar, his commander. So it seemed we were back where we started.

Col. Ansari was a medium built man about 5'7", partly bald and enjoyed smoking his cigarettes. He also was a fast talking character! He welcomed and received us well, ordered some hot tea and personally went to look for my file since his assistants could not find it right away.

He opened my file and said: "Mr. Saiid, everything in your file seems to be in order and was completed for you four years ago. We are far ahead of the game and will not need to make any requests for numbers or amounts from any departments".

He was saying all this with lots of smiling, and in a pleasant manner. Nader was my spokesperson, so he asked him what was inside my file.

Col. Ansari disclosed that there were two things recorded in my file against me:

1) A three-year imprisonment that needed my attention, but it might fall under the amnesty given by the leader of the country.

2) Two or three figures which amounted to about 20k dollars, which is the amount of money the Navy had spent on me and needed to be paid back.

Col. Ansari then called Captain Hassanvand who supposedly specialized in and was familiar with the law, to come to his office. He agreed that sometime in 1979, right after the revolution, the leader of the country gave a general amnesty to all those who left the country and who worked for the government, including those who did not finish their military service. Nonetheless, I needed to go after that letter of amnesty and clear my name for good. As a result, they would have to introduce me to the military court by way of a letter. Col. Ansari ordered a letter to be written and to be signed by the commander in their department.

This letter took four and a half hours to be written and signed. We were there at the base from 9:00am until 2:30pm, waiting at Col. Ansari's office for the most part. He was very friendly toward us, but it appeared that his helpers were too slow and lazy. A few times, he had to chase after the letter he had delegated to others to type. He finally was able to obtain the signed letter at 2:00pm, which was right before they closed their office. The commander who signed the letter had been busy with meetings, a funeral, prayer at the mosque and lunch. But finally we had accomplished what we came for.

Even though this was a step in the right direction, I still was not sure I could trust them. It was too early for me to determine if they were scheming behind my back. I had to trust what they were telling me. Col. Ansari put on a good show to impress us with his fast talk and led us to believe that he was working very diligently on my behalf, but we did not know how much of that was real or fake.

We left Col. Ansari's office with lots of hope. I felt very good about the outcome of our visit, and it encouraged me to continue doing whatever needed to be done in order for me to get home and to be able to make future trips to Iran. However, because of the Iranian New Year, we found ourselves dealing with many days when the government offices were closed due to the national celebration.

The 13th day of the first month of the New Year, Farvardin, is one of those days where all offices are closed. It is called "Nature Day" and is the last day of the two-week long Iranian celebration of Norooz (New Year). Most everyone gets out of their house with their families for a picnic. It is also a tradition for single ladies to tie grass leaves together and to make a wish to be wed (tie the knot!) in the year to come. We also decided to get together at Nader's house, since it was located out in the country. The roads were bumper to bumper with cars, buses and motorcycles. The streets that normally had little traffic on them were packed with cars and people. It seemed that every part of the countryside that you might find streams or rivers were occupied with families drinking their hot tea, smoking on water pipes and relaxing under shaded trees. Kids were playing, young people walking, talking, and enjoying the countryside.

We also got together with our families at home and enjoyed eating good food, played cards, danced and later walked in a huge vineyard close by. We sang songs and joked about life today compared to what life used to be like 30 years ago. Hamid and I purposely planned our trip to correspond with this national holiday. It was a joyous time for our family reunion!

On Monday, April 4, 2005, after eleven days into my vacation, Ali, Nader and I started out early in the morning and went back to the military court. The traffic was heavy as usually, and the acrid exhaust fumes of cars and buses made breathing uncomfortable.

We finally arrived at our destination where the military court was located. After driving from one street to another and making a few circles, we found a space between two houses to park our car. Nader used a big padlock to lock the steering wheel to prevent anyone from "hot-wiring" it and driving it away. Then he set the car alarm and took the removable faceplate to his car radio, and with a prayer, we left the car. We had to walk a few blocks to the entrance. We went through a gate guarded with a few soldiers, and then to the reception room where they checked our identification cards. We received our passes and then went through a metal detector and a basic body search before going into the main lobby of the building. The building had six floors, so I was glad Nader was with me to read the signs to help us get to where we needed to go. Speaking and reading Farsi wasn't easy for me anymore.

We went straight to the clerk of court with the sealed letter Col. Ansari gave us and gave it to the clerk. The clerk sent us to see someone else in another office. She searched for my name in a file drawer, which they kept alphabetically, looking for my name, but could not find it. She then suggested for us to go to the lowest level (the basement) where they keep all the older files. We went two floors below the main lobby to the basement and waited a long time for this office staff to search for my file. They could not find my name in any of their paper records or in their automated records by computer. They finally referred me back to the Navy.

By the time we left, it was about 1:00pm and there was not enough time to get to the Navy base since they closed their offices at 2:00pm. So, we called Col. Ansari using a cellular phone and told him about our dilemma. He prepared a copy of the naval court order, which included the three year imprisonment, and gave it to us so that the next day we could take it back to the military court.

We later learned that thirty years ago, the Navy had signed my discharge papers, but had attached a three-year imprisonment to the discharge. We obtained a copy of the court order and brought it back to the military court who then hand delivered it to the clerk of court. The ball started to roll. We went from one office to another so people could okay and sign the amnesty paper. Thankfully, no one gave me a hard time.

One person at one of the offices wanted to know the reason for my AWOL. I told him that it was a long story. With curiosity, he asked me to give him a brief version of it. So I briefly explained to him about my dissatisfaction with the school system, as well as my resignation from the school. I could tell by the look on his face that he was not satisfied with my answer, but I knew that the choice was not his to make since the amnesty paper had already been signed by others ahead of him.

Before the last person signed the amnesty papers, I was told that someone else wanted to see me, so Nader and I went to his office. There were actually two men there. Nader was told to leave the room, but when Nader objected by telling them that I might not be able to communicate well enough, he said, pointing to the palm of his hand, that he would make me talk. I could tell that Nader was a bit nervous by leaving me alone, but he had no choice but to obey. So Nader left the room and I was asked to sit down.

I did not know what to expect but I wasn't worried. They offered to bring me a cup of hot tea, but I declined and thanked them for their hospitality.

One of the men asked me when I was born, so I told him my birthday.

They both had a peculiar look on their faces. I didn't know what to make of it and waited to hear what the next question was going to be. Then the one who seemed to be the older enlightened me by saying "The reason I asked you to come in here was that your birth year is the same as mine and I wanted to meet you". They both chuckled and wanted to know what I did to stay in the shape I was in!

He looked like my father with a wrinkled face, missing a few teeth, and with gray hair. I was hoping not to say anything that would be insulting, so I told him it was the exercise! He immediately responded by saying, "Aha, that definitely helps one to stay younger." Then they both wished me well and we said goodbye to each other.

We finally had the last person sign and I was provided my amnesty papers in a sealed envelope to take back to the Navy. We left the military court and called Col. Ansari to

165

tell him about the amnesty papers, but he told me to bring it to his office the next day since it was getting late and we would not get there before he left for the day.

My experience there made me feel there were some good people in the government who desired to be compassionate and helpful toward others, and it seemed to be the nature of their hearts to be like that.

While we were still at the military court, I decided to introduce myself to a particular judge whom a good friend of mine had suggested I should meet for advice. He had dealt with many situations like mine and knew the problems that I may face.

First, he advised me that I should agree to pay the money they spent for me. He believed that the Navy would work with me in order for me to pay them back. He also forewarned me that they may require me to pay the money at the rate of thirty years ago, which I will explain later. He said that this is the sticky part because to this day no law or legislature had been passed concerning this subject and how to handle this issue. He said that it would be to the best interest of both parties if you could resolve this issue between you, but if an agreement was not reached, you may have to bring the matter before the court so we can settle it for you, but it may take a longer time.

The Judge advised me that if it came to that or if I felt that they were being unfair, I should object to their demands, and bring it to the court. He was very candid and to the point. I was very grateful for his advice and thanked him for his time. So I left the court house, full of hope and expectation.

The next day, Ali, Nader and I got up early in the morning and made our two hour trip to the Navy base in order to finish our work. I took this opportunity while traveling to and from Tehran to share what the Bible teaches about Christ with my brother-in laws.

As we traveled, Nader pointed to the writing right above a mosque that said, **"Islam is the only path to God"**. He seemed to always have an answer for everything I said, but Ali on the other hand, was responding more positively concerning our discussions, and in many cases, he was even helping and agreeing with me.

At the Navy base, Col. Ansari sent a message to the gate to allow only one of us to go in with the letter of amnesty, so Nader went in for me. He gave him the letter and requested a copy for my records.

Nader had served in the military and knew what questions to ask. He objected to the $20,000 Col. Ansari had given us previously and asked to see the signed and detailed documents in my file to see how they reached that amount.

Col. Ansari agreed right away that we had the right to see the documents, but he would need some time to write another letter to the education department to request a list of the expenses in more detail. On that note, Nader left his office and told him that he would call and check on things in a few days.

While my brother and I were in Iran, we visited many of our relatives and friends. I was not in the mood to do much shopping considering the situation I was in. I needed to save all the money I had just in case. Spending time with my family and friends was a joy and very comforting.

167

It was during one of those visits that I met my uncle for the first time. My aunt had remarried since I had been in the US so I had never had the chance to meet him. His work involved traveling in and out of the country and he had done this most of his adult life, therefore I had never had a chance to meet him when I was younger. With his travels, he had many opportunities to meet other people with other faiths. When he heard that I was a 'born-again' Christian, he immediately wanted to talk to me and ask some questions.

He told me that he had read the Bible several times and fell in love with Jesus Christ and his qualities. In his own view, and based on what he had read in the Bible, he could not believe that the God of the Bible was the same as in the Quran. He believed that maybe the ones who wrote the Quran changed many things in it and that is why it was so different from the Bible. I asked him how he came to this conclusion.

He said that what you read in the Quran and the history of mankind in Islam is so different from what the Bible teaches. Secondly he said Islam is a religion that came upon the nation of Iran by force of the sword. The people of Iran, before the Arab's aggression, had a great religion with good and basic creeds such as, good talk, behavior and character. But today Islam has 'two-faced' religious leaders who proclaim that they care for their people, but instead they bring poverty to them while making themselves rich. There has been nothing fruitful from this tree, only thorns, even after more than twenty-five years of domination. This is what my uncle believed, and right or wrong, his perception was reality for him.

HOW ISLAM STARTED AS A RELIGION

In the seventh century, an Arabian named Mohammad claimed to have revelations from God, which ultimately gave rise to the Quran and the faith of Islam. Mohammad claimed that this faith was the final revelation of God, though he recognized the genuineness of earlier revelations given through Moses and Jesus, both of whom he considered great Prophets. Yet, they wish to kill their followers at the same time. **He enforced this new faith through the power of the sword** and eventually conquered many of the lands that had been largely Christian. These events eventually led to the Christian Crusades of the 11th through the 13th centuries, which led to even more bloodshed.

I asked my uncle, what he liked about Christianity and Christ. He told me that he sees the true God in the life of Jesus Christ. He always cared for humanity, he always loved mankind and no one ever came to him leaving empty handed. He never used His power against people. He drew people to Himself not by force or sword but by showing them love and compassion. I was so glad to hear my uncle talking like this because this was also the way I was drawn to Christ! **I asked him if he had shared this with his wife and children.** He said that he had not yet.

So when Hamid and I were invited to his house the following week, we shared the good news with the rest of our uncle's family.

On another occasion, I was in one of my sister's house and the subject of religion came up. Ali, one of my nephews brought his Quran to point out what it says about Jesus. His Quran was written in both Farsi and Arabic languages. I welcomed his effort. The whole family was there, listening to what transpired between us.

He started to read from the chapter of Maryam, named after Mary the mother of Jesus. As he was reading, the first person of interest he talked about was Zechariah, the father of Yahya (John the Baptist), who is recorded as being a promised son in comparison to Jesus who was the Holy Promised Son, yet both are considered to be prophets in Islamic theology.

"O Zechariah, We give thee good news of a son, his name shall be Yahya. (Sura 19: Ayah 7)

But since Zechariah and his wife Elizabeth were in their old age and past the age of child bearing, they needed assurance. The Quran states that Zechariah was told that he would be speechless for three nights, though he was not dumb, as a sign. Ayah (verse) 10

I told my nephew to stop and I asked him this question. In our Holy Scripture it is recorded that Zechariah was speechless for the entire time of Elizabeth's pregnancy. Without questioning the Quran, which one do you think is a greater miracle from God?

He responded "Yours of course." He continued reading until he reached ayah (verse) 19, where the angel is announcing to Mary **"the gift of a holy Son"**, which the word 'holy' was translated as "pure" in theFarsi language.

I asked him to stop so we could discuss the difference between just saying someone is pure and God saying Jesus is pure or holy. I asked him if he would agree that due to man's limitations and knowledge we can only compare the purity of one person to other. However, when God says that Jesus is holy (pure), that word carries a meaning beyond man's personal experience. It means that there is no sin, flaws or imperfection in Him. Just as God is Holy.

My nephew acknowledged my reasoning.

Therefore, this verse speaks of exactly that, the purity of Jesus, which corresponds with our Holy Scripture. Furthermore, **God has never called anyone else Holy or pure after the fall of Adam and Eve in the same way as Jesus.**

In ayahs (verses) 7-10, we see a miracle has taken place for Zechariah, yet the good news was only about a son, not a holy son!

God has called "good" to the things He has made. The creation story is an example, **but holiness only goes to His Son.** People through the ages have called other Prophets or Apostles holy, but I do not recall God calling anyone, except Jesus Christ Holy (Pure).

{Note: the word holy has two major meanings.

1) Divine, "for the Lord our God is holy"

2) Set apart, "holy temple" or "holy Prophet"

Except for Jesus, all have sinned and fall short of the glory of God. I went farther and explained other writings in the Quran that have not been explained correctly to people which I have already covered in my previous chapters. Unfortunately they could not understand me due to the preconceived state of their minds!

It is interesting that the Quran gives a few very distinctive qualities to Jesus that was not given even to Muhammad such as:

1) *Jesus is the Word of God (kalimullah in susa 3:45)*
2) *Jesus is The Spirit of God (Ruhullah in sura 21:91)*
3) *Jesus is born of virgin Mary as a Pure Son*
4) *Jesus will reappear to mankind again*

None of these unique claims were given to Muhammad whom they consider to be the last and the most superior to all other Prophets!

My brother in law finally asked this question; so, you mean "Jesus the Son of God" is not the result of a physical intimacy between God and Mary <u>as we have been told!</u>

I responded, of course not. Mary never had any physical contact with anyone. She was a virgin and remained a virgin. She married Joseph after the baby Jesus was born. He then told me that he understood.

Later he showed me a book of poetry he had and started reading it to me. He said that it was one of his favorite books. As he was reading, he came to a verse that mentioned Jesus as the Son of God. I said, There it is in your own book too!" Then he realized what he was reading and told me that if his family knew he was reading this and what it actually meant, they would consider him an infidel. What a shame!

Chapter 12

Hamid's Departure

It was Friday, April 8, 2005. It was the day Hamid would be leaving to go back home to the United States. We had traveled together to Iran and were supposed to go back home together, but it was not working out as we had hoped. So, it was not the greatest day for me. I was grieved and happy at the same time. I was happy because Hamid was going home to his dear wife and children, but sad knowing my wife and children were disappointed by this obstacle in my path; not being able to see each other as expected. I also felt Hamid's dissatisfaction that I was left behind.

I felt certain I would gain my freedom and that it would be delayed for only a short time, but I had to overcome my depression by being calm and patient and rely on God's faithfulness. My soul was disturbed and it was hard to face the reality of Hamid' departure without me. Therefore, instead of going to the airport to see Hamid off, I stayed home with Mom and Dad and prayed for his safety and the rest of my own journey here in Iran. I opened up my Bible to hear what God had to tell me concerning the rest of my journey, for I needed to hear more assurance and comfort from Him. I was hoping that His words would bring peace to my disturbed soul. I came across this passage in the book of Psalms, chapter 43:

> *"Vindicate me, O God, and plead my cause against an ungodly nation; Oh, deliver me from the deceitful and unjust man! For You are the God of my strength."*

I read this psalm several times and it spoke to my heart. I wanted to hear more and wished to hear Him audibly, telling me what to do next. That night, I tossed and turned, and had a hard time sleeping. All kinds of thoughts were going through my mind. I would grab a pen and paper and jot them down before I forgot, hoping that it was from my Lord.

In Iran, with the situation I was in, you either hire a lawyer to do the running around for you or you do it yourself if you expect anything to be done. So, early in the morning at 6:30am, Nader and Ali came over to pick me up and we headed to the Navy base. We got there at about 9:30am, and called Col. Ansari from outside of the base. Ali spoke with Col. Ansari, but the response was that he needed a couple more days to finish the work that he had already started. Col. Ansari also said that he had been busy working very hard on my behalf and was able to reduce the expenses down to about $10,000, half of what we had earlier been told.

Ali was happy about the news, but not me. My heart was telling me that something was wrong, but I could not put my finger on it. All I knew was that we had just driven three hours in heavy traffic, inhaling lots of exhaust fumes to get there and for him to tell us to come back in a couple of days was very upsetting. So I decided to call him back. I sensed that Ali did not agree, although he did not voice his feelings, but I went ahead anyway.   I told Col. Ansari that I was not satisfied with his conversation with Ali and that I must see him since we drove such a long way. He agreed, and Nader and I went in while Ali stayed behind in the car.

We went directly to the building where Col. Ansari was. He welcomed us and began with his "fast and charming talk" singing the same song by saying, "I have been working so hard on your file, sending and receiving letters from the education dept. finance dept., the budget and credit dept. etc. and of course everyone has to sign the papers."

He told us that he had done a lot on my behalf and that he could not tell us everything over the phone. Then he proceeded to tell us that he was actually able to reduce the expenses to almost $4,000 **plus some expenses in Rial, which amounted to about $330.00**. So all together the adjusted repayment figure was about $4,330!

Nader and I looked at each other and could not believe what we were hearing! Nader wanted to trust everything Col. Ansari was saying, but I had mixed feelings about it. I needed to go along with what Nader wanted to do, since he was making every effort to help me.

The news made me happy and eased some of the stress I was under.   I thought that perhaps my problems were almost over and the grace of God was falling on me. And again, but for a short while, I felt that these people I was dealing with seemed to be Godly and truly wanted to help resolve my situation.

But later, I realized that something was indeed fishy. I wondered why he did not want to tell me the truth about the *reduction to $4,330 over the phone! What did he have to hide by telling us $10,000 and later changing it to $4,330 in less than half an hour?*

I also was suspicious of the fact he was trying to stop us from looking into my file because later on, I was told by Mr. Javadi that many documents from that far back were destroyed.

Someone else suggested that perhaps he wanted some bribe money! Or perhaps he simply was giving me a hard time by trying to intentionally delay me, therefore dodging me. I had been trying to think positive, but it was very difficult!

Col. Ansari told me all that was left to do was to have the commander of the personnel department sign the document, and then I would be done. I thanked God, thanked him and shook his hand acknowledging that I was happy with the results. I left that day with a smile!

I was so excited from our conversation and thought that it should not take any more than a couple of days for the commander to sign the letter. Therefore, with no time to spare, we went straight to the KLM office in Tehran, rescheduled my flight for two weeks later, paid the exit fee of 10,000 Toman ($12), and my flight was reserved for April 23.

At first the KLM agent told me that there was no seat available for the next month in the seating class that I was in, but after speaking with a supervisor, she was able to change my seating class in order to find me a seat. I thanked God for that too and phoned home to tell my wife the good news! I also called my supervisor, Terry Kipick, at work and told him about my situation and to let him know that if God was willing, I should be home soon. My wife had been in touch with my co-workers and had kept them up-to-date about my status. I figured that if everything went as planned, I would be late only two weeks. I still had extra paid vacation days left so I could use them as part of my income.

It was great to visit my family and friends in Iran, but I was more than ready to leave and come back to my own family in America, which is where my heart was.

The next step was to collect enough money to pay my debt. So the following day, my mother went to see her sister,Zahra, to ask her for a loan. I only had about $1,000 with me. Hamid left $1,000 for me to use if needed, and my Aunt Zahra lent the other $3,000. Now I had the money necessary to take care of what I needed to pay the Iranian Navy.

Later that week my mom and sisters took me shopping at the central bazaar in Tehran and to some shopping centers in Karaj. They purchased many gifts for all of my family back home. Soon, my suit cases were packed and ready to come home to my loved ones.

After two days I called the Navy to see if the commander had signed the letter, but was told to call back on Saturday which was three days later. I then learned that the commander would not be in his office on Saturday, and Sunday was a holiday, and Monday was Military Day and he would be busy with a parade that day. On Tuesday April 19, the commander was on a mission and out of town.

Finally, on April 20th, I learned   that the commander, Col. Mirshekar, and his boss, General Ghots, rejected the letter!

"Why did he do that?" I cried out to my God!

Have you ever felt like you were on a sinking ship? That's the way I felt upon hearing that news.

The reason they gave was that they wanted the expenses in Rial, which amounted to about 330 US dollars and claimed to be for "special mission expenses" to be converted from Rial to Dollar at the rate of 30 years ago.

In other words, a $330 conversion would increase the total repayment to $40,071. This is how it was calculated:

Today $1=850 Toman, but 30years ago $1=7 Toman so,

330 X 850=280,500 Toman already written in my file

280,500 / 7 = $40,071 conversion at a rate of 30 years ago.

Nader went to see Col. Mirshekar and questioned him about this conversion of the money. Col. Mirshekar showed him a file of someone named Mr. Hossaini whom he claimed had similar circumstances as mine. They intended to use his situation as a legal precedent for the conversion of the money in my case as well.

Col. Mirshekar then said that they had requested more clarification   from the courts on this other man's case, and they were still waiting for the answer, but, in the meantime, they were following the order from the leader of the country. He did not however disclose that they had been waiting for an entire year for that clarification of that request. Nader then took notes of the file number that he was referring to and left his office.

So, since the letter for my case was rejected, it was sent back to the budget and credit department for a redo. Nader went to the Navy base and spent all day there, carrying the new letter to different departments to speed up the process. While he was there, he also went to the information dept. and complained about the way they were taking their time and sending us back and forth causing extra anguish for us. Over the past few weeks, I had overheard some comments being made about me from some of the officers saying, "He has been in America enjoying   life for the last 30 years, let him run around and suffer for a little while in this country."

The budget and credit department sent back the second request to the personnel department without any changes. I asked, "What do we do now? It was exactly the same figures as the first. Why did they not change the amount?" We were not sure what to do next.

We then decided to go to the budget and credit department to meet with Mr. Goodarzi and to ask him why he did not change the numbers as requested. Mr. Goodarzi was a very calm and soft-spoken person. He was working there as a civilian. After a short pause, he tried to choose his words very carefully, saying that he could not do that for a few reasons:

1)   *He did not have an order to change the numbers even though he had requested it from higher up in his department.*

2)   *There was a card in my file indicating that the money that was issued thirty years ago was in Rial and not in*

179

US dollar, therefore he could not change it to the rate they requested.

3)   *He did not have the exchange rate as it was 30 years ago.*

4)   *It sounded like too much money from a small amount in Rial, which they had recorded in my file, and he felt that it was not a justifiable request.*

5)   *It was against the law and he did not want to be part of that. If they wanted to change it, they could do it themselves!*

We went back and forth between the budget department and the personnel department to clarify what to do next. When Col. Ansari kept giving us his assurance by saying that our final days of coming and going were almost over, he gave me enough confidence to re-reschedule my ticket. I was confident about leaving Iran and had banked on his words.

Capt. Hassanvand, the lawyer for the Navy, came over and we discussed our dilemma with him, and these are the exact words he told us, "If you still have your passport in your possession along with the copy of the amnesty letter, then you should be able to leave the country without any problems. Then, Nader can act as your lawyer on your behalf to finish where you left off and settle the financial matters at a later time."

Now when I think back, I believe they intentionally tricked me, knowing that I would be leaving the country soon and that I would be stopped by the airport security who had the authority to confiscate my passport, and not the Navy. When I had given my passport to Mr. Ahmadi at the Information Department, he gave it back after making a copy of it, which proved to me that they did not have the authority to confiscate anything, only to file a complaint. They somehow wanted to punish me without being blamed. But first they needed to tempt me to do something wrong or illegal in order to accuse me and keep me there at their mercy indefinitely!

Another thought I had was since other border cities in Iran do not have the sophistication of Tehran's airport, anyone could leave the country through those border cities with their passport in hand and without being detected. This was a clever tactic on their part to obtain my passport!

I had already reserved my flight for the 23rd of April to leave Iran. Capt. Hassanvand had already deceived me by telling me that it was okay to leave the country. Other friends were also encouraging me to get out at whatever cost. I remembered from the Bible the way Peter was able to escape from prison and the angel of God was with him, opening every prison door. I thought to myself, could it be like that God? Would you do that for me? Would you close the eyes of the authorities in order for me to leave Iran? I was doing a lot of praying and asking others to do the same. Prayer chains had already been started in both Iran and the USA as I was getting ready for this departure. I was already delayed for two weeks from my original departure. So, with those thoughts, I mustered enough courage to try to leave Iran, hoping to be free from this "prison!"

"Over the next days and weeks, I was in touch with our local congressman's office and our state senators' offices. They were mostly compassionate and were willing to do anything they could, but the reality of it was there wasn't much any of them could do as long as he was in Iran. Saiid and I both were doing everything we could under the circumstances. Everyday we would wake up with renewed hope that there would be a breakthrough and this nightmare would be over, but the day would come and go and there would be another obstacle. It seemed there was no end.

But in my heart I knew God had a plan and I felt in time He would bring Saiid home, but the waiting and uncertainty was hard. I found myself so many times on my face before the Lord, praying for my husband and for his safe return, and for His strength to get us through. This is one of the verses that gave me comfort:

Psalm 5: 1-3 "Give ear to my words, O LORD, Consider my meditation. Give heed to the voice of my cry, My King and my God, For to You I will pray. My voice You shall hear in the morning, O LORD; In the morning I will direct it to You, And I will look up."

It was especially hard for Saiid with the run around he constantly got from the navy base, and the fact that he was the one trapped and separated from his family. I could tell he was discouraged from time to time, and I tried to cheer him up the best I could. I think the thing that helped the most was the encouragement from our family and friends. I always made sure to let him know about the cards, phone calls, visits, and emails that were coming in from all over! I usually forwarded the emails to him so he could read them for himself. We will never forget the love, the concern, the prayers and the generosity that came from so many people during that time."

Ursa

Chapter 13

First Attempt to Leave!

It was Friday night, the evening before my scheduled flight. I was confused, yet hopeful; cautious, but willing to take chances. I packed my suitcases and prepared to leave my dad's home. Early on Saturday morning, we left and headed toward the airport.

All my sisters were there to see me off. We did not know what the outcome was going to be that night, except to trust God for my rescue and hoping that He would cover the eyes of those authorities for me to slip by. I checked in my luggage and after saying goodbye to all my sisters and in-laws and my nieces and nephews, I proceeded toward the exit and passport check. Three of my relatives were with me to make sure that everything went smooth.

There was much comfort in knowing so many people were praying for me, but I was still a little anxious and concerned. All kinds of things were going through my mind, but I tried to remain calm. The officer stamped my exit passport, and I saluted good-bye to Nader and a couple of my relatives who came as far as they could to make sure of my departure. But, I had not walked more than 200 feet when I heard someone calling my name through the loud speaker and echoing through the hallway:

"Mr. Saiid Rabiipour!"

My heart sank when I heard my name.   Then I heard my name being called again, "Mr. Rabiipour!"

Then I saw a man headed in my direction, holding a two-way radio in his hand. Part of me wanted to keep on going, but I stopped because I did not want to create a scene.   He then asked me if my name was Mr. Rabiipour, and I acknowledged that I was.

He asked for my passport. I gave him my Iranian passport, which was used to leave the country.   Then he pointed his index finger at me to follow him and asked me to identify the officer who checked me out at the passport booth. I pointed to the officer who checked me out. He then voided my exit by using another mark on my passport, and told me that I did not have permission to leave the country until my name was cleared from his computer.

He kept my Iranian passport and gave me a receipt with instructions on the back to go to the passport office on Africa Avenue in order to get my passport back. I attempted to show him the copy of the presidential amnesty letter I kept with me, but he was not interested in listening to me or seeing anything. Then he went to the KLM agent and requested to have my luggage returned to me and proceeded to cancel my flight.

Nader and my other relatives were still there when they heard my name being called. They tried to intercept and beg on my behalf but to no avail. It took quite a while to get my luggage back, and finally we left the airport. It was 4:30 in the morning when we got back to my parent's home.

Was I disappointed? You bet you.

Why didn't God answer my prayers?

Why didn't He allow me to leave the way He allowed Apostle Peter to get out of prison?

Should I get angry at my Father since He chose not to do what I wanted?

This is one of the reasons many Christians stumble in their walk since they don't get their prayers answered the way they wished and for His protection on earth. In fact the Quran makes mockery of People of the Book (Jews and Christians) for being punished by saying, then where is your God to protect you if you are called His children!

So, should we stop praying all together since we may not get our prayers answered the way we wished?

Oh no, prayers reflect our humility before God the Father. He has already done everything that needed to be done to redeem His children. We need Him no matter what our circumstances may be. He is worthy of our worship and praise regardless of our condition.

So, I thought to myself that perhaps my Father had a different plan for me. So, I thanked Him and patiently waited for His next move.

The next day we went back to the Navy base and found out that the commander of the personnel department rejected the financial settlement from the budget and credit department for the second time and for the same reason.

It was so obvious by then that they were treating me like a ping-pong ball, paddling me between the two departments of the Navy. We did not know what to do except to try to knock on every door for help for the possible answer.

I thought about getting a lawyer, but was told that would drag things out even longer. It would be much faster if I went after it myself. Frankly, I did not have much money or time to rely on others, which is why we were attempting to do the running around ourselves. With that in mind, we visited the finance department to check on the method of disbursement of the money thirty years ago. We were told that the person who was familiar with files that far back was Mr. Javadi.

We waited for him to return from his break and he welcomed us into his office and ordered some hot tea. He was not feeling well that day but he was there working anyway. He was a man with a gentle attitude, soft spoken and seemed to be very meek. He listened to us carefully as we explained our problem to him. He said that there was no meaning in what they were doing to us. We asked him about my file and details of how the expenses were paid during those years. He told us that all files from 1988 and before were voided and destroyed. He even checked with someone else in the same department and both said the same thing.

He suggested that the only place that they may have any records kept that far back was the Central bank, but he

188

would have to call them some other day in order to find out the answer for us. He said he would also like to speak with Col. Mirshekar to see how he could help solve our problem. So we left with the hope that we would hear from him soon.

Day 22

On April 26, after twenty two days, my struggle was not improving much. They still had me stalled between two departments in conflict with each other. One was demanding to change the so called "mission expenses" to be calculated at the rate of thirty years ago while the other would say that they could not do that unless they had an order from their own department head, which both were part of the Navy base. So we were stuck between a rock and a hard place without any answers.

Col. Ansari was no longer working on my case. His boss, Col. Mirshekar, told him that from now on Capt. Hassanvand and he would handle my case. He told me that Col. Ansari did not know anything about the conversion of the money when I questioned him about the figures he gave me. Apparently Col. Ansari objected to his boss about the changes in figures, but was told to leave his office and that his work work was finished on my file. Whether they were telling me the truth or not, I wasn't sure.   Obviously, the judge who had earlier advised me knew all about the conversion of money and the tactics that were used in cases like mine.   There was at least one unresolved case that we discovered ourselves and noted the case number as a reference.

The following day was the Prophet Mohammed's birthday, another holiday. According to some Muslim Imams, the prophecy of his coming is mentioned in our Holy Bible. One of my sisters also brought that to my attention and asked, "Doesn't the Bible talk about Mohammad?"

The Quran also makes the same reference in **Sura 61:6**

"And remember, Jesus, the son of Mary, said: "O children of Israel! I am the apostle of God (sent) to you, confirming the Law (which came) before me, and giving glad tidings of an Apostle to come after me, whose name shall be Ahmad."

Note: Ahmad is understood as Mohammad by Muslim Scholars.

Of course there is no such a statement in our Bible and Jesus would not have any reason for saying that since He is the end of the law. Jesus came to free mankind from the law, through grace. Muhammad would put us back in the law again, which would make no sense at all!

There are two other passages in the Bible which Muslim scholars think are referring to Muhammad. They are:

1) Deuteronomy 18:15 "The LORD your God will raise up for you a Prophet like me (Moses) from your midst, from your brethren. Him you shall hear," And again in verse18, "I will raise up for them a Prophet like you from among their brethren, and will put My words in His mouth, and He shall speak to them all that I command Him."

Since the Quran is allegedly a recitation of what the angel Gabriel recited to Mohammad, Muslims considered that as God's word being put in his mouth and prophecy being fulfilled. But he is an Arab and a gentile, not a Jew! (A small twist in language)

2)   John 14:15-18, "If you love Me, keep My commandments. And I will pray the Father, and He will give you another Helper, that He may abide with you forever— the <u>Spirit of truth</u>, whom the world cannot receive, because it neither sees Him nor knows Him; but you know Him, for He dwells with you and will be in you. I will not leave you orphans; I will come to you".

Muslims consider Mohammad as the "spirit of truth" and a helper, who came after Jesus. Therefore, they think that the above verses are talking about Mohammad.

Just for the record, a Baha'i friend of mine pointed to the same passages in the Bible as a reference to the coming of their Prophet Baha'u'llah, after Mohammad.

So, I asked my sister if she thought the Prophet Mohammed was with her forever, and she said "NO."

Does Mohammed live within you? She said "NO"

Then the Bible is not talking about Mohammed, for he died and was buried, and his tomb is in the city of Medina, Saudi-Arabia. But what the Bible is talking about is the "Holy Spirit" or "Spirit of truth", who lives within His children.

While in Iran, I always had a handbag with all the necessities such as extra cloths, toothpaste, toothbrush, my notebook and my Bible with me. Every day after going places, I spent my time at either my sisters or parent's house. I felt like a nomad going from one place to the other!

The first three weeks of my vacation was good, but two months was a bit uncomfortable for me, especially since my focus has changed. My Mom and Dad were in their old age and I did not want to cause them too much work by being there all the time. Sometimes I even had to witness their disagreements over mostly simple issues, and they wanted me to take sides with them, which was not easy for me to do.

Suffering from arthritis, my Dad complained a lot about his legs. He kept himself close to a heater and we occasionally would help him with a massage, applying some ointment on his knees. My Mom's back was also giving her a hard time sometimes, yet she never quit working or cooking. They kept their heater on high all the time. I had to keep a window partially open and stay close to it for fresh air unless I wished to be in a sauna!

My sisters had teen-age daughters and I did not want to intrude on their privacy. They were all very nice to me and made me feel right at home. I would try to teach them English, played cards, or watched TV while in their homes. They often watched me reading my emails coming from my wife and friends, and frequently saw me as tears were running down my face. I would share with them the importance of my relationship with my wife and family and the value we had for each other. I would try to show them how the love of God had affected my life by my actions and conversations while living among them. None of my sisters have ever seen my wife, yet they were in love with her because of my relationship and the way I talk about her to them. I tried to show and tell them that our marriage relationship is after the example of Christ for His children.

One day we had gone downtown window-shopping. After walking around for an hour or two, I suggested for us to walk back home. They agreed. My sister's feet were hurting as a result. Later that evening, I offered to show my brother-in-law how to give his wife a foot massage. Boy! That felt good to her! Now every time we talk over the phone, I ask if Ali (her husband), is still massaging her feet, and she laughs about it!

On Thursday, April 28, we all went to a park in Karaj (not far from my parents' home) to have a picnic. My Mom cooked as usual and we all played, ate, and rode the ferris wheel at the park. I always shared the love of God with my family, whether in the park or at the house or on our way to the navy base. I never blamed anyone for my situation, even the people at the navy base, just the system in which they were operating under.

I had a great time with my visits, delicious foods and fellowship, but my time was up and I needed to get back home to America where I belonged. Nader and Ali tried very hard to keep me busy, and made sure I was having a good time by taking me sightseeing or to other places.

One day we made a trip to Beheshte Zahra (Zahra's heaven), which is a huge graveyard. I remembered that place from my childhood when it was dusty, smelly, hot, and hardly any trees or flowers. You did not wish to stay there for a long time. Now the place was exceptionally clean and beautiful. The streets were paved and clean. There were flowers and trees everywhere and the tombstones were kept clean making this a very desirable place to bury your loved ones.

My brother Parviz was also buried there, so we went to see his grave and I prayed for him and remembered him before the God of Mercy and Grace. He was only a year and half older than me and was very close and dear to me. During the summer he would take me to work with him and other places, such as picnics, movies, etc. I could not help but remember all the good times we had growing up and tears filled my eyes as my heart cried for him.

I also saw the graves of many soldiers who died during the eight year "Iraq-Iran war' which took place between 1980 and 1988. There were a total of 188,000 soldiers, militia, and civilians killed. They were all decorated beautifully with pictures and flowers. Many of them were young people. Families who lost their loved ones were there with trays of home-made cookies or other pastries to give to the people in honor of their dead. It is customary to accept the cookie and then pray for the soul of the person who has passed away, since Muslims believe in 'purgatory'. I suppose this action brings peace to the one who is offering the cookie and honor on behalf of the dead, similar to putting flowers on the grave.

On another day, we made a trip to "Imam Zadeh Davood" which is located north of Tehran. He is the brother of Imam Reza, the 8th Imam of the Shiite Muslims. We went there to pray and to do some sightseeing at the same time. I did not have any problem going to other locations to pray, for I always carry the Holy Spirit within me and pray "in the name of Jesus".

I remembered the words of the Apostle Paul, saying into my ears: "I have become all things to all men that I might by all means save some. Now this I do for the gospel's sake, that I may be partaker of it with you." (1 Cor. 9:22-23)

On our way there, we stopped at a restaurant by the road to use the restroom. We saw a nice waterfall and stopped to take some pictures. Two attendants there took care of the place and cooked for those who wished to eat there. I opened up the conversation with both of them and told them where we were going. One of them asked me to pray for his sister. She was having some internal bleeding and was very sick.

I asked him where he lived.

He answered that he lived in a city called Zanjan, which was about five or six hours away from where he was.

I asked, "Do you have a family"? He said, "Yes, I have a wife and some children."

"Why are you here?" I asked.

"For work, there are no jobs there where I live", he responded.

"How often do you see your family?" I asked.

"I work here five days out of the week and then I go home for two days." He answered.

I asked for the name of his sister and wrote it down on a piece of paper so I would not forget to pray for her, the man, and his family.

During this time, I never made any suggestions as to where to eat or what to do. Whatever decisions Nader and Ali made was fine with me. I believed that God was in control of my situation and my whereabouts, and my conversation with the man at the restaurant was not by accident. God knows everything and sometimes He uses us in a way that only He will receive the glory!

On our way back, we stopped at the same restaurant for lunch and I gave both of them a tip for good service, and to help the one from Zanjan with his trip to see his family. It is not customary to give tips at most restaurants there, but I wanted to do that for them. I wanted to show them the unconditional love and compassion since I was in need of it so desperately myself. I felt at peace for them, but for some reason or the other, my stomach was like a knot about my own situation due to the uncertainty of my future.

On our way back home, I could not help but think about my own dilemma. I just could not understand why the navy personnel were giving me a hard time. I somehow felt that I should talk to them directly in order to get to the bottom of the problem. With that in mind, I decided to see Col. Mirshekar, the commander of Personnel. So one morning while we were there at the Navy base, we went to his office. Col. Mirshekar, Mr. Javadi (from the Finance Dept.) and two other men were also sitting in his office. Mr. Javadi was there for the same purpose as I was, wanted to ask him about my situation.

After saying hello, I asked him boldly why he was causing problems for me.

He responded, "What problem?"

I asked him about the conversion of the money.

He said that the order was from the leader of the country and he was only following his order and there was nothing he could do about it.

I said, "Sir, I have my job and my family to go to and do not have time to stay here. "Then he responded. "That is not my problem."

I said "Sir, you said that if I come forward on my own and introduce myself, you will take that into consideration and work with me. Besides. Col. Ansari, your assistant, gave me the amount of the settlement and I even had to borrow that, but now you are changing it."

He told me that it was an order from his superior and that the money for the 'special missions' had to be converted to the way it was paid and Col. Ansari did not know about this change.

- I said "Sir, my file shows that the money was paid in Rials, not in dollars.

- You have said that you requested for the clarification of that order almost a year ago, but you have not received the answer to that yet.

- You are attaching a file that belongs to someone else to my file, even though that file has not been resolved yet.

- Lastly, your budget and credit dept. will not change the amount."

After hearing what I had to say, Col. Mirshekar said that he was only following orders, and I should speak with his boss, General Ghots. He said if he wants to change the order, then that would be fine with him.

At that moment, I realized that Col Mirshekar only wanted to give me a hard time, along with most everyone else I had dealt with. If he really wanted to help, all he had to do was pick up the phone and call General Ghots.

Later, as I was pacing in the personnel building, a colonel approached me wanting to know who I was and what I wanted. When I told him my problem, his response to me was that Iran was not a poor country and the navy did not need my money. With that thought he went directly to Col. Mirshekar to ask him to help me to get back to my home country. But Col. Mirshekar refused to even to listen to him. He would not waiver at all. He tried to get other people involved but to no avail. He then said he was sorry that he could not help me. I thanked him for trying. He seemed to be such a nice person, but he just didn't have the right amount of authority.

Chapter 14

The End of My Rope!

It was Day 26, Saturday April 30th, and things were not getting any better. Therefore, we spoke to my friend Nader #2 who happened to be the brother of one of my friends in the USA. He is a well known and respected individual by many people in Tehran and that is why I will not mention his last name. Incidentally, Nader #2 was the one who introduced me to this Judge earlier. I asked him to speak with the Judge about my situation one more time since I was not getting anywhere. He finally called me back at 11:30pm to tell me that I should go back to the base and ask to speak with Admiral Farzaneh, because he had the authority to make things work.

I always got up in the morning with a small ray of hope that something good was going to happen that day, but by the end of the day I seemed to always hit a brick wall. But I tried not to get too discouraged, remembering that God was with me.

The next day, Nader and I left Karaj at 6:30am and arrived at the base at 9:30am. At the gate, everyone knew us and called us by our name without looking at any identification card.

"Whom do you want to see today?" The guard asked. (Sometimes they would phone the person we wanted to see.)

"Admiral Farzaneh!" we answered. He looked at us and repeated, "Admiral Farzaneh! I cannot call him" (talking to himself.) So, he gave us a pass to go inside.

We were really getting tired of going and coming so many times. The base was so large, and we had to walk to the offices on foot. It took us at least 15-25 minutes of walking uphill to get to some of the offices. They did not allow cars on the base unless you worked there. That day Nader was having problems with his breathing and heart rate and I could feel his frustration. So, I hitch-hiked a car in order to get us closer to the buildings we needed to go to.

The Admiral was not in his office but was expected to be back at 4:00 pm, so we requested from his office manager, Mr. Jafar, to meet with the Admiral that afternoon when he came in. He made a note and invited us to check back with him later that afternoon.

In order not to have to go all the way back to Karaj, I called my aunt who lived in Tehran and asked her if we could stay there until 3:30pm. She was more than happy to welcome us to come spend our time there at her house. She even went to the trouble of fixing us lunch.

At 3:30pm, we called the office of the Admiral and spoke with Mr. Jafar again, but he told us that the Admiral could not see us at that time and made another appointment for the following day at 9am.

My aunt insisted for us to stay at her house that night which was wonderful for us. She also asked if after our business at the base the next day was done, we could take her to Karaj with us. Of course we told her we would be glad to. That evening the three of us decided to walk to a shopping mall for a couple of hours. I saw many beautiful items I wished to buy as souvenirs, but that was only a wish because I could not afford to misuse any money in case I needed it for other unexpected expenses. Then we went to a fast food restaurant and ordered a chicken sandwich, fries and drink. It was different from home cooking though, yet delicious! My aunt paid for all of us.

The next day, Sunday, we arrived at the base at 8:30am and went straight to the Admiral's office. His office manager was a different person that day! He wanted to know the nature of our business and who had sent us. Then, he asked us to write down our request on paper and after reviewing, he would direct us as to what to do next. Obviously, the Judge had not spoken with the Admiral about our situation as I had wished. Therefore, he did not know who we were, and as a result, he was not interested in speaking with us.

As we started writing our request on paper, the office manager went inside and spoke with the Admiral. Thankfully he agreed to see us. Nader and I went into his office, but he would not allow Nader to stay. I introduced myself and mentioned the judge who told us to come and see him. He was already on the phone talking with someone else, and after he hung up, he told me I would need to go see Admiral Vahmani who was over the Education Department. He would do whatever was lawful for us.

Admiral Farzaneh was not interested in talking with me at all and when I mentioned the name of the judge again, he immediately said that it was not any of his business and would not allow me to ask any questions. I thanked him and left his office to see Admiral Vahmani at the next building.

Admiral Vahmani received us well, listened to what we had to say, and made a few phone calls. He called Col. Mirshekar, but he was not there. He called General Ghots and talked to him via cellular phone since he was not in his office, and at last he spoke with Col. Ansari.

Col. Ansari told him that the Navy gave us a break by cutting down a lot of my educational expenses, and their hands were tied in regard to the conversion of the money from Rial to Dollar since it was an order from the leader of the country himself.

As I was explaining my side of the story and how I decided to stay in the USA, not coming back to Iran to serve in the Navy, Nader whispered to the Admiral that I was telling him the truth. Admiral Vahmani said, "I know that he is, for I received my education in Italy. People from the west do not usually lie. We are the liars. It is sad, but true. We lie as if we drink water and do not even realize it. We are used to this manner of conversation."

Admiral Vahmani told us that it was not important why I chose to stay in the USA. What the Navy was interested in was for me to pay back the money spent for me, and that the amount of money was correct and perhaps the Navy had spent maybe even more than that. He continued by saying that when he had his education in Italy, the cost was about the same or even more.

We questioned him regarding the two departments, personnel and budget; that they were not cooperating with each other. In addition, there was not any law written concerning this conversion of the money from Rial to US dollars at the rate of thirty years ago. That is why we were there seeking help. Finally, he said that Col. Ansari indicated that the order was from the leader of the country, and if that is the case, no one can question his authority. The matter would have to be resolved in the Personnel Department. So we left there without any result or change in our situation.

I called two of my friends, Hassan and Mohsen, who live in the USA and asked them about the money we used to get paid while we were at the Citadel, as I did not remember the amount. According to Mohsen, it was two or three hundred dollars a month as part of our salary. We used that money to take care of our expenses since we had no other means when we were off school. That amount may have gone up to five or six hundred dollars by the end of our school. But Hassan who came later and with a different group, said they got paid even more. We used the money to live on during the summer or when the school was closed. We did not have any other means of survival and that was part of our salary while we were employed by them.

Hassan went back to Iran after graduating from the Citadel, which happened in the early years of the revolution. He then served in the Navy for two weeks when Banisadr, the new president of Iran announced that they had too many people in the military and was allowing anyone who wished to resign from the military to do so without any penalty. Hassan jumped at the opportunity, resigned from the Navy, and left the country for the USA. His airplane had just taken off when the announcement came of the war between Iran and Iraq, in September of 1980.

Hassan gave me his sister's phone number, Naheed, who happened to be a lawyer and lived in Tehran. She had helped his brother Hassan and was familiar with some of the issues pertaining to the Navy. Therefore, that evening we went to see her at her house and I shared my problems with her. She treated me like a brother and we talked about our families, friends, and what she had done for Hassan during the time when he was getting out. Then, she told me the same thing Admiral Vahmani was telling me, that if the order was coming from the leader of the country, then no one could change it. However, if they were misusing the order for a different case wrongly, then we could complain to the high court. But unfortunately, it would take more time. If I paid what they wanted, I could still complain to the high court; but whether I got my money back would be doubtful.

We were trying to knock on every possible door for some possible answers to my dilemma, but it seemed as if every door led to a dead-end. Frankly, I did not know what God had in store for me; nevertheless, I did not lose my hope in Him. I knew that He was going to do something. As a result, I was trying to be sensitive to the Holy Spirit and the opportunities that might come my way.

From there we went to see my friend Nader #2 to see if we could get one more appointment with the Judge and to ask him more advice as to what to do next, and if I had any other options left at all.

The next day we met with the Judge at his office. We explained to him our new discovery about the fact that the leader of the country may have ordered the conversion of money on someone else's case file which was similar to mine; as a result, they used this as the legal precedent for the same decision on my case. The Judge listened carefully and told us if that was the case, his hands were tied too. But before we jumped to any conclusion, he wanted to see this particular file first. He called downstairs and had the file delivered. Nader and I waited almost an hour while he read the file. He finally finished and called us back into his office. This is what he told us:

- No decisions had been made so far on this case.

- The Navy has requested a clarification as to what to do concerning the conversion of the money. They are still waiting for the answer and so far, after one year no decisions have been made.

- The assistant to the court responded to the military before the court handed down its decision, by a letter quoting Mr. Khatami, the supreme leader of the country.

- Mr. Khatami had given his own opinion about the issues concerned but he did not issue any orders

- The Navy is following a letter rather than a lawful order.

The Judge suggested that since the Navy was not willing to cooperate and was trying to force me to accept their terms and conditions, I would need to go to the courthouse and file a complaint against their decision. He gave us the name of a person in the inspection department of the courthouse and told us to offer them collateral, and the $4,330 they had previously requested. If the law is passed in their favor, then you will arrange to pay them on a monthly basis. However, if the law did not pass, then you would get your collateral back, everyone would be happy, and the case would be resolved.

I was happy with the answers and the assessment of the Judge. We went home with renewed hope that tomorrow was going to be a better day. I was constantly praying and asking God to show me a sign that He was with me in my efforts, and when something good like this happened, I could not help but think that God was in it.

I communicated all these events with my wife in the USA via email and phone calls and told her the good news. She was constantly praying for me and shared my situation with my brothers and sisters in Christ located in several States and asked for special prayer for me.

The next day, May 4th, was full of hope and excitement! I asked my Mom and Dad to get ready to go to the courthouse and to bring the title to their house which they had wholeheartedly offered to me several times to use if needed for collateral. Hopefully this would be our final trip to the courthouse.

You often hear that parents disown their children if they leave Islam for another religion, but not mine. They loved us unconditionally and my feeling toward them was the same.

At any rate, Nader and I went inside ahead of my parents to see the Judge while Ali parked the car and waited in the reception area along with my parents until we came for them.

The Judge sent us to the office of Mr. Sharifee, one of the inspectors, and he asked us to write a letter of complaint and bring it in to his office. I wrote and rewrote the letter and finally gave it to them.

Mr. Sharifee was busy at the time but someone else assisted us. He told us to come back the following week after the inspectors reviewed and investigated the complaint. Then they would let us know what to do next. We were prepared to finish the job that day and insisted on staying until everything was done, but the office manager said that there was no way they would do anything that day. So, we left there at 11:30am with disappointment.

The whole idea was for me to talk to one particular person to get the job done, but no one was specific or clear about who that person was and as a result we ended up talking with the wrong person.

I was angry for dragging my parents there, and very angry for the false hope. I was also disappointed for giving false hope to my wife. My Dad told me not to "count your chickens before they hatch" in this country, because things never go smooth. On our way going home we stopped at an outdoor restaurant, relaxed, ordered kabob and rice, and tried to enjoy the rest of the evening for the sake of my parents.

The offices were closed for the next two days and when we called on Saturday to check on our complaint letter, we learned that the persons in charge in that office were on some kind of mission trip and they would be back on Monday, May 9th.

Day 46th

It was Monday, May 9, at 8:00 in the morning. Nader and I left home, picked up Ali from his house and headed toward Tehran to the military courthouse to follow-up on our complaint from the week before. Mr. Sharifee was busy in a conference room. We sat in his office until about 11:30. We finally got tired of sitting there not knowing if we were ever going to talk to him or not, so I spoke to one of his office workers about my case. He went into the conference room and obtained our file from Mr. Sharifee and directed us to another room where two inspector Judges were sitting. They were Mr. Ahmadi and Mr. Razavi.

Mr. Ahmadi was short, a bit fat, and almost bald. Mr. Razavi on the other hand was a bit tall and thinner, with a beard, but half bald. They asked Nader and Ali to stay outside of the room while they were going to converse with me. I told them that my Farsi language was not so great, and might not be able to communicate well with them. They insisted that it was okay and they understood me. Then they asked me about the problem or concern that I had.

I started to explain to them what happened when Mr. Ahmadi interrupted and told me that I was in the wrong place and needed to go elsewhere for my case. The question about the file number came up that was attached to my file. I told them that Nader had that information and requested to allow him to come in with the file number and other information because I could not explain it well. So they allowed Nader to come in.

Nader explained my situation in more detail as to what took place and where we had been. Mr. Ahmadi was convinced that we should go to the office of Mr. Montazari, the assistant to the courthouse. Then he asked, "Who told you to come here?"

We told him a particular Judge who knew about my situation and had directed us to them for help. Mr. Ahmadi said, "Well the Judge knows his book." We suggested that
208

he call the judge if he needed more information. We realized later that it was a mistake on our part to let them know who the judge was, for he did not appreciate us getting him involved. He was only our advisor and guide, hoping to direct me to someone who would help to resolve my problem. I regretted what happened because later on he expressed his disappointment about us using his name. I just wished that he had been more clear about that, but we learned to be more careful in the future!

Mr. Ahmadi came to the conclusion that we must first see Mr. Montazari (since he was the one who issued the letter of suggestion on behalf of the leader of the country concerning the conversion of the money) to solve our problem. Perhaps his letter to the military was meant only for Mr. Hossaini (who's file number we had), and if he could not solve our problem, then I could come back to them for help. He felt that they did not want to step on someone else's toes. He picked up the phone to call his office, but Mr. Montazari was not in. He then told us that I should call him tomorrow after he conversed with Mr. Montazari.

In the back of my mind, I was beginning to visualize a long stay in Iran, perhaps forever! The thought of that was beginning to bother me greatly! I did not want to let anyone know how I felt. I needed to stay strong. I hinted to my wife that there were other means to leave the country but she did not like that idea at all, and asked me to promise her not to do anything dangerous that would bring harm to me. Nonetheless, there were risks involved no matter which road I decided to take. The thought of being locked up and away from my family and grandchildren was my worst nightmare and brought many tears to my eyes.

We left the courthouse and went to my aunt's house, ate lunch and brought her with us to Karaj. She was interested in buying a house for herself as an investment, and wanted it to be closer to my Mom's house also.

The next morning at 10am, we called Mr. Ahmadi. He said,

"Oh call me back in half an hour for I have not yet called Mr. Montazari".

When I called him again, he answered, "Mr. Montazari is not in his office, but I spoke to some other workers there and they said the same thing that the Navy has been saying."

Mr. Ahmadi had not read the file of Mr. Hossaini in order to understand the content of the file before making a decision. He was simply taking the words of someone else and making a decision based on that. When we were in his office the day before and talked about the conversion of the money, he was talking with more sense and making a comparison to the value of the 'mehrie' (money that a man agrees to pay his wife as part of the contract when they get married). In addition, he was saying that a mehrie of a woman, which the husband promised 30 years ago, might not have much value today. Therefore, the courts had decided to adjust it by some means that would be fair to both parties, and we agreed with his example, but not with the outrageous rate hike the Navy was planning to charge me.

When we went to see Mr. Ahmadi the following day, I asked him if we could use my Dad's house as collateral until the law prevails. I told him the judge suggested we come to him because he had the authority to exercise this action and

210

because the Navy could not lawfully accept any type of collateral. It had to be done through the court system.

Mr. Ahmadi then asked: "Do you have $80,000 as collateral? As they want twice of what they are asking as payment." I did not, of course!

Then he picked up the phone and asked for the file of Mr. Hossaini, to be sent to his office.

While we were waiting in his office he started having casual conversation with me. I do not know if he was joking or serious when he asked me, "why don't you just stay here?"

I said, "I have my job, home and family waiting for me."

"You can get a job and start a new family here." He responded.

"I am already married." I said.

"You can have another wife and stay here." He suggested.

I thanked him for his suggestion and told him "No thanks, for I am satisfied with my marriage!"

He then asked me if I knew anyone in the USA such as a Senator or a Congressman. I jokingly said I knew lots of them! Then he redirected his questions toward atomic energy. I started to respond, but Nader's foot touched mine as a signal not to go there. I stopped immediately. Later Nader told me that even joking might lead to the wrong assumption and they might hold you for the purpose of getting some useful information or on espionage charges!

A soldier brought in the file of Mr. Hossaini and gave it to Mr. Ahmadi. After studying the content of the file, he said, "Mr. Saiid, this is going to take time."

How much time? I asked.

"I do not know," he said.

"We have to have a meeting about this matter with many people and it may take weeks or months."

Nader said, "He needs to go back home to his family and to his job, as he is going to lose his job if he does not go back soon." but we could not get any promises from him. We thanked him and left.

I had called the Navy and spoke with Col. Ansari during the past week while we were trying to see if we could make some headway from another direction. Col. Ansari said that my new letter was ready and if I wanted to speed up the process, I should come there and be the mail carrier myself, otherwise he would have to do it through the mail system. (The offices were only a building apart from each other!).

The reason Col. Ansari was back on my case was perhaps because Admiral Vahmani spoke to him and asked him to do so, but I felt that the whole ordeal was to give me a run-around. However, at this time, I could not come to any conclusion as to why they were dragging their feet, plus I was trying to think positive and remain hopeful. I wanted to make things work out in order to continue my future trips to Iran. Then I was faced with another lie.

Chapter 15

Another lie

I would like to share with you, the reader, why I feel it necessary to go into so much detail about this part of my story. Dealing with the Iranian government was an unending circle of frustration and dishonesty. A friend of my brother who used to work in one of the government offices in Iran said they would use different color pens when they signed a document in order to send messages to each other. For example, if they used blue ink, it meant to stall the person. If they used red ink, it meant to refuse their request. This way they could silently work together to cause hardship for certain individuals, and sadly, I was one of them!

One of our relatives, Hossain, a ranking member in the military, met two Navy Colonels in a meeting and talked with them in reference to my situation. He then asked them to check with Col. Mirshekar to see if there were anything they could do to resolve my problem so I could leave the country and go to my family. Hossain himself had spoken with other military lawyers and found out that there was no merit in the demands of the Personnel Department about the conversion of the money in my case.

Later on when Hossain spoke with one of the Colonels again, he said that Colonel Mirshekar expressed **that the problem was not with him, but with the Budget and Credit Department. They had created all the problems**

and were asking for more money in US dollars. He told them everything he had done was to help me!

I was taking notes about all these misrepresentations by different people and pointing them out to Nader. He often bragged about Iran, and how much they have achieved and how he believed in the system of their government. Though I was already at my wits end, I did not want to discourage him about his country. I tried to patiently wait to see how much longer Nader could take the lies and trickery of those people.

The following Friday, my aunt came to Karaj to purchase an apartment house and I went along to see how things would go. Being away all these years, I was very curious about how dealings and transactions went on a day to day basis. The next day, I went along with Nader to take his daughter, Mahdieh, to a hospital because she was not feeling well and she was due to have a baby any day. Her mom (my sister) was with us as well. We took them to the hospital, and then headed back to the Navy base.

We went straight to the Budget and Credit Department and spoke with Mr. Goodarzi and Captain Salehi, his boss. They already had a letter prepared and changed everything from Rial to Dollar at the rate of 30 years ago, it was calculated for $43k. Nader looked at the letter and found some mistakes. They converted all the money instead of only a portion that was characterized as "mission expenses". These were probably related to the summer training I attended with the U.S. Marine, Air Force, and Navy each year I was at the Citadel. Nader questioned the calculation and showed them the correct conversion of the expenses. They corrected the calculation and it changed to $37,300 all together, then they gave us a copy of it. Now it needed to be signed by their department head! (Another un-necessary run-around!).

From there, we went to see Col. Ansari at the personnel Department. He did not act like the same person as before toward us and started complaining by telling us that he had prepared this letter two weeks ago and except for a phone call from me, no one came to take care of it. I told him to be happy and smile, for we had been busy and told him about our discoveries and whom we talked to, as well as our letter of complaint against the parties involved. He then became calmer and said perhaps the next person would not have to deal with the same issues any more.

Now, here is what surprised me about those letters that they had to write back and forth to each other, which made me very apprehensive:

- *The letters were not on any official papers with headings such as: "Iranian Navy or the Personnel Department, etc."*
- *Most of their communications could have been handled by a phone call or using one of their soldiers to courier for speed and reliability.*
- *They had created this method of communication to deliberately give me a run-around and to prolong my stay there, for some unknown reasons to me.*

Perhaps they wanted a bribe from me since they kept hinting about it in many indirect ways. Col. Ansari many times expressed that I should not offer him anything as a gift, not even something as small as a pencil because he would not accept them, as he was only doing his job. He also said that if he paid too much attention to my case, some people in his office might think that I had brought a bag of money into his office. One of my relatives told me that it sounded like he wanted bribe money by the way he talked, for this is the way they talk when they want something under the table. It is an indirect way of telling you what they want and it is a common practice by many in Iran.

On Monday, May 16, I called the Navy and spoke with Captain Salehi in the Budget and Credit Department. I told him my name and that I was calling to see if the letter was ready and signed by the department head."

He responded, "Oh, I just talked to the commander about signing the Letter of Approval, and it should be ready for you to pick up today." But later on, I learned that it was neither signed nor reviewed by anyone yet.

I was getting tired and agitated, and as a result we did not go back to the Navy base for a couple of days. Furthermore, Nader needed to take care of his wife, his daughter and the new born baby too. However, when we did go back to the base and spoke with Captain Salehi, he said that he had sent the letter to his commander but he had not received a response yet.

I asked him where his commander's office was located at, that we might go there to help finish the process. He pointed to the building in the same base and the name of the person to see.

I asked him to please call his commander and let him know that we were coming to see him. This time Ali was with me to help take care of these matters.

We went to the engineering building where the commander's office was and spoke with Mr. Alemi. He was tall and skinny, but in civilian clothes. He looked for the letter but could not find it. He then asked us for the file number. We did not have that, so I asked him to please call Captain Salehi and get the number or whatever else he needs.

These people were making me so irritated on purpose by acting so irresponsible, and the reality was, they had us by our tails and we could not do anything about it except to play their games. I had to stay calm and in control of my emotions, for I did not want to let them know that what they were doing was bothering me.

Then he called Captain Salehi, got the number, entered it into his computer and was able to find the letter he wanted. He then brought it to where we were and started by telling us that the conversion of the money may be wrong. Just as he began to question us about it, I interrupted him by saying; "Mr. Alemi, I do not wish to go there. We are accepting the letter just the way it is and this is also the wish of the Personnel Department, so go ahead, approve it, and let us go on with their plan."

After 30 minutes he came back with another letter consisting of two lines saying "We approved this letter and here is our signature". (What a joke!)

We then took the sealed envelope back to the Budget and Credit Department and asked Captain Salehi, What was left to do? This is what he said:

1. We now need to send this letter back to the Personnel Department for approval.
2. Then it goes to the Finance Department, and from there, it goes to the bank.

3. Once paid, I would then come back with a receipt and they will send that back to the Personnel Department, then from there to the Information Department.
4. They would send another letter to the Military Courthouse to clear my name.
5. Then the court will let the airport know that I am free to leave the country.

I could not believe what I was hearing! I knew that each one of those steps could take days or weeks but before I could respond, Captain Salehi turned to his lieutenant, Mr. Jafari, and asked him to hurry up the process by writing another letter to the Personnel Department to help keep me from making this long trip again.

The Lieutenant agreed but made his biggest mistake by telling me while we were all still in the same room, "Mr. Saiid, your letter will not be ready today; you need to call or come back tomorrow!"

That was the moment I was waiting for. I now knew for sure what I had suspected for quite some time. They had no intention of letting me go easily, if ever. Every day that I was

there was making it easier for them to attach something to my case. Even if I had paid the money they were demanding, I doubted that they would let me go.

I was not sure what to do next, but something was about to happen that would change everything. God's hand was moving!

Chapter 16

Strange Phone Call!

Change of Plans

"**G**od please help me! I am running out of options and ideas. I felt like my ship was about to sink! I cried in my heart, and fervently searched the scriptures for something to hold on to. I found this passage that spoke well of my situation:

Psalm 107:23-28

"Those who go down to the sea in ships,
who do business on great waters,
they see the works of the LORD,
and His wonders in the deep.
For He commands and raises the stormy wind,
which lifts up the waves of the sea.
They mount up to the heavens,
they go down again to the depths;
their soul melts because of trouble.
They reel to and fro, and stagger like a drunken man,
and are at their wits' end.
Then they cry out to the LORD in their trouble,
and He brings them out of their distresses."

A few days earlier while I was at my aunt's house, I received a phone call from one of my sisters saying that someone from the <u>Retirement Section of the Navy</u> had called and wanted me to call him back.

At first, I contemplated, "Whom do I know at the retirement section who would want to talk to me?" Nader asked if I knew anyone there. The only people that came to my mind were my classmates from the Citadel who may have recognized my name and wanted to see me, but wouldn't they have told me? Or perhaps, someone was playing a trick on me.

Frankly, I did not have time for anyone's jokes or tricks under the circumstances that I was in. So, I called the number my sister gave me, but no one was there to answer my call. A couple of days later I called the number again, and the person that answered asked me to meet with them at the old Navy Base, section 1943, because someone there would like to meet with me. He made the appointment for 9am on the following Saturday but would not disclose who they were or what the nature of this meeting was. The more I thought about it, the more it bothered me. I could not imagine what they could want from me. The tone of the man's voice on the phone was calm while at the same time serious and left me in suspense!

I had heard that other people who had also been trapped in Iran all had the same common denominator. They usually were taken into a room where they were interrogated and accused of being a spy. The interrogator would drill them and require their cooperation in return for letting them go and giving them the freedom to leave the country.

What I mean by cooperation is that they simply ask you to write a statement that you are indeed a spy from the country that you came from and sign it. Most people get trapped by the word "promise" and agree to sign. Unfortunately, their problems have just begun. Usually that means prison, abuse and sometimes torture while waiting for their court time so their voice can be heard by a judge. But if you do not cooperate, the interrogation becomes more forceful and abusive. Either way you are at their mercy!

Two day later, as we were leaving the military courthouse, I asked Nader if he knew where the old Navy Base was. He pointed to the next street right above the military courthouse. So, since we were so close, we decided to stop by and check on it, to save ourselves a trip if possible.

As we approached the building, I noticed that it was surrounded by an eight foot iron-bar wall with several signs that said: "No Photography Permitted". Seeing those signs made me realize we were in a secure area and I became very cautious.

When we approached the gate, there were a few guards who were there to help direct people to where they needed to go. One of the guards greeted us and asked how he could help. "We would like to meet with someone in section 1943", Nader responded.

The guard immediately answered, "Security Section, Ha?"

Nader said, "No, the Retirement Section."

The guard answered, "The Retirement Section is not here, it is on another street."

Then he directed us to a room within the compound to get further help. The guard there recognized the code 1943 as the Security Section. At this point I became very suspicious and began to feel like I was about to be trapped. I was careful not to let on how I felt and decided to go a little further.

As we were directed to the next room, my heart started beating faster and I felt uneasy. I thanked God that Nader was doing most of the talking for me since I was very nervous!

Another gentleman greeted us and asked how he could help. Nader told the man that we were looking for Section 1943, the "Retirement Section".

The gentleman said "the Retirement Section is not here, but, since you are here, let me call Section 1943 to get some answers for you." He then picked up the phone and called, but no one was there to answer. Thank God!

I immediately jumped at the opportunity and told him that our appointment was not until next Saturday. We just happened to be close by and decided to stop and check on it, but we would come back at our appointed time. On that note we said good-bye and left quickly!

When we got out of the building we both realized that our Saturday appointment was unquestionably a trap and could have resulted in an unwelcomed interrogation or other unpleasant events. And my fear was that I might not see daylight again after that encounter.

I believe that the Iranian Navy did not have the jurisdiction to punish anyone, yet at the same time they felt that I should be punished. I believed that they secretly asked another department outside of the Navy to find a way to punish me. That is why I was summoned to this unknown department for interrogation. Iran is well known for its human rights violations. People face torture or just disappear into a prison in Tehran **without ever going before a court of law. In that country, you are guilty until proven innocent. There are many well documented cases where individuals were taken to prison and ultimately given the death penalty without any trial.**

The horrifying tales of some Iranians who came to Iran from abroad for a visit were still floating around in the country. They faced many difficulties when they went to visit their families. Among them was the story of a man who taught Iranian dance and made some videos while in the USA. When he went home to visit his ailing Mom and Dad, the Government harassed him severely for making those videos. They fined, imprisoned, and abused him before he was able to get out of the country! They also treated some other actors, actresses and musicians with the same type of treatment. Many people in Iran talk about these humiliating issues and hate the way the government of Iran treats some people, while at the same time calling themselves, a 'peaceful Islamic Republic'.

I had been very patient with the Navy and the people in the courthouse up to this point, but now it was time to take a different course of action. I was waiting to see how long it would take for Nader to lose his patience with them since he believed in his government and its leadership as the one who is appointed by Allah. He often said that the marriage of government and religion was the best thing since Allah's way is always the right one. But when he finally saw the deceit and lies by the people in the government on numerous occasions, he gave up.

Meanwhile I had been approached several times by a few people concerning the possibility of a rescue attempt to get out of Iran. It was scary and dangerous and if I was caught, the punishment would be severe!

Among those whom I spoke with was a man who had a brother who had made a similar trip to Iraq. We got together with him at his house to talk about our options. We talked about the pros and cons of leaving the country through Iraq. He first tried to discourage me because of the mountainous terrain. He began to tell us that when he went through there a few years ago, he was young, but he would never do it again. The terrain was rough and he became so exhausted that he ended up crawling on the ground. But when he realized that I was serious about this option, he volunteered to go with me. He also told me of another option. He knew a friend who could make me a fake passport so that I could leave from the airport, but we were not able to contact this person.

I also spoke to another person who had made several secret trips to Turkey through the mountains a few years ago, but he needed time to contact his connections to see if that was a possibility.

Then my cousin called me from Shiraz to introduce me to one of his friends, who also could take me out of Iran through Afghanistan or Oman which are located east and south of Iran. We actually met with him in Tehran at his brother's house. I liked his personality and he offered to take me all the way to a US embassy in Kabul, Afghanistan. He also said that he knew a few people that could help me in this escape and they were very capable and confident. After detailing a few routes and possibilities for our escape, we parted, but planned to get back together again at a later time.

I was praying to seek God's guidance in what I was about to do. Don't you just wish God would open His mouth sometimes and audibly tell you what to do and throw away any guess work? Well, it just doesn't happen that way!

The following day a neighbor friend also put me in touch with someone else to get me a fake passport to get me out of Tehran. He came by my dad's house and we talked, but he wanted a lot more money than I could afford at that time. Then at last, another breakthrough!

Thursday May 19th

While visiting one of my relatives a few days later, I met a man who was the operator of a convenience store. He spoke Turkish and had connections with some friends who actually lived on this side of the border as well as some relatives who lived on the other side of the border in Turkey. He told me that his friends were here the day before and had just left heading back home, but he could call them to return. I told him that would be great, so he picked up the phone and called his friend's cellular phone and asked him to come back to meet with me.

So, on Thursday, May 9th, I met Majid and Ghader at my parent's house. They said that they were brothers and convinced me of their strategy and plans. I asked for Majid's driver license. I took notes of his name, home and cellular phone numbers as a precautionary step and gave it to my mom just in case. Ghader claimed that he did not have his

227

with him. Then I asked them to give me until tomorrow to think about it, and they agreed.

I was very excited about our conversation and was almost certain they were the ones that I would be going with, but I needed time to pray and discuss the plan with my parents in private. We had also discussed the financial matters and the method of its dispersion. I agreed to pay them $1,000 up front and when they delivered me to the US embassy in Turkey, they would be given $1,500 more and when I arrived in the USA they would get the second $1,500. It was agreeable to all.

I went to see my sisters that night to see how they felt about all of this. They felt that this was the right thing to do. My family knew I had done everything I could to do the right thing here in Iran, and I had been separated way too long from my family in America. Knowing this helped give me the peace I needed about my decision.

Ali volunteered to go with me on my journey. That encouraged and comforted me to have him come along. He wanted to make sure of my safety, and if possible, to do some sightseeing in Turkey as well.

I wanted to take them all with me but I could not! Nader had been by my side the whole time. He had given up his work for the last two months to be with me. In the beginning he believed in the Iranian system of government and often bragged about it. He expected that everything would go well and that the door would be open for me for future trips to Iran. He often told me that he wanted to be there for me to the very end and I liked his attitude very much. But, toward the end he lost his faith in the people in the Iranian government and the Navy.   He could not think clearly and would say things that I did not agree with. He was troubled with the idea that something might go wrong with my alternative plan and everyone in the family would blame him for that. That is why he was going against my wishes and several times attempted to discourage my decision to escape in this way. But my decision was firm, with no turning back. Even my Mom and Dad were in favor of my decision and gave me their blessings.

Surprisingly, I received a call on Friday, the day of my departure, from the person who was going to take me through the southern part of the county to Afghanistan or Oman. He was planning to make a run toward the south since he was in a business of cloth trade and wanted me to go with him. I asked him to give me a couple of days to make my decision and he agreed.

But ultimately, I chose the route through Turkey because it was closer to where we were, but if I did face some obstacles, then I would still have time to reroute my getaway through the southern part of the country to Afghanistan or via the Persian gulf to Oman.

That Friday, most shops were still open. I exchanged $1000 of my American dollars for Iranian Toman at a jewelry store, said my goodbyes to my relatives that lived close by. Then I went to my parent's house and packed my bags.

About three weeks earlier, an Iranian friend of mine came to Iran from the USA to attend a funeral of one of his relatives. I went to see him at his mother's house in Tehran. I discussed my ordeal with him and asked him if he would mind taking one of my suitcases back with him when he went back home. He said that he did not mind at all. The suitcase contained mostly gifts and souvenirs that my family had purchased for me, my wife and children back home. This way I only had deal with my personal stuff such as my clothes and essentials. And with the journey I was about to embark on, it would have been impossible to carry anything more.

Chapter 17

The Rescue

Finally, I made the decision that I would be going with Majid and Ghader by way of Turkey. I made it clear to my family that no one was to blame no matter what happened. But I could not tell my wife about what I was doing. She had pleaded with me from the beginning not to try anything that could jeopardize my life. Deep within my heart, I knew that she was right. I might be killed, robbed or stabbed and left in the middle of nowhere. Nevertheless, God was giving me the peace I needed about this decision, and was providing the means. All I had was my faith in Jesus Christ to carry me through these mountains. I was giving up my logic for faith. I did not want to stay in Iran anymore and experience its unexpected surprises. If I were killed, I knew I would go to heaven to be with the Father, and if I lived through it, God would use me for His glory. He had been there with me every step of the way since I had been in Iran, and I had no reason to believe He would choose to leave me now! He is a Great and Mighty God!

His promise in Psalm 91 says:

*"He who dwells in the secret place of the Most High
shall abide under the shadow of the Almighty.
I will say of the LORD, "He is my refuge and my fortress;
My God, in Him I will trust." Surely He shall deliver you
from the snare of the fowler, and from the perilous
pestilence."*

So, on Friday, May 20th at 11:30pm, we left Karaj and headed toward Urumiye (previously called "Rezai-yeh" during the Pahlavi regime). Majid and Ghader rode in the front seat and their nephew, Farsheed, Ali and me in the back.

After a brief stop for a snack and some water, we traveled toward our destination while listening to some Persian music from the selection of cassettes they had.

I kept my eyes open all night as Majid drove. I felt I needed to stay alert at all times.   When I exchanged my $1,000 to Toman, it was a large stack of bills and I could not keep it all in my pockets. So, I kept it in my suitcase in the trunk of Majid's car. This was always a concern to me when I had to leave the car for any reason.

The gauges of the car Majid was driving were disengaged, so I could not tell how fast we were going or how much gas was in their car.

After a couple of hours of driving, we stopped at a gas station for gas and a restroom break. I stepped outside of the car to get some fresh air and to stretch my legs. It was cold and breezy. I told Ali to be cautious and to stay alert, and that only one of us should leave the car at any given time since all of our belongings were in the trunk of their car.

There were many stores open all night, and they had their hot tea ready for those travelers who commuted at night.

Ali, Farsheed, and Ghader slept through most of the night but I could not close my eyes even for one minute. I wanted to know where we were going, which roads we were taking and who we might meet. I did not want to be surprised at anything. Besides, Majid needed someone to keep him company in order to stay alert and awake while driving.

After hours of traveling and right before entering the city of Tabriz, we made one more stop for the restroom and hot tea. Inside the store I saw Majid and Ghader looking at some knives. This made me very nervous. I went inside the store with the intention of keeping a closer eye on them. Majid asked me if I wanted to buy a knife to take back with me. I told him I did not need one and from that point on, I stayed very close to them wherever we went. I wanted them to know I was watching.

When we got back on the road, Ali, Farsheed, and Ghader went back to sleep until we reached a checkpoint. At the checkpoint, two road police dressed in soldier uniforms stopped our car for inspection. Majid stepped out of the car and spoke with them in his own native Turkish language. Most people in that part of the country spoke "Turkish" as well as "Farsi" including Majid and Ghader. "Farsi" is the official Iranian language which is also called "Persian" in English.

They looked inside of the trunk and pointed to a loose pair of glasses laying there. Then they told Majid that those glasses might break throwing there like that. But he told them they are fine as they were. According to Majid, this is how, in a round about way, they were asking you  to give them something. I supposed that they check some vehicles for "drugs or guns" as well as just routine inspections and question the traveler's intention since they are going to a city located close to the border. Majid's license tag was from that area so coming and going for him was not any problem. So they let us proceed.

We approached the city of Tabriz at about 5:30am. Tabriz is a beautiful city with many mountains covered with a lot of greenery. Trees and flowers were budding everywhere. I was surprised because the mountains in Tehran and the surrounding areas were still rocky at that time of the year.

We drove slowly through the town. The streets were busy with traffic, even though it was still very early in the morning. The guys were hungry, and began looking for a restaurant, but could not find many open. After making a couple of circles around the town, we finally stopped at a shop where they were serving "Kalleh-Pacheh" which is a soup made with the head and skin of sheep. Just thinking

234

about that kind of Middle Eastern food was not pleasant, but the fact was I wasn't hungry at all.   But they insisted on me trying it. So, I tasted a small piece of the brain poured in a bowl of soup with a piece of wheat bread. The soup and bread tasted good but the brain was slimy. One of the things that I was struggling with was trying to find a clean restroom, so in order to avoid having to use one I needed to refrain from eating much!

After breakfast, we continued our trip. Ghader decided to drive so Majid could rest. We had not gotten very far outside the city limits when I noticed there was a red light on signaling there was something wrong with the car.   I pointed it out to Ghader and about the same time, the car's power started to reduce.   Realizing that the car was having mechanical problems, we stopped on the side of the road to figure out what to do.   Majid got out, popped the hood open, and immediately spotted a broken fan belt. I looked to my right and to my left, and saw nothing but miles of bare land. Since we were not far from the city, I figured that we might have to go back in order to repair the car. I did notice a few very old buildings made out of clay about a quarter of a mile ahead of us. However, from that distance they did not look like stores or shops that would have what we needed.

I started to pray, asking God for his help. I knew that something good would happen. I just did not know what it could be, and was anxious to see what God would do next.

We drove the car on its battery to where the old buildings were. Fortunately, and to my surprise, one of them was a mechanic shop with many belts hanging from it's side walls!   But the shop was not open yet since it was still too early in the morning. I figured that we might have to stay there for an hour or two before the owner came, but suddenly, we spotted a private car nearby which was being used as a taxi. Majid approached the man and asked him if he happened to have a spare belt. He had one! Jesus was trying to tell me with little but important signs that He was with me and I thanked and praised Him nonstop for the way He was watching over me. Majid paid the man for the belt and repaired the car himself and we continued our journey.

We still had several hours to travel to get to our destination, but since Majid was familiar with the area, he knew a quicker route where we used a ferry to go across the calm Orumieh Lake. It took only thirty minutes to cross the lake and that saved us a few hours. We were in his territory, and he knew all the side roads as well as the main highways. He told me that there would not be any more checkpoints on the route he was taking us, even though we were much closer to the border of Turkey.

Before we left Tehran, Majid and Ghader had told us that they were in the business of buying and selling sheep and goats. They told us that someone was tending their herd for a sum of money, so they needed to get home as soon as possible to prevent having to pay them extra. This was their livelihood, buying and selling livestock, but I never saw any sheep or goats that belonged to them.

Majid also told us that when we got to the city of Orumieh where he lived, we would meet his wife and children and rest a while in his home while he contacted his sources to make arrangements for the rest of our trip. That did not happen, but it was okay because I was not worried. I knew God was guiding every one of my steps!

Saturday May 21

At about 10:30am, we arrived in Orumieh. We stopped at a café for more hot tea.   While we were sitting there, Majid and Farsheed quickly told us that they were going to go buy some chickens, make some phone calls and would be back in about 10 minutes.   They did not give us time to object, and I must confess that it made me a bit nervous to see them leaving suddenly and with all our belongings in the car, including my suitcase with all the money!   Ali and I looked at each other, trying to hide our concern from Ghader who had been left behind with us.   Since Ghader stayed behind, it gave us some comfort to know they would most likely be back.   But we couldn't help but be concerned at their hasty move!

We sat there at the café drinking more tea and tried to keep the conversation going among ourselves to ease our mind. I was relieved when I saw them back within 15 minutes. They had purchased two whole, uncooked chickens! Then we all hopped back in the car and headed toward the village.

The landscape and view of the mountains was breathtaking! We saw some Kurdish people dancing on the side of the road, a few local country shops, and the beauty of God's perfect creation. We finally arrived at a large house, not far from the mountains, with an enormous living room and several bedrooms.

Majid told me that it only took 30 minutes to go across to the Turkish side. When I looked at the mountains up close, it appeared they would not be hard to cross, but I would soon find out that was not true at all!   For some unknown reason, they did not tell me the truth about how long and hard it would be to make this journey. Maybe it was because they thought I would back out if I knew. But at this point, nothing could have changed my mind. I had to get home to my family.

I had not slept for the last thirty hours and was not feeling the best, so in order to refresh myself I took a hot shower, which made me feel much better. I also shaved off my beard so my appearance would be much neater. I tried to sleep, but for some reason beyond my control, I could not make myself go to sleep peacefully. I would close my eyes, but any movement would trigger my eyes to open. I suppose it was because of the uncertainty of which I was with, where I was, and what was to come.

The women of the house prepared lunch with the chickens we brought, along with white rice and homemade bread. We were waiting for the rest of the family to come in, but they told us they would come when they were hungry, so we should go ahead and eat. It had been quite some time since I'd had a good meal, so needless to say I was very hungry! So, we sat down and enjoyed a wonderful meal.

Later, I met Jamsheed and the rest of the people who were working outside on the farm. Jamsheed was interested in hearing my story since he was the one who was planning the rest of my trip. He seemed to be a very compassionate person or perhaps it was because of the money, or maybe he did not care for this religious government. Either way, he told me that he was willing to help me.

Majid distributed the first payment of the money among them. Then Jamsheed told me to rest there at the house while he was going to meet some people who were going to help us make the rest of this trip possible. Ali went along with him in case they needed to use his cellular phone.

I was exhausted to say the least! Everyone was gone except me and Majid. We laid down to rest, but I had one eye open. While we were resting, one of the farm workers whom I had not seen before, tip-toed in and came toward me. He quietly tapped me on the shoulder and whispered for me to get my things together because we may not be coming back. I found out later that they wanted to leave Majid behind because Jamsheed had some bad dealings with him in the past. Majid had told us that he and Ghader were brothers but that was not true. I already knew that Majid would not be going across the mountains with me. He had told me this earlier and he said it was because he had a wife and children to take care of, but that Ghader would be with me the rest of the trip. So I was not surprised when he did not come along.

At any rate, we got in the car and left the village house, heading closer to the mountains. In the back of my mind, I was still thinking about what Majid had said about the distance we would be traveling to get to the village in Turkey. He had said it only takes about 30 minutes, so I figured the border was right behind that first mountain. It looked like only a hill and not hard to cross at all, but I was about to find out the truth!

As we approached the mountains, the paved road turned into a dirt road. We continued on into the mountains for a little while, and soon I saw Ali and Jamsheed sitting down on the side of a hill, waving us to where they were.   To their left stood two horses, and with them were Ebi and

239

Javad who were going to be my guides through the mountains. After a short visit, we said our goodbyes. Ali and Jamsheed were planning to drive across the border and meet us on the other side. They both had their passports and were carrying my suitcases. We were to eventually meet at the home of one of Jamsheed's relatives across the border.

We got back in the car, including some young men who came along to help if needed, and Ghader drove up the hill, deeper into the heart of the mountains. The road was not made for cars but for tractors, and was not in the best condition. The bottom of the car sometimes would hit the rocks on the road, but he did not seem to be bothered by that at all. We had to cross a small creek at one point, so we all got out of the car and pushed it to the other side. If they had tried to drive across, it would have made a lot of noise, especially if it got stuck, and they did not want to alert anyone living nearby. After about 300 yards of going upward we stopped. The men gave me a bag with homemade bread, cheese and mashed potatoes for our trip. Ghader stayed with me while the rest of the guys drove the car back down.

We found a small spring of water on the side of the mountain and sat down. I splashed some of the cool water on my face to refresh myself and to help keep me awake. Soon, we spotted Ebi and Javad riding their horses towards us. It was time to continue my journey to freedom.

Chapter 18

A VIEW FROM THE MOUNTAINTOP

Our journey began at about six in the evening. I rode one of the horses and Ghader rode the other. Our guides would walk most of the journey. There were no stirrups to rest my feet, but they had thick blankets on their backs which made it very comfortable to sit on; that is as long as they walked! They also did not have regular bridles with a bit in their mouths, only a rope halter with reins, so controlling them was not easy for me.

The horses would walk most of the time and seemed to know the trails well. Sometimes my horse would stop to eat some grass or perhaps it was just tired, but when I made him move with a small kick to his side, he would take off fast and I would yell for help! Fortunately, Ebi and Javad were walking ahead of us, so that when this happened they could stop my horse!

The trails were narrow, the mountains were steep, and sometimes rocky, which made me afraid that the horse would slip. However, it appeared that these horses had traveled these trails before and knew where they were going.

Ebi and Javad knew the mountains like the palm of their hands. Just like the horses, they knew this trail and had traveled it many times. During the entire trip, they only rode the horses with us a few times, and then it was only because of the terrain.

As we were traveling, we ran into a group of teenagers, who were heading back toward their home. They all seemed to know each other and were there to pick wild vegetation for food. I also noticed a farmer plowing a field with his tractor on the side of the mountain a distance away. Although this land did not belong to any one it was being used by all the people there. They were far from any town and their livelihood was mostly farming.

Before we left my parents' house, I didn't even think about checking to see what the weather forecast would be for the next few days. I suppose I was expecting our guides to be in charge of that and to tell me how to dress accordingly since they were familiar with the climate and terrain. But they never told me how to dress or what to expect. During the daytime it was calm and pleasant, but as night approached, it became very cold! Fortunately I had a light jacket with me, which was helpful in keeping me warm as long as we were moving.

At 9:00 pm, the sun left us and a beautiful full moon lit our path. It got cooler but was still comfortable. The stars were out and you could hardly see any clouds in the sky.

During the trip, I was constantly thanking and praising God, and at the same time praying for His protection. I felt His presence the whole time.

When we got across the first mountain, it became darker and harder to see since the moon was not shining on that side. However, it was not any problem for our guides or the horses, as they knew every inch of those mountains. I was not worried at all even though it was there that we saw a couple of wolfs. One of our guides spotted them and told us what they were. Our horses were also sensitive to their presence as you could see their ears perk up and their heads turn toward them. Javad threw a rock at them and spoke loudly to let them know we could see them, and they ran off. They never came closer or created any danger for us. Thank God!

We continued up and down the mountains, walking over the snow and watching streams of water going downhill. At times, we had to get off the horses and walk because of the steepness of the mountain and at other times we doubled up on the horses to move faster. We had to pass over at least three mountains to get to our destination. Before we climbed the last mountain, Ebi proceeded ahead of us by using a shortcut in order to catch up with a group of people who were also traveling ahead of us. They were carrying merchandise to the other side. He was also prepared to pay off the border patrol if needed.

After a couple of hours, we finally caught up to Ebi. He was sitting down on the side of the last mountain. He told us that we needed to be cautious from this point on and very quiet. Therefore, we quietly went up to the top of the mountain and saw the rest of the horsemen there. I counted at least thirty-five of them, all gathered in one place, waiting for the final run. I was not sure who they were or what they were doing at first, but later I learned that they were trading commodities their own way.

It was about 12:30 am, just after midnight and I could see the Iranian border patrol building that was behind us, but there was no movement or activity. In front of us, I could see the Turkish border patrol building, and there were some lights on and I could see some activity. The border patrol would go back and forth with their vehicles equipped with a searchlight, shining it toward the mountains.

So now all we could do was wait. The temperature had dropped and it was getting colder by the minute. We were not moving and I was not dressed appropriately for this weather. I was experiencing my weakest point, and at times ready to give-up. I was so tired and sleepy that I could not think rationally, and wished to end this fight. I also felt like a failure because if I had to face the Iranian interrogators, I was afraid I would not be able to be courageous or bold enough to confess my new faith knowing that if I did it could results in severe punishment or even death. I could tell them a lie just to save my neck, but then I would be lying to myself and my God by denying Him. Either way I was not ready to be tested. A soldier is tested after having much practice before going to war in order to mentally and physically face tough challenges, even death as war demands. But not me, I have never been tested nor faced that kind of challenge before. All I could do was pray that God would give me the strength I needed if it came to that.

But then, my wife, my children, and Roman my grandson, would come into my mind, which would give me more hope and desire to fight harder against that dreaded cold morning a bit longer. They were waiting for me and I did not want to disappoint them. I had so much to be thankful for in my life and was not about to give it up so easily!

Javad gave me a blanket to cover myself with to stay warm. I was okay as long as I walked around, but as soon as

244

I stopped, I would be miserable.   Everyone there had several layers of clothes on except Ghader and me. We had not been instructed on how to dress.   Javad told me to be careful not to fall asleep or I would get sick, so I then started to move around again to keep myself warm and awake.

I wondered how long we would have to stay here, or if we would have to go back.   These questions came to my mind, but no one knew the answers.   I could not speak their language to communicate with them, but it seemed our guides were not sure exactly what was going on. All we could do was to wait.   At some point, we spread a blanket on the ground, gathered together with a few other people, and shared what food we had brought in the bag. I was not hungry at all, but just to keep my strength up I ate a small piece of bread with cheese.   I did not know what to think or what to say. I was confused and did not even know how to pray. At that moment it felt like we were against the Red Sea, with nowhere to go.

One of the guys in the group told us he had received four messages on his satellite phone, but did not know what it meant since they were all in English. They were talking among themselves, wondering what the messages said as he checked his satellite phone to call back those on the ground. Ebi told them to bring the radio to me to read since I spoke English. The messages indicated they were all missed calls. We assumed they were trying to call us to let us know it was ok to come down, but could not reach us because our satellite radio was turned off or on silent! On the mountaintop, they had to be very careful not to have anything light up because it could be seen from miles away and the satellite radio had a backlight. As I read the messages, several of them made a circle around me to keep the light from being seen.

In the meantime, a small group of men and their horses decided to go down the mountain first and once they got there, sent us a signal by their two-way radio that everything was safe for the rest of us to go down as well. We set out on foot, leading the horses as we began our downhill journey towards the border. As soon as we started down, the rest of the group started to follow us. Javad whispered into my ear to slow down and let the others to get ahead of us just in case we had to run if faced with a trap. I made an excuse, went to the side to tie my shoelace, and as a result, we ended up getting behind several others.

This trail was very difficult and slippery to walk on as we were rushing downhill. I slipped a few times, falling on my hands and knees. At times I found myself walking sideways, but we managed to get down and to a smoother terrain. There we mounted the horses, Ebi and I on one and Javid and Ghader on the other. We started out at a fast trot and then Ebi told me to hang on because we were about to gallop very fast for the rest of the trip! We rode downhill till we reached level ground. We then crossed through a very

**cold and rushing river to an unpaved
road where we rode for about another
1/4mile. There our rides were waiting for
us.**

I stood off to the side while they were transferring their goods from the back of their horses to the trucks and vice-versa. I saw some of the horses by the river drinking. I also was thirsty, but I was afraid to drink the water which could have made me sick. They loaded up the trucks with the merchandise they brought, and after a short rest, all of the horsemen went back home the same way we came in. I was introduced to a truck driver who later was going to take me to my destination. [No name provided for security reasons]. I thanked Ebi and Javad and they too, departed and went back home with some goods on the back of their horses.

All the trucks were loaded and had left the area except the truck that I was in.   I was already sitting on the front seat when I was told to get out because the truck would not crank! They seemed concerned, yet were calm about the situation. They popped the hood open and drained out the excess gasoline from the carburetor, which was what caused the truck not to crank. It was flooded. They worked hard, sweating even though it was so cold.   Then they put everything back in place and cranked it up!   Praise God!

Our truck was the last one to leave the area, but we did have a lead car with us with a few armed men.   I saw at least two individuals with rifles; one kept it on his shoulder and the other had it hidden under his long overcoat. The lead car was ahead of us for protection and to give us signals.

They could not afford to lose the valuable merchandise they had in the back of their truck. Finally, our truck moved forward with its headlights turned off, waiting to see a signal from the lead car. Once the signal came, we moved forward and out of the area.

Our first stop was a warehouse where they emptied some of the goods they had in their truck. The next stop was at one of the men's home where they unloaded some merchandise, reloaded some other goods, and headed toward the village. By this time, it was about five in the morning and the sun was beginning to come up. I asked the men for some water to drink so I could take some ibuprofen for my backache. Ghader and I were both exhausted and barely could keep our eyes open. I would barely open my eyes occasionally to see where we were. When we got closer to the village, we went to another house where they unloaded the truck, switched to a car, and headed to the village and to a house where we stayed until I could call the US embassy.

Chapter 19

Border Town

It was Sunday, May 22nd and about 7:00 am when we arrived at the house. The family was expecting us. Ghader spoke with the lady of the house in his native Turkish language and I followed him to the kitchen floor where breakfast was served. The breakfast consisted of homemade bread, white cream cheese mixed with mountain vegetables, homemade plain yogurt and hot tea. I was not too concerned or fussy about the food. I was just in a state of perplexity, and did not know if I was dreaming or if it was real. After the meal, we were directed to the guest room where we could relax, watch TV, or take a nap. I chose to lie down for a short nap until Jamsheed and Ali arrived.

The house belonged to a man who had several children and they all were very kind to me, but none of them spoke any other languages except Turkish and Kurdish. One of the older children started telling me that he would like to go to a university in America, and brought his English book to show me what he had been studying in high school. He spoke a few words in English but mostly in Turkish, so Ghader interpreted for me. I used his book to open up a conversation with him and he liked the idea of communicating with me in English.

Most houses, including the one we were staying in, were equipped with a satellite for TV viewing, but the electricity was not very reliable as it went off several times during the day. Occasionally, Ghader would translate what was being said on TV.

Ali and Jamsheed finally arrived by cab two hours later and joined us at the house. We rejoiced to see each other and were very happy to have overcome such an obstacle! Ali started telling me about the ordeal he faced while going through customs. Security had decided to check our suitcases and started looking through all my notes and pictures, reading and asking questions about the notes and wanting to know to whom the pictures belonged. Most of my notes were in English and they could not read them, otherwise they would have even caused more problems for Ali for no apparent reason. Customs security kept them for at least thirty minutes going through the bags, but mostly reading my personal stuff.

Later, another customs agent came to see the reason for the hold-up at their booth. Ali finally told them that these notes and pictures were the life story of one of his relatives named Saiid and they were from thirty years ago and that he was delivering them. He asked Ali if he was delivering them to me or someone else. Ali replied: "Does it matter if I am taking them to Saiid or someone else, since they were notes going back thirty years ago?" He responded, "No, it does not matter."

Then the custom agent pointed to my picture, asking if I was the one he was taking these things to. Ali told them yes.

When Ali saw their concern and the cause of the holdup, he turned around, gathered all the notes and pictures and handed them to Farsheed, one of Jamsheed's relatives who had driven them to this point so that he could take them back to Iran with him. Ali did not want them to think they were of any value or for them to find someone to interpret them since they mostly were written in English. This would have taken more of their time and could have possibly caused the officers to have reason to deny them entry into Turkey.

As Ali was passing all the notes and pictures to Farsheed, he accidentally gave the custom officer's notebook to him also. (This is a notebook where they logged in any incidents.)

Finally, as Ali and Jamsheed were cleared and were on their way through the exit gate, someone tapped Ali on the shoulder. It was the customs officer again! Ali was terrified and turned around asking, "What is it now?" The officer wanted his notebook, claiming that perhaps he put it inside my suitcase by mistake.

Then they opened the suitcases again searching for his notebook, but it was not there. "Where could it be?" The officer asked. Ali answered, "It could have been with the things I gave Farsheed, the one who drove us here. You will have to go after him if you want to see if he has your notebook." So they proceeded to chase after him to see if that's what had happened.   By the way, we never found out the outcome of that!

It was terrifying and funny at the same time!   For he deserved what he got in return for giving Ali such a hard time, not to mention reading through my personal notes!

251

After Ali and Jamsheed had arrived and we had some time to catch up, we decided to rest while waiting for the owner of the house to come home from work. As we talked, we found out that the lady of the house was related to Jamsheed and had been born in Iran. She was married at a very young age and had moved to Turkey with her husband to live.

At noon, they brought a long tablecloth in and spread it on the floor for us to have our lunch on. The lunch consisted of homemade bread, plain yogurt and potato soup. They all spoke Turkish except for Jamsheed and Ghader who spoke both Farsi and Turkish, so they became our translators.

Now that we had overcome our first obstacle, we started to talk about our second obstacle; how to approach the US embassy. We had been told that the United States had a consulate in the city of Van, which was a few hours away from where we were staying, but we found out that was not true. We also found out that there were several check points between the two cities as well.

I began to read my passport for possible help. Under "tips for travelers", it was written that American citizens who were traveling abroad could call the nearest Embassy or U.S. Consulate if they got into any trouble. It was very encouraging to know that, but I didn't have the phone number!

At about 5:00 pm, the owner of the house finally arrived with one of his co-workers. They were both shepherds and were arriving late because they had to carry some of their sheep to another town. We sat around the room and continued our discussion about how to approach the U.S Embassy.

There was a phone in the house, but we were told that it was used for incoming calls only. Ali had his cellular phone with him and was able to communicate with his wife along the way. I was waiting for an opportunity to call my wife, but Ali wanted me to wait until he was able to purchase a prepaid SIM-card for his cellular phone before I made the call. He thought that it might cost a lot less than calling direct, so I went along with his wishes.

That afternoon, Ali and Jamsheed went into town. They wanted to visit some friends and exchange their money. Ali said he would purchase the SIM-card while he was out, but found out he could use his cellular phone just as economically as prepay would have been.

When he returned, he allowed me to use the phone to call my wife. I tried our home phone first, but no one answered. It was a little after 7:00 am there and I figured she was probably on her way to work, so I called her cell phone.

When she answered, I said, "Hello darling!" We had not talked for several days, so she was excited to hear my voice and asked me how I was doing. I tried to hold back my emotions because I didn't want those around me to see me with tears in my eyes, but I could not help it!

I took a deep breath and asked, "Where are you?" She said she was on her way to work.

"Could you please pull over for a minute so I can talk to you," I asked?

She pulled over and then asked, "What's going on?"

"I'm in Turkey!" I responded.

She screamed with excitement and said, "I knew you might be up to something since I hadn't heard from you in so many days! Are you ok?"

"Yes, I'm fine. Ali and I are inside the Turkish border in a family's home. There are some things I need for you to do for me."

I gave her the phone number to the home I was in as well as Ali's cell number. I asked her to get me the phone number for the U.S. Embassy in Turkey. I felt that the U.S. Embassy was my best route to freedom since I entered the country illegally. She then told me that she would change her plans that day in order to make a few phone calls and that she would be in touch with me later on.

We were both excited and anxious at the same time, praying that everything would go well and without any problems!

As I looked back and thought about the events that had happened, I could not help but think how God was with me as I faced so many obstacles and danger. I had no choice except to trust Him when I chose to take this route, and I wanted to continue with the same assurance for the rest of my journey even though I felt like I was walking on some hot coals at times!

For the next hour, the owner of the house and the rest of the family sat down and drank hot tea and smoked on their cigarettes nonstop until the dinner was ready to be served.

We had soup, chicken, plain white rice and salad, which consisted of onion, tomato, and cucumber diced up and mixed together. It was tasty and delicious! Then we watched Turkish TV while we continued our conversation about our next step.

After a little while, I became so tired and desperately needed to rest. There were individual sleeping mats already prepared for each one of the guests in another room, so I excused myself and went to bed.

I slept well that night! At about 5:00 am I woke up. It was daybreak and the light was beginning to shine into the window. The owner's co-worker, who was also their friend, woke up, prayed his morning prayer and went back to sleep. At about 6:30 am I noticed the sun was way up high and shining through the windows of the house. The owner and his friend left for work, for they had to tend to their flock. The rest of us got up around 9:00 am. After eating breakfast, Ali and Jamsheed departed for the town and left Ghader and me behind.   There was nothing to do except watch TV or drink hot tea. The electricity would come and go as it pleased, usually about four times a day. The place we were staying was so peaceful and beautiful.   There were mountains all around us. Outside of the house was farmland with cows and hens roaming around. There was a spring of fresh running water for their personal use, as well as for their animals and for watering the crops.

Ghader occasionally would keep himself busy by getting his opium out to smoke. Apparently, it was all right to smoke opium or other drugs similar to that without trying to hide it. One of the women staying in the house brought him a small propane cylinder to be used as fire. He then used a small rod on the fire. When the rod got hot, he touched it to the small piece of opium where it created smoke, and with a straw he would inhale the smoke through his mouth similar to smoking a cigarette.

While we were traveling through the mountains, Ghader offered me a small piece of a type of opium called "Sheereh" (left over of the smoked opium), but I declined. He said that he used it to help him with his backache. I had a backache too, but I decided my Ibuprofen would do just fine!

The children were all very nice and hospitable toward us and they kept the hot tea coming almost every two hours. The mother of the family was born in Iran but she only spoke Turkish, so we could only communicate with each other through simple sign language. Ghader would interpret when it was needed. I had brought a bag of tea and some candy from Iran with me, which I gave to her for their hospitality and kindness they had shown toward me.

I guess the children in the community, especially the girls, had not seen anyone who spoke different languages before, so they would come to the house one by one from the farmland, school, or work, and attempt to see and talk to me with sign language. On one occasion while I was shaving, I noticed three of them standing by the door giggling as they were watching me shave my face. That reminded me of some of the old western movies on the big screen where everyone was watching the strange cowboy who just came to town. It was funny though!

Back in the US, my wife went to work to let them know that she needed to be off in order to help me. Everyone was so understanding and told her to do what she needed to do.

She still worked at the same doctor's office she had started in 15 years before when we first came to Asheville, but it was now called Parkway Family Physicians.   Dr. William Hamilton was one of the doctors there. When he heard the news, he told Ursa that Eric Ager, his nephew, was in Turkey at that time and gave her his phone number. Eric's parents, John and Annie Ager are also good friends of ours, and live in the same town as we do.

At the time, we did not know how or in what capacity Eric would be involved, but God knew, for he was there to help in a way that we could not even imagine!   Romans 8:28 speaks well of this:

Romans 8:28 "And we know that all things work together for good to those who love God, to those who are the called according to His purpose."

My wife went home and started making phone calls. She called our Congressman and Senators' offices. They suggested she call the U.S. Embassy in Ankara to let them know of my situation and that we needed their full support. She then called me back and gave me the phone number for the U.S. Embassy in Ankara, Turkey.

I called the Embassy in Ankara, introduced myself and gave them my U.S. passport number.   I told them of my situation and asked for their help to get back to the United States. The gentleman that I spoke with told me that I needed to turn myself in to the police and they probably would send me back to where I just came from!

"Oh No!" That was not what I wanted to hear! It felt like a knife going through my back and I could feel the pain all over my body!

"Please do not tell me that! I have read the information in my passport which states that if any American citizen is in trouble on foreign soil, to call the U.S. Embassy immediately for help... and now I am calling you; but you are telling me that they will send me back to Iran!"

The gentleman said, "You have broken Turkish law by entering the country illegally and this is what you have to do according to their laws."

I told him I was not satisfied with his answer and thanked him for his time. I immediately called my wife.

"It was Monday morning and I was on my way to work. My cell phone rang. I answered it and heard my husband's voice on the other end. "I'm in Turkey," he told me. I couldn't believe it! I was so excited when I heard the news and relieved to hear he was out of Iran! The last time I had talked to him was three or four days before, and I hadn't heard from him since. He had been talking to me about the possibility of escaping, but I would always plead with him not to try that because of the incredible danger. But honestly, there was a part of me down deep that wanted him home whatever it took. He knew not to tell me and just did what he knew he had to do. And by the grace of God, he had made it into Turkey safely!

I pulled over and took down the telephone numbers where I could reach him, and went on to work. I excitedly told everyone the news and they were all so happy! The doctors and so many of my co-workers had seen what I had been through over the past few months and had been such a support for me. I have worked in this family practice for almost 20 years now, and am blessed to work in a place where people truly love each other and lift each other up in times of need. It is also a place where we are not only allowed, but committed to be a place where we show love and compassion to our patients through the love of Jesus Christ. It is truly a wonderful place to work!

One of the doctor's I worked with at the time was Dr. William Hamilton. When I told him about Saiid being in Turkey, he was so excited and began telling me about his nephew, Eric Ager, who was serving in the military and just <u>happened </u>to be stationed in Turkey working at the embassy there! You could say, "What a coincidence!" But oh no, this was no coincidence! It was the beginning of many miracles that would bring my husband home.

I stayed at work only a few hours that day. I realized quickly after making a few phone calls that I needed to be home and near the phone. And it truly took almost every minute of every day for the next week, and sometimes night as well, talking to   many different people; politicians, the Turkish embassy, the Turkish police, Eric Ager, the airlines, and family and friends. I knew he

259

wasn't out of the woods yet, especially after an official at the Turkish embassy told me that he should turn himself over to the police and that they would most likely send him back to Iran! That was a moment I will never forget! I felt like a 'cement block' had been placed on my chest and I couldn't breath. But after they realized that he had his United States passport and had an airline reservation home, they were very helpful, staying in touch with the Turkish police making sure he was treated well.

I praise God that my youngest daughter, Elizabeth, was able to be with me most of that week. She had just graduated from nursing school and had some extra time. My daughters Crystal and Alyson were a great support to me as well and they did what they could. Crystal lived in West Virginia at the time. Alyson lived close by, but worked full time along with having to care for our first grandchild, Roman. We are very blessed to have three precious daughters on whom we can depend and who love the Lord. We have also been blessed with 3 wonderful son-in-laws who also love the Lord and take good care of our girls. And now we are blessed to have 5 beautiful grandchildren, and one on the way! Saiid and I are both convinced that being a grandparent is one of the greatest blessings from God above!"

<u>*Ursa*</u>

I believed that going back to Iran was like signing my own death certificate! For him to respond the way he did made me wonder if he believed at all. I was not in any position to argue or disagree with him, so when I called my wife back, I asked her to please call the Congressman and Senators' offices in North Carolina and ask them to telegram the U.S. Embassy in Ankara to help me.

It turned out that my wife had also just spoken with the U.S. Embassy in Turkey and they told her the same thing! She was crushed, but would not take that as an answer either. But another lady there seemed more understanding to our needs and was willing to help. She wrote down her name for me to talk to and gave it to me.

I called her and introduced myself, but was not sure at that time if I was calling the same building as before or if it was in a different building. First she told me that I should speak with the same gentleman that I spoke with earlier, as he was in charge of those matters.

I told her that I had already spoken to that gentleman and was not satisfied with what he had to tell me.

She then said the same thing the gentleman had already told me.

I told her that I needed help from the Embassy!

Then she responded: "Let me connect you to someone else."

That person was another lady that seemed to be more sensitive and compassionate toward my need. Although she told me the same thing as the gentleman did, she gave me more explanation as to what I would need to do. She told me that if I had a confirmed airline ticket to my destination along with my passport, I would need to go to the nearest police station which was called Amniyat and they "usually" will deport you to your destination. She also told me that my wife had called them as well and that they were aware of the situation.

After that conversation, I felt like a weight was lifted off my shoulders, and it sounded a lot better than before. As a result, it gave me more hope and I understood the correct course of action to take.

I asked Jamsheed if he had a police friend that we could talk to and get some advice from in order to go to the right section of the police department. I did not want to just walk in the police department without knowing which section was going to handle my situation and I did not want to get shuffled around by the wrong group of investigators. I had seen in some movies and even heard that if you are not careful, you could get into the wrong hands where you could be treated improperly.

By this time, the owner of the house was home from work along with a couple of his friends. They sat in the guestroom for three hours talking, smoking and drinking their hot tea.

Jamsheed, after thinking about who he might know in the police department and talking to some people, told me that he believed that he might know someone who could help. He then asked the owner of the house for his mobile phone to call his police friend. An hour later, two police officers in their civilian attire came to the house, drank hot tea, and talked. They were speaking in Turkish of course and I could not understand what they were saying, but occasionally I understood a word or two. Then the two officers left the house to speak with another detective who specialized in this type of situation. They said they would call Jamsheed on the cellular phone at a later time.

That night, we were invited to a friend's house for dinner, which was only a few blocks away. There were twelve men at the dinner table including Ali and me. The women stayed in the kitchen. Their conversation was over a piece of farmland they owned and the problems they were facing.

We were almost finished with our dinner when the cellular phone rang. The phone was for Jamsheed and after a short conversation he went outside to meet with the caller. It was the same police friend who came by the house earlier. He asked for me and Ali to take a ride with him. He did not tell us where we were going or what we were going to do. I did not ask either; I just knew God was not going to get me out of "Egypt just to drown me in the Red Sea!" He is so faithful!

We got into his truck and drove around. Jamsheed sat in the front seat while Ali and I sat in the back. As we were driving around, he took us on some back roads away from the main street. I did not know what was going through his mind and since I did not know the language could not understand what they were talking about. I have to admit that I felt a bit uneasy since we were in the middle of nowhere!

After driving around for half an hour (though it seemed a lot longer), we finally went to a house to pick up the police officer's son, took him to another location and dropped him off. I felt much better after that since we were now on busier streets. Then he picked up a detective that we were supposed to meet with. They continued their conversation as we were riding around. They drove by the police station and pointed out to me where I should meet with the detective the next morning. He would take me in to the proper authorities who would then create a file for me. He said the paper work would probably take about an hour and then they would give me a certified paper that would give me permission to travel anywhere in the country and so I could pass through any checkpoints without any problems. (He had good intentions but things never go that smooth when you have to depend on others!)

Then they drove us back to the house. We thanked them for what they were doing to help and they went on their way. Jamsheed then told us that the officers wanted some money for their troubles and were asking for $1,000. I told Jamsheed that I did not have that much money to spare. I needed to hold on to most of what I had because I had no way of knowing how long I would be in Turkey or what I would need to use my money for. I told Jamsheed that the most I would be able to give them is $100 each. The owner of the house heard our conversation and did not like what he was hearing. He saw their greedy intentions and told Jamsheed that it was the police officers job to help and that they should not be asking for money. He said if they are going to behave like this, then we will go in ourselves without their help!

I also wondered if it was the police officers who had asked for money or if it was Jamsheed who was really trying to collect more money from me. I would never know the answer to that!

Ali chimed in and reminded Jamsheed of the agreement we made from the beginning. If we had to pay any extra now then it would be deducted from what we already owed them. He agreed, and we gave them $200 dollars. On that note, we ended our conversation about the money. It was getting late and I was tired. I had a long day ahead of me, so I excused myself and went to bed in the other room.

Chapter 20

Another Challenge

The next morning, Tuesday, May 24th, Jamsheed left the house in a cab at about 8:00 am to meet with the police officers to discuss the details of how I would turn myself in and to whom. He would be back to get me and Ali as soon as he could.

While I was waiting at the house, Ghader started to cause problems by asking for the balance of the money. He told us that he had done all the work and he should be the one to get the money, not Majid who stayed behind. Ali tried to convince him that we had made an agreement with Majid and could not give him the money unless we talked to him and he gave us permission.

Ghader claimed that Majid did not have a phone at his house and his cellular phone had been cut off because he had not paid his bill. Ghader was making excuses to get his hands on the balance of the money we agreed upon. He said that he wanted to purchase things while he was in Turkey and that was the reason he needed some money right then. He then told me that if he didn't get it, he would not allow me to continue my trip to the next level.

Ali and Ghader went head-to-head for almost two hours about how to disburse this money and finally they came to an understanding. If they were able to speak with Majid, Ali would tell him the situation; that because there was not a U.S. Consulate or Embassy in Van as he had promised, it was causing him to have to spend more money on taking care of me and getting me where I needed to go.

I somehow believe that they had intentions all along to try to get more money from us. Majid had told us that he would take me right to the door of the U.S. Embassy in Van, but there was no Embassy or Consulate there. He had told us that Ghader and he were brothers, but they were not. There was so much inconsistency and untruth that it was hard to believe anything they said. But they had gotten me this far and for that I was grateful. I had to trust them to a certain degree, but God was my true guide!

Also, Jamsheed later told Ali that he saw Ghader going through my suitcase the night before while I was asleep trying to steel my passport. I always kept my passport on me because of that very reason, so praise God he didn't get it! He took some other papers that didn't matter instead. His intention of course, was to try to keep me from leaving until I paid him the money.

Finally, Majid called the house at about 10:00 am. Ali talked to him about the money, and he was okay with us giving the money to Ghader. This $1,500 was the second part of the money we agreed to pay them once they delivered me to the U.S. Embassy. So Ali called my sister back in Iran and authorized her to give the money to one of Ghader's relatives to hold for him until he returned. He was happy with that.

I was dressed and ready, anxiously waiting on Jamsheed to return. I went outside to wait, pacing back and forth and praying that all would go well as I turned myself in to the Turkish police. Finally, he came back in the same yellow cab and the three of us left for the police department. We went straight to the front of the building where the detective was waiting for us. We all got out and the cab left. The officer helped me with one of the two bags I was carrying and we went inside the station. Jamsheed and Ali stayed behind on the street and said they would wait to hear from me, hopefully in a few hours.

The detective took me to one of the offices on the second floor where they started a file on me. There were two other detectives in the office when we arrived. The officer, who took me in explained to them my situation. While one of the officers was making some phone calls, the other officer tried to start a conversation with me in his broken English. They seemed to be very nice, offering me a soft drink or hot tea, but I declined since I was planning to be there for a short time. In order to "break the ice" and be friendly, I attempted to continue an exchange by teaching them a few English words as we shared things of common interest.

I finally asked, "What are we waiting for?"

He answered, "We are waiting for the Captain. He has gone to another town and should be here within a couple of hours." Then I told the officer I would accept their hospitable offer concerning the soft drink since it was going to take much longer. They gladly brought one.

Then they looked through my bags and documented all my possessions, and at noon took me to lunch at the officers' mess hall. The dining room area was small. It only fit about ten small wooden tables with two chairs around each one. There was a small window where you would order and pick up your food. Next to the pickup window was a person at a desk that would collect the lunch money or record names based on the prearranged status.

After lunch, we went to another building close by where many officers and staff were gathered for fellowship. All the officers I had seen so far wore civilian clothes and no uniform. I thought that a bit strange, but it put me more at ease. They all were gathered there drinking hot tea, smoking their cigarettes, and some were playing card games, etc. The room was full of smoke from the cigarettes, but I stayed close to the entrance of the door to get fresh air.

It was there where I met the Assistant Captain. The officers who had brought me in briefed him on my situation. After he heard my story and studied my appearance, he motioned to the officers to do whatever was necessary to help get me home. Then the ball started rolling! The officers took me back over to the office where I was before and started the process. They took a mug shot, (just a front facing picture with a smile!) fingerprinted me and sent me to a local medical clinic for a check-up. I believe they did the check-up so there would be proof I had not been abused in their care.

While all this was taking place and we were going from one building to another, I saw Ali and Jamsheed pacing back and forth on the street, but was not able to talk to them. There was no one to let them know what was going on and I couldn't say anything to them for fear they would get in trouble for their part in helping me escape from Iran. There was nothing I could do and I felt so bad for them!   But it was comforting to know they were there for me, especially Ali. And I even believe that Jamsheed, even though he was being paid to be there, cared a little about what happened to me. I prayed that soon I would be able to somehow let them know that everything was ok.

The U.S. Embassy was aware of the whole situation and gave my wife the phone number to the police station in case she needed to speak with me. As a result, we talked several times when she wanted to check on me.

When I found out the airline would not accept my old ticket and while trying to find the solution to that, my wife called me, (she was one step ahead of what my needs were) and gave me the confirmation number of a newly reserved airline ticket. WOW!

I was delighted and overjoyed, for I saw my Father in heaven in action by putting my need in my wife's heart! She had called the airline to check on my old ticket, but they told her that the old ticket was no longer in their computer and we had to purchase a new one, therefore in order not to delay any longer she took it upon herself to buy a new ticket. Praise God!!

While going through the necessary paper work, a phone call came in to let me know that two detectives who spoke English were coming to question me. Then they explained to me that they must take me before a judge to authorize my deportation. The two detectives came and questioned me about my background, my wife and children, my work and the length of time I had been with the company, as well as where my wife worked. They also wanted to know how long I had been married and the purpose of my visit to Iran.

Then they asked, "How did you manage such a trip through the mountains?"

I answered, "I had help."

"Did you know them?" They asked.

I answered, "I did not know any of them."

They responded in amazement by asking: "Did you ever think about the danger of going through such mountains that were unfamiliar to you and traveling with people whom you did not know? Do you realize that what you did could have cost you your life?"

Frankly, they were right about the danger, but during those uncertain times I clung to such comforting words from the scripture such as Psalm 23:4 which reads: "Yea, though I walk through the valley of the shadow of death, I will fear no evil; for You are with me; your rod and Your staff, they comfort me."

I told them that I knew my actions were not the best and that I considered myself fortunate to have made it safely, but I was desperate and had to make a choice if I was ever going to leave Iran, as I was not sure how much longer they were planning to keep me there against my will.

I would not advise anyone to do what I did because I truly could have disappeared and never been seen or heard from again. But my love for my family drove me and my trust in God sustained me as I crossed those mountains. It was the only thing that made sense to me at the time!

The detectives took notes of our conversation and before they left told me not to ever come back to Turkey illegally. I thanked them and told them that not to worry; my next trip to Turkey would be with my wife and family. They smiled and left.

Later, they brought in a lady who was an English teacher and who would be my interpreter when I went to court. She helped me with the rest of the paperwork, explaining it to me and telling me where I needed to sign. When I finally went before the judge, very few words were spoken between us. The judge looked at my identification, such as my driver license and passport, and asked a few questions. He then gave his stamp of approval and I received the court order for my deportation! Haleluia!

Next, I needed to be handed over to the Foreign Affairs Department in Hakkari. About 4:00 pm, I left with two detectives who would be transporting me. The two detectives sat in the front seat while I sat in the back. As we were leaving the town, I spotted Ali and Jamsheed who were still pacing the street, waiting for someone to let them know what was going on. At that moment, the car slowed down because one of the detectives saw someone he knew and wanted to speak to them. God had provided an opportunity at last! They saw me and Ali came a little closer, hoping to get a chance to find out what was going on, so I rolled my window down. With excitement and a smile on my face, I said,

"Freedom at last! I am going to America!" When Ali heard the news, he backed up, and with a big smile on his face waved goodbye. Jamsheed had kept his distance, but motioned me goodbye with a bow and a smile!

We traveled by car for two hours, going through at least two police checkpoints before we reached the city of Hakkari. The officers turned me over to the foreign affairs officer and then returned back to their own town. There in Hakkari, I met two other officers in civilian clothes. Later, another officer who spoke English joined us. They were required to establish their own file on me, so again I had to be "booked" like before. Another photo opportunity! Seriously though, it was not an unpleasant experience under the circumstances. They were treating me with kindness; just following procedure. The officers worked late and diligently to expedite my paper work.

I patiently sat in one of the offices while I waited for them to finish the paperwork. The phone rang and low and behold it was my wife! She was calling to see how things were going and how I was. My daughter, Elizabeth was there with her as well. They were calling to be my encouragers! I had not talked to any of my children during this ordeal, so Ursa asked me if I wanted to talk to Elizabeth. I told her I wasn't sure if I could maintain my composure, but Elizabeth wanted to talk to me so I agreed. As soon as I heard her voice she began to cry, and of course, that's all it took for me! When the detectives saw my emotions, they left the room to give me some privacy. We were not able to speak long, but it was wonderful to have the opportunity to hear from the ones I loved and for them to know I was fine.

Eric Ager, (one of my angels from God!) whom I mentioned earlier was from my hometown and was stationed at the U.S. Embassy in Ankara, also called to check on me. He wanted to know if there was anything he could do for me. I thanked him for the phone call and his offer, and told him that they were being very kind to me and doing a very good job. He gave me his phone number and told me to call if I needed anything at all.

At about 9:00 pm, we sought the commander in charge to review and sign off the paperwork. He was at a private dinner with some important people, but took the time to come outside for a moment. I was standing at a visible distance, dressed in black pants, a white shirt and black shoes. The officer began to tell his commander about my situation. After a short conversation, the commander wanted to know who the person was who made such a trip through the rugged mountains. In order to be polite, the officer did not point his finger at me, but rather made motions with his head. The commander looked toward me, then to the left and right, but he only saw me! So he asked the officer,

"Is that him?"

The officer nodded "Yes".

The commander laughed, because he could not believe his own eyes that someone like me would cross those mountains! (Perhaps he was looking for someone who looked a bit rougher than I did. Believe me, I had a hard time believing in what I did too, and to this day, everything that happened appears to be like a dream to me. It was definitely the adventure of my lifetime!) Then, with much relief, the commander signed the deportation papers!

It was getting late, so the officers took me to a nice restaurant and fed me whatever I wanted. Later they took me back to the police station in order for me to rest. They would not allow me to be by myself since they were responsible for my safety, so that night I slept in their jail cell, but with the door open so I could be free to move around. Before I went to sleep, we sat in the front office and watched a soccer game on TV with the rest of the policemen while drinking hot tea. None of them spoke English, so we didn't talk much! I soon became tired and decided it was time to get some sleep, so I retired to my cell.

In the jail cell there was a narrow platform on all three sides covered by a thin mat. I needed to try to get some rest because of the long day ahead of me, so I washed up, shaved and brushed my teeth, then laid down to try to sleep. There was no pillow so I used my hand bag to lay my head on and no blanket so I used my jacket to cover up with. Thus needless to say I didn't get much sleep. I will tell you, that was the closest to being put in jail I ever wanted to be!

The next morning the officers came for me. We went straight to a travel agency in order to make reservations for a bus to Van and a flight from there to Istanbul. Getting our bus tickets was no problem, but there were only two flights daily out of Van to Istanbul, and they were both booked for that day!

By bus, the travel time to Istanbul was 30 hours. It was Wednesday and my flight was scheduled out of Istanbul to America for Friday at 4:00 am. If we took the bus, we would not make it on time. So I immediately called my wife and asked her to call the airline and see if she could change the day and time. She was able to get it changed to 4:00 am on Saturday, one day later. At that time, I was asked to purchase the two detectives tickets also! I was not prepared financially and surprised to know that the responsibility of purchasing airline tickets for the officers was mine, but at the same time I was so grateful to God that I was willing to do even more if I could. I had $360 in cash as well as my credit card. Ali had kept most of my money for security purposes while we were traveling, but after going to the police station, we never made contact anymore. The cash I had was not enough to purchase all of our tickets.

I offered to use my credit card, but their computer rejected it! There was a bank next door to the travel agency, but they would not honor my credit card either. I called my wife again using one of the policeman's cellular phones. It was about three in the morning there and I woke her up. I asked her to call my credit card company to see why I could not use it there. She called me back after speaking to the 24-hour bank representative. Their computers were down and she would have to call back later. At first, I wasn't sure what to do next.

Then I remembered Eric and his offer to help. My wife called Eric and told him the situation, and asked if there was any way he could lend me the money I needed to buy the tickets. Eric immediately called me to get the details. He was more than willing to lend me the money, so he tried using his credit card but it was rejected too. Then he went to a bank near where he was and within 30 minutes, the $700 I needed was transferred to the bank next to the travel agency! Wow!

Is God awesome or what?
He is so faithful and true!
What is the possibility that someone who lived in the
same town as I did was half-way around the world at
the same time I was! I know in my heart that God
made that possible, knowing my need before I did.
He is truly amazing!

With that money I was able to purchase the airline and
bus tickets we needed. We would be taking a bus to Van,
and then a flight from there to Istanbul. The bus was
scheduled to leave at 3:00 pm, and we barely made it. We
were the last ones to board the bus and headed to Van.

It happened that Eric's mom, Annie, was already in
Turkey visiting her son, and John, her husband was going to
be flying to Turkey within the next few days, so Ursa took
the money to him so he could take it to Eric and pay him
back.

We were all so excited that Saiid was finally in Turkey
and seemingly on his way home, but I would not rest until he
crossed into American airspace! I kept thinking that there
was some possibility the Iranian officials would realize what
he had done and would try to come after him. He could not
get to the Istanbul airport fast enough for me!

But it was comforting that I was allowed to keep in touch
with him by calling the cell phone of one of the officers who
was with him, as well as being in touch with the embassy,
who were also keeping up with his progress. It was a true
miracle all that was taking place. The fact that the Turkish
officials were treating him with kindness and respect was
not something you would expect, but I knew in my heart that

278

God was the One paving his path and protecting him from harm

Ursa

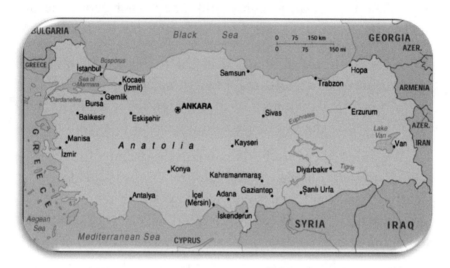

We arrived in the city of Van around 7:00 pm. The officer who spoke English had lived there some years ago and was very familiar with it. It was a small city, but people were as active and busy as you would see in most big cities. We stopped at the first hotel that we came to. The hotel looked good from the outside, but turned out to be poorly maintained.

The officer said: "Since we are not going to stay here more than a night, I don't see any reason to spend more for an expensive one."

I didn't object.   They had what was left of my money, as well as my passport, so I had to trust them to make a decision.   I was just looking forward to a place to rest. So, we checked in and put our luggage in the room.

The room had three single, narrow beds with a 13"
remote TV as well as a broken and non-functional telephone.
The space between the beds and the wall was so small that
after I put my luggage on the floor there was hardly room to
walk. The room had a musty, old smell, so I chose the bed
next to the window so that I could open it for fresh air.

After a short while we decided to leave the hotel for
dinner. Before we left, the English speaking officer called
one of his friends whom he had not seen for a while to come
meet us. When she got there, we all went to a restaurant.

We enjoyed each other's company as we ate dinner, even
joking around a little. After dinner, we walked down the
streets of Van and did some window shopping. I wasn't
sure what to expect to see while I was in Van, but there were
some things that surprised me and got my attention.

One was that most households were equipped with a
Satellite dish, regardless of the condition of their house.

Secondly, most people had a cellular phone on their
sides. Sim-cards (for prepay cellular phones) were very
popular and sold on every street corner.

Thirdly, I saw "Internet cafés" and "Phone Booth
Stores" almost at every street corner, packed with customers
who wanted to talk or chat to people around the world. I
decided to take advantage of one of the phone booth stores
and called home to talk to my wife. A desk timer kept track
of how long you talked and you paid the attendant the
amount after you finished your conversation.

Before we went back to the hotel, we stopped at a
grocery store and purchased a few things. I picked up some

fruit; nuts, soda and some shampoo, but the officers wanted beer for themselves.

When we got back to our hotel, I jumped at the opportunity to take a good hot shower. I had not had a shower for a few days and was feeling very uncomfortable. I had to let the water run for a long time before it got hot enough. The shower curtain was broken, but I was able to manage with a little creative ingenuity! The sheets on the bed were not clean to my satisfaction, so I slept on top of the covers and used the extra blanket to cover up with. This certainly wasn't the best hotel I'd ever stayed in, but it sure beat my accommodations the night before! It was the first good night's sleep I'd had in days and I slept like a baby.

Friday May 27th

The hotel offered a continental breakfast, so we made our way down to the lobby. As we ate, one of the officers checked the expiration date on the jam that was placed on our plates and noticed that it was already expired. We all agreed that this is what you get in cheap hotels!

Our flight out of Van would be leaving later on that day, so we had some time to kill. We decided to walk and window shop again and that took most of the morning. We found a place to eat lunch and, then went back to the hotel to get our luggage. Finally we left the hotel by cab and headed to the airport.

As we were traveling, I was getting calls often on one of the officer's cell phone. The gentleman from the U.S. embassy called to check on me several times. My wife called me, as well as my brother, Hamid. When I talked to Hamid, he asked me three times if I was okay! He had been forced to leave me behind in Iran and that was not easy for him at all, and he needed to know I was okay. I assured him that I was and told him I would be home soon! So many people from all over were praying for me, showing their love and concern in so many ways. That was very comforting for me and I know was a very big part of how I made it home!

Soon, we arrived at the airport and checked in. When security realized the officers had guns with them, they made them turn them in and were told they would get them back at the airport in Istanbul. They willingly turned them over and we boarded the plane.

We arrived in the beautiful city of Istanbul at about 6:00 in the evening. Istanbul is indeed a beautiful city! The city is lively twenty-four hours a day, seven days a week with so many tourists from all over the world. There is a beautiful bridge connecting Asia and Europe together. The famous Blue Mosque is located in the center of the city adding even more beauty. Opposite the Blue Mosque is a large church bringing two major religions, Islam and Christianity, closer together and in peace with each other. One of the officers commented on how proud he was of that fact; that Muslims and Christians can live side-by-side with respect for one another in that country.

We traveled to town by metro from the airport. Then we took a cab to a place where we met a friend of one of the officers who owned a rug shop. He also spoke good English. I had been looking at some small handmade carpets as we window shopped in Van, so I took this opportunity to purchase one from this gentleman. After making the purchase and visiting a little while, we all went out to dinner.

Given that we were going to need to leave for the airport at 2:30 am the next morning, we really did not want to spend the money for another hotel room for such a short time. So the gentleman whom I purchased the rug from was kind enough to put us in touch with a good friend of his who owned a hotel. With no charge, his friend allowed us to spend the rest of our time on the balcony of the 4th floor where there were tables and chairs for us to sit and enjoy the beauty of Istanbul at night. So until we had to leave for the airport, we sat on the balcony, enjoying some snacks and drinks we had purchased, and talked. We talked about our families, children, and Christianity. They were very open-minded and eager to listen. They asked many questions and they received the answers well concerning things that I had to share with them.

One of the police officers asked me if I would share with the American people that the people of Turkey despise terrorists and those who use Islam to advance their own cause, killing innocent people as you see on television and in newspapers. He told me that he had once visited the USA and had a great love and respect for the people there. He said he wished for the day when all the terrorist activity would end.

Bosphorus bridge, Istanbul-Turkey

At 2:30 in the morning, we called for a cab to take us back to the airport. The airport was very large and was divided in two sections. One section was Domestic and the other International. At the airport, we had to check on a couple of things. One was to find the place where the officers could pick up their guns, and second was to go to an exclusive custom and security department to stamp my exit on my passport. Since the Turkish officers were escorting me out of the country, we were able to use police privileges to bypass the normal interviews, gates, etc. It was interesting to see all the things that were going on behind the scene at an airport to ensure a safe flight for everyone.

From time to time as I traveled on this unexpected journey, I would find myself thinking back on the events that had happened the past two months, and I would be overwhelmed with so many different

284

emotions. On one hand I would feel excitement and joy, and on the other I would feel afraid and alone, uncertain of the unknown.

The unknown was the fact I had come this far in my journey and had been faced with many unpredictable circumstances, and I wondered if there were more ahead. My heart would be filled with anxiety, but then I would open my wallet and look at the pictures of my wife, children, and my grandson, Roman. My heart would ache and my eyes would fill with tears, longing to see and hold them in my arms!

Chapter 21

Victory

Heading Home

WEll, the time for my check-in had arrived and after my tickets were confirmed, I picked up my boarding pass. My tickets were First Class, which was a surprise to me! I found out later that when my wife called to make my reservation, it was all they had left for that flight, and as she told them the story, talking to several different agents, they gave it to me for the same price as coach! Another small miracle!

I received a free breakfast pass to use at the VIP lounge in the airport before boarding, so my officer friends and I took the opportunity to go and have a good breakfast together. After we ate, I bought them both a souvenir and gave them any extra Turkish money I had. We had been through a lot together and they had truly become my friends. They were right there with me the whole time making sure I was safe and did not encounter any problems.

When it was time to board the plane, the officers and I gave each other a hug and said goodbye. They also asked me to call them when I arrived safely in America. I told them I would. Then I boarded the airplane to Amsterdam, Holland.

When I arrived in Holland, there was a four hour layover until my next flight to Detroit, Michigan. In Amsterdam, every passenger was required to go through an interview before he or she could board the plane to the USA, and I was the first person in line for that interview.

The airline security asked me, "Where are you coming from?"

"Turkey," I answered.

"Were you in another country besides Turkey?

"Yes sir, I was in Iran visiting my family."

"Do you have an Iranian Passport?"

"Well sir, I did, but they took it away from me."

I then proceeded to tell him the truth about what had happened. I showed him my American passport and showed him where there was an exit stamp, not an entry stamp.

Then he consulted with his supervisor about my case. The supervisor came and asked a few of the same questions. He smiled at my interesting story and then he let me pass through without asking any more details.

Months later after my return to the USA, an FBI agent came to my workplace to check on me. I do not know the real reason why he came to see me, but I volunteered any information he asked about my ordeal. I suppose there must have been something that triggered an investigation for security purposes, but his visits didn't bother me at all. He returned several times and eventually we became friends.

Our airplane was an airbus. It was very nice and appeared to be new. In First Class, all the seats were far apart from each other with plenty of leg room. They would turn from a seat to a bed with a push of a button! Each seat also had a private TV and a massager built right into the seat. All of these comforts were so nice after all I had been through!

As the airplane took off, I dozed off, dreaming of the events of the past few days. I was resting so comfortably when suddenly the Captain came over the loudspeaker and informed us that we had to go back because one of the instruments on the plane was not working properly. He considered it a minor problem, but didn't want to take any chances. So we went back to the airport in Amsterdam so the technicians could fix the problem.

After they realized the problem would take longer than expected to fix, we disembarked the plane and relocated to another gate to wait for another plane. All of this delayed my trip for four hours, but I was okay with it all. I didn't mind a delay as long as I was safe. And as it turned out, there was a 7 hour layover in Detroit and I was able to make that flight with no problem!

I was now in the air to my final destination! I was going home where all my family and friends would be waiting for me. Although I had no idea how many there would be! I arrived in Asheville at about 10:15 pm. As I started down the escalator, I could see the large crowd, many holding welcome signs and American flags. It was a marvelous sight! There were at least 35 or 40 of them and I was humbled to see so many people there to greet me!

I was first greeted by my wife and then my children and their husbands, and my grandson, Roman. It was a wonderful reunion! Then I went around to each one of my friends who were there and gave them hugs and kisses and expressed my gratitude for their love and support for me and my family while I was away. I was so fortunate knowing that so many of my family and friends were on their knees praying for me. I truly rejoiced in the Lord, offering Him praise and thanks for the way He and His children showered me with so much love! This outpouring of love will remain in my memory for the rest of my life, and it will be shared with many as part of my testimony. It was especially wonderful to hold my wife in my arms again; my gift from God who now completed my soul.

Saiid Rabiipour

"Finally, the day of Saiid's homecoming was here! I had been tracking his journey with the airlines from the time he left Istanbul till now. I knew he should be on that plane, but after all we had been through, I was afraid to get too excited until I saw him with my own eyes!

So many of our family and friends gathered at the airport to welcome him home. And because of the crowd, I think the airport employees thought that there was someone famous about to get off the plane!

The plane landed and we all stood in the waiting area anxiously waiting. Person after person came down the escalator until finally, there he was! It was a wonderful sight to see my husband for the first time coming down that escalator. I knew he was weary and worn from all he had been through, but when he saw the crowd that had gathered, he knew why he was home, safe and sound. All those people, and so many more, had diligently prayed for him.

During the time he was away, he had many opportunities to share and he took advantage of every one. God had him in His hands every minute, guiding his steps and protecting him from harm.

I think I knew in my heart that ultimately everything would be ok; that God would take care of him and bring him home to us. I knew He had a plan and a purpose for him being in Iran; it was just hard to

291

see sometimes. It was hard not to be afraid, or to question why, but now I know that this was an opportunity God gave us to learn to depend on Him, to trust Him, and to have the kind of faith that moves mountains! A passage from James says it well: "My brethren, count it all joy when you fall into various trials, knowing that the testing of your faith produces patience. But let patience have its perfect work, that you may be perfect and complete, lacking nothing." (James: 2-4)

Saiid and I both now have a new appreciation for what it means to be loved and cared for and to see God's love in action. So many were there for us, supporting us, loving us, and most importantly, praying for us! If I tried to make a list and mention each one, the list would go on forever! We want you to know we love you all and pray God's richest blessings on you and your families!

And to God we give ALL the Praise, ALL the Honor, and ALL the Glory for who He is and for how He loves and cares for His children!"

Ursa

Arriving at the Asheville airport

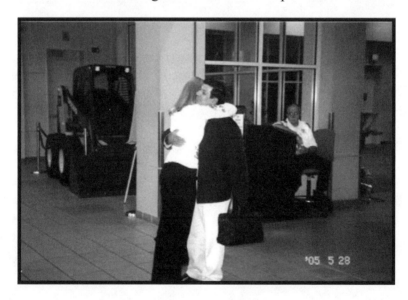

Greeted by my dear wife, Ursa

My daughters Alyson, Elizabeth and my wife, Ursa

It was wonderful when I was finally able to see and kiss the faces of my daughters. When I was away, I was very emotional, and could not speak to them over the phone without tears running down my face.

And there he was; my grandson, Roman! I proudly showed off his picture to everyone during my adventure. At the time, he was the only grandchild I had, but now I have five! What a blessing they are.

I hugged my son-in-laws, and all those who were there to welcome me. All of them had been such an encouragement while we were under so much pressure.

Most of all I want to thank GOD for being my deliverer twice.

For I am twice born and twice saved!

My grandson, Roman, at age two

GLORY BE TO GOD
FOR HE IS GOOD

Chapter 22

Conclusion

After reading my story, I hope you have seen how Christ influenced my life from the time I was born to where I am today. Of course, the revelation of Christ was not revealed to me until the day conversion took place in my heart, as I mentioned in chapter seven. Now, I would like to finish my book with an ending that will explain the reasons why I left Islam to a true relationship with the One who is *"the Way, the Truth and the Life."* Today, I am indebted totally to Jesus Christ for His love, grace and mercy that he has offered so freely.

As a Christian, I am a better 'Muslim' than when I practiced my faith as a follower of Muhammad in Islam.

I happened to become a <u>Muslim</u> by birth because I was born in a country at a time when Islam was, and still is, the main religion of the land. The majority of the populations including my parents were practicing Islam as their religion. But today, I am a <u>Christian by choice</u> after realizing who Christ is and what He did for me. I was in awe at the teachings of Jesus Christ and I preferred them over the teachings of Mohammad. Here is why:

For years, I searched and questioned both religions in order to find the Truth. My family's fate was in my thoughts and mind since they were still practicing the doctrine of Islam. Because of their lack of religious freedom, peer pressure within their society, and lack of education about other faiths, they had no choice but to trust those Imams and Mullahs as their spiritual leaders. Although there was some education about other religions, it was mostly one-sided and incorrect.

When I came to America, I was faced with a challenge that I had never encountered before. I noticed that people were at ease to discuss any matters they wished and that the manner of their conversation and thinking were different from mine. My curiosity was raised, and I desired to know more, but I didn't want to jeopardize my own character or identity that made me who I was.

As I was growing up, I was taught to believe that Islam had many, good moral values, and these became a part of me. But, there was still something missing in my life. When you don't know what to compare it to, you might be content with what you have, but the more I learned, the more I knew there was a "void" in my life that only Jesus could fill. He gave me hope and assurance with a clear understanding that I could not attain as a Muslim.

As I was searching, this freedom that belonged to Christians fascinated me and I wanted to be like them. I felt free to ask questions or discuss any subject in public or private without fear; something I could not do in Iran. You never question or challenge an Imam! I was also curious to know why so many people in the United States were not practicing Islam as I was, yet they possessed pure hearts!

As part of my research, I spent a great deal of time listening to Muslim professors and scholars such as Dr. Jamal Badawi, Sheik

Ahmad Deedat, and Dr. Zakir Naik in debates with Christian teachers and pastors. I also read many books from well respected Islamic teachers, i.e. Ayatollah Noori from Iran and others, as well as the Quran, in order to be certain that I did not miss anything. Here are some of the points I learned by listening to those debates:

1) You cannot convince any Muslim in a debate because they are not willing to listen and understand what the Christians are trying to say to them, as they choose to close their ears! One example is this: Christians believe in one God manifested in three persons (the Father, Son and Holy Spirit), while Muslims are conveying the opposite by saying, "No, you believe in three gods!"

2)   There are statements or words in the Bible that Muslim scholars have wrongly interpreted, yet no one is willing to acknowledge it and say, "Perhaps I do not understand that; please explain!" Here is an example. Muslim scholars look at the statements in the Bible as they are written literally, interpreting them in such a way that changes their meaning to something very different. The Bible is full of figurative words or statements that require more explanation than literal interpretation will allow, yet they are not willing to listen and they often misquote by using a part of the scripture, or they take it out of context. A good example is in the Book of Numbers 23:19, which often is quoted by Muslims and where they claim "God is not a man or the son of man". But the scripture says, "God is not a man that, He should lie; nor a son of man that he should repent."

3) Due to the lack of the Holy Spirit as their guide, Muslim scholars often refer to their own Quran as the source of correction for the Bible since they claim that the Bible is corrupt. But, the Quran claims that God is the protector of the scriptures including the Torah and the Gospel.

(Sura 6:34 says: "There is none that can alter the Words and Decrees of God". Sura 35:43 says: "But no change wilt thou find in God's way- God's Laws are fixed." And Sura 10:94; 4:136; 6:115-116 all confirm the before books (meaning Torah and Gospel).

I have concluded that the religion of Islam, with Muhammad as their Prophet and the Quran as their scripture, are part of historical events. These historical events, whether I believe in them or not, occurred in 610 A.D. and there is nothing any person can do to change it. Many good people practice Islam and are no different from those who practice Judaism or Christianity. They love their families and would do their best for them. Many of them hate war, confrontation, or ill feelings toward others, however, at the same time, most are trapped by a whirlwind of a lifestyle that is chosen for them, such as my family in Iran, and thousands of other like them. However, there are some exceptions, such as those who live in a free country like the USA, and still practice Islam. I actually have more respect for them since they are free from the peer pressure of their closed-society and the influences of their government. But at the same time, thousands have left that faith for Christianity, including Mullahs, Professors, and Imams. I have seen some of their baptismal videos, as well as read their testimonies over the Internet and their published books.

While growing up as a teenager in Iran, I was faced with many teachings and slogans that are humorous in this day and time! We were brain-washed to say the least! We were chanting words and phrases that could only have come from a mad-man or an evil-minded person! One of those slogans was, "Omar-Omaru, sag-pedaru" meaning Omar's dad was a dog. (The word, "dog" represents a dirty and pathetic animal.) Here is the reason for that slogan:

300

"Omar was the second Sunni Caliph following the death of Abu Bakr, and is thus regarded by Sunni Muslims as one of the Rashidun (righteously guided Caliphs) after Mohammad. The Shiites regard Omar as an usurper, or bully, citing his refutation of Ali as Mohammad's heir, his role as a fugitive from the battle of Uhud and Hunayn, and his threat of violence against Ali, to induce him to submit to Abu Bakr. Omar is said to have caused the death of Muhammad's daughter, Fatima Zahra, and her unborn child, Mohsen.." (From Wikipedia encyclopedia)

When I went home to Iran in the spring of 2004, I spoke with a few teenage boys and I asked them what they thought about America. They immediately started chanting the "Death to America!" slogan. I pictured myself as one of them, as we used to shout the same type of slogans many years ago without realizing what we were saying. Where did these teenagers learn these hatred slogans? No one should ever subject these innocent children to such harsh words!

For the last thirty years, the slogans, "Death to America and death to Israel" have been painted on several walls in Tehran, including the walls of the former U.S. Embassy in Tehran. Now, you can imagine who the culprit was behind these hateful slogans in a country which claims Islam as a peaceful religion under the Islamic Republic!

Here is another example: There is a chapter in the Quran called "Sura 112 Lahab", concerning Abu Lahab, uncle of the Prophet Muhammad, who disagreed with Muhammad and his Prophet-hood. Many people, including me, used to recite it in Arabic, not realizing what we were saying since Arabic is not our mother language. It was brought to my attention recently by Ali Sina's website, another Iranian who lives in Canada, that this is a cursing verse. I looked at that particular chapter in the Quran and sure enough, Ali Sina was correct, yet I never thought of it as a curse. It was just another slogan we learned to recite out of our ignorance! This is the translation of that chapter {Lahab, or the Father of Flame} in English:

1. *Perish the hands of the Father of Flame! Perish he!*

2. *No profit to him from all his wealth, and all his gains!*

3. *Burnt soon will he be in a Fire of blazing Flame!*

4. *His wife shall carry the crackling wood as fuel!*

5. *A twisted rope of palm-leaf fiber round her own neck!*

Muslims believe that the Quran verses are the exact words of God! But why would God find it necessary to curse Mohammad's uncle? It sounds as if God is chanting those hateful slogans Himself! This is one of the reasons I believe that the Quran is written by men and not God, though it contains some beautiful passages for mankind as a guide and for encouragement. Furthermore, it does not have the same message as the Bible as many Muslim scholars claim.

As I have listened several times to the recorded audio version of the Quran, I can't help to hear so much damnation and hell fire and fear tactic messages. The chapters jump from one subject to another without a definitive beginning and ending. It's content is full of hatred and mudslinging toward anyone who does not follow Allah and his messenger, Mohammad.

You may ask why I find it necessary to question Allah or his writings since I have been taught not to do so from an early age. My answer is that it is okay to question Allah if you don't understand it. In fact I believe Allah loves it when his people question him. I am not arrogant in my questioning. I just don't understand why there is such a huge difference in the message and in the teachings from the same creator!

Side remark from "Answering-Islam.org"

"That is one of my problems with Muhammad, who according to Islam is the greatest prophet, because his message is the final one, the one for ALL mankind, while the earlier ones were just of 'local' significance. So then, if the Messiah, Jesus, was only of 'local' and 'temporal' significance, how come, that there are over 300 fulfilled prophesies about the Messiah in the Old Testament PLUS several hundred more prophesies about his second coming, but nothing clear at all about Muhammad?

Did God get his plan for the correct religion so woefully wrong and out of balance? Or did He change his plan after the Bible was already written? Seems to be unlikely to me, and it is one more indication for *me* that maybe Muhammad was not being sent by the God of the Bible. And how come that all over the Bible, representing a 1500 year period of God talking through prophets, we have many thousands of prophecies on historical events, many already happened and verified, and many more to come, but somehow God suddenly chooses to speak a 'different language' and there is basically *nothing to be found in that respect in the Qur'an? Unlikely again, to my taste."*

In many Muslim countries, such as Sudan, Christians are being killed daily simply for believing in Jesus Christ, not to mention those who left Islam for Christianity.

You can easily find many sources of persecution over the Internet that exposes these disgusted countries and individuals. The "Voice of the Martyrs" magazine is one of those sources which expose and describe the persecuted church since 1967.

Incidentally, Jesus' name is held in "great honor" in the Quran. The One who did nothing wrong but showed mercy and love to mankind, forgave the sinners, even those who persecuted Him, and taught others to do the same.

Why would anyone want to kill the followers of the Prince of Peace?

Unfortunately, to the Muslims, Jesus is only a great Prophet and nothing more.

I asked one of my sisters what she thought the difference was between the Sunni and Shiite, in reference to the rulers of Islam after the death of Muhammad. She told me that according to historical events, there were four, so-called guided rulers; Abu-Bakr, Omar, Ali, and Othman. However, Shiites do not accept, nor recognize them all, only Ali, as their legitimate ruler.

The reason for my questioning her was this. There are some historical facts that are not being recognized by some.

The Crucifixion of Jesus Christ is another example. The crucifixion of Jesus Christ is a historical fact, and billions of Christians have put their trust in that fact. It does not matter whether Muslims, or any other religion 'leaders', want to accept it or not. Christians believe that "God the Father" has accomplished everything He has willed through the person of Jesus Christ. Salvation was sealed and achieved on the Roman Cross.

Don't make any mistake about it, that which was meant to disgrace and humiliate Jesus by going on the Roman cross, was changed to honor and glory by the power of His resurrection, and Jesus Christ rose bodily and is alive forever more! And one day He will return.

"For the message of the cross is foolishness to those who are perishing, but to us who are being saved it is the power of God. For it is written: "I will destroy the wisdom of the wise, And bring to nothing the understanding of the prudent." *(1 Cor. 1:18-19)*

There is nothing more that needs to be added to what Jesus Christ has already said to mankind.

Jesus said in Matthew 5:17 "Do not think that I came to destroy the Law or the Prophets. I did not come to destroy but to fulfill".

Also, it is recorded in John 19:28-30; "After this, Jesus, knowing that all things were now accomplished, that the Scripture might be fulfilled, ... He said, " It is finished!" and bowing His head, he gave up His spirit. There is no need for any other Prophets, books or mediators between man and God.

Jesus warned us about the false Prophets; that some might come claiming that they are exalting Jesus as 'the messiah' or the most honored Prophet, yet they reject Him as Son of the Most High. Jesus Christ is the One who will judge the world (John 5:22-23), and is coming back again. He is the 'Lamb' who is worthy to open the scroll (Rev. 5), and reveal the end time, for He is the "Alpha and the Omega".

One more thing before I move on. We all are the children of God by the means of creation (Luke 3:38). In addition, Christians are the children of God by adoption (John 1:12). This group is exclusive to those who believe and trust in Jesus Christ as their savior.

Jewish people were the chosen ones, but due to their disobedience, they have been temporarily pushed aside until the Davidic covenants take place. Christians have replaced them as the chosen ones. This new chosen generation, royal priesthood, includes many from all walks of life, such as Jews or Gentiles, free or slave and from any color, or ethnic background.

"For God so loved the world that He gave his only begotten Son, that who so ever believeth in Him should not perish but have everlasting life." (John 3:16)

Lastly, Jesus is the only begotten Son of God. This **does not** mean that God the Father had an intimate relationship with Mary as some Muslims believe. God forbid!

He is much more supreme than that. In Muslim theology, the authority and the written word of Allah is expressed in the whole Quran. In Jewish tradition, the Law was given to Moses. But in Christianity, the authority of the Word of God is expressed and manifested in the person of Jesus Christ.   **In other words, the Quran is the written word of Allah for the Muslims, while Jesus Christ is the living <u>Word of God</u>.** (John 1:14)

GOD'S SUPREME REVELATION:

"God, who at various times and in various ways spoke in time past to the fathers by the Prophets, has in these last days spoken to us by His Son, whom He appointed heir of all things, through whom also He made the worlds; who being the brightness of His glory and the express image of His person, and upholding all things by the word of His power, when He had by Himself purged our sins, sat down at the right hand of the Majesty on high, having become so much better than the angels, as he has by inheritance obtained a more excellent name than they." (Hebrews 1:1-4)

Now, since the Quran is the written word of Allah for the Muslims, then the next series of questions are:

Are Allah and God the same?

Who is Muhammad? Is he one of those false Prophets Jesus was talking about?

What are the writings within the pages of the Quran?

How can Muslim scholars prove that the Quran contains the exact words of Allah?

These are some of the questions people are eager to know since Islam is known as the second largest religion in our world today.

No one can deny history when it tells us that Islam surfaced by the person of Muhammad in about 610 AD. His revealed book is the "Quran", while "Hadith and Sunnah" are considered the words and deeds of Muhammad and are used daily in almost all Islamic countries as their example and role model, even their laws.

We also cannot deny that more than a billion people put their trust in that religion. The only puzzling part of the issue is how their revelation, as it is written in their holy Quran and hadith, collaborates with the nature and character of Jehovah God, as it has been revealed to us and to past generations, thus recorded in the Bible.

If we reject the truth of the past as false, corrupt and unacceptable, then the future events will also become unacceptable since ultimately God is the author of the scripture. With that in mind, let us examine the source of Islamic revelation, Allah, and what the community says about him:

"Allah (Arabic: الله, *Allāh,* is the standard Arabic word for "God". While the term is best known in the West for its use by Muslims as a reference to God, it is used by Arabic-speakers of all Abrahamic faiths, including Christians and Jews, in reference to "God". The term was also used by pagan Meccans as a reference to the creator-god, possibly the supreme deity in pre-Islamic Arabia.

The concepts associated with the term *Allah* (as a deity) differ among the traditions. In pre-Islamic Arabia, Allah was not the sole divinity, having associates and companions, sons and daughters.

In <u>Islam</u>, Allah is the supreme and all-comprehensive divine name. All other divine names are believed to refer back to Allah. Allah is unique, the <u>only God</u>, transcendent <u>creator of the universe</u> and omnipotent. Arab Christians today, having no other word for 'God' than 'Allah', use terms such as <u>Allāh al-ab</u> (الآب الله) to mean <u>God the father</u>. There are both similarities and differences between the concept of God as portrayed in the Qur'an and the Hebrew Bible." (From Wikipedia, the free encyclopedia)

By the way, in the above statement, "In <u>pre-Islamic</u> Arabia, Allah was not the sole divinity, having associates and companions, sons and daughters." it is where one of the sources of the <u>false trinity</u> came from; the second source of false trinity came from another group. In the 5th century, the same heresy surfaced among a sect of Christians called the "Maria-mite sect.", where the talk of an intimate relationship between Mary and god and having Jesus as their son was floating around. These talks concerning God and Jesus were pure heresy and false, and were strongly rejected by the orthodox Christians altogether. The Quran interestingly includes both "The pre-Islamic false association and companions and the Maria-mite sect" within its pages when it says, "Do not say trinity!" This trinity is different from what the Bible teaches, "Father, Son and the Holy Spirit."

Unfortunately, there are many other verses in the Quran where it talks about Christ not being divine, or it is a monstrous idea for God to have a son! And so on...

We know from history that the name of Muhammad's father is Abdol-allah, meaning, "servant of Allah". Abdol-allah died before Muhammad was born. Therefore, Allah pre-existed before Islam came to existence, which could lead us to the pre-Islamic Arabia or pagan Meccans ,as mentioned earlier. The reason I bring that up is this. Most people, especially the ones in the west, thought that Allah surfaced with the beginning and introduction of Islam through the Prophet Muhammad. But the name Allah was known to the Pagan Arabs way before Islam. We know from history that Pagan Arabs worshipped 360 deities, including the "moon god" as their deity before Islam. This is the reason why Muhammad, when he came to power, went to Mecca to destroy all those false deities. He never went to a Christian Church, claiming that their God or Scriptures were false. In fact, it was the opposite. He was told that if he had any doubts or questions, he should go to the People of the Book, meaning Jews and Christians, for answers. Did he? Yes he did, but with his sword unfortunately! Several Jewish tribes were slaughtered; wives and children taken as slaves, and all their belongings taken as booty! Why did he attack them? This is how Ayatollah Montazeri answered:

Ayatollah Montazeri

"As for the raids at the merchant caravans of the Quraish, this caravan comprehended several wealthy Meccan enemies of Islam, and was accompanied by Abu Sofyan, the renowned arch enemy of Islam and the Muslims. In that year, the hostilities of the Quraish and their instigations against Islam and the Muslims had intensified. Medina had just become the political and governmental center for the Muslims and was under attack of its Quraish enemies from every direction.

Many Muslims were forced to abandon their homes due to the Quraish persecution and immigrated to Medina. These people wanted to retaliate and reclaim their properties from the Quraish. They had been informed that this caravan carried a lot of wealth. The leadership of the Muslims was also planning to render the highways that were providing economically and militarily the enemy, unsafe. The main objective of this sudden attack was to render insecure the arteries so that the enemy would be weakened in their war against the Muslims. These wars continued until Mecca was conquered.

Obviously, when two countries or two forces are in war, and while there are no peace treaties between them, each side is justified to harm the economical and the military strength of the opposing party and to threaten their security.

This was, and still is, an accepted practice in the world. Highway robbery, however, is something completely different. A highway robber is a thug and a hoodlum that endangers the lives and the safety of the people that live peacefully in their own city or country, without showing enmity to others or stealing their property."

Now this was the climate of that time as clashes between the Muslims of Medina and the Quraish of Meccan took place. The reason the Jewish tribes were attacked by the Muslims as it is alleged, was because they sided with the Quraish by passing the information to them about Muhammad and the Muslims. Here is a response by another Iranian "Ali Sina" (not his real name) in a debate.

Responded By Ali Sina in his debate:

"The truth is, despite the fact that Muhammad constantly insulted the religion of the Quraish and infuriated them with his abrasive behavior, there is not a single incidence of physical violence or persecution against him or his followers recorded in Islamic annals.

Muslims today would not tolerate any criticism against their religion. They would kill at once any person who dares to question their belief. This is what the Prophet taught them to do. But Arabs, prior to Muhammad, were more tolerant. They used to live with the Jews and Christians in harmony without any sign of religious animosity between them. Yet the ultimate test of tolerance came when Muhammad started to taunt their gods. Despite that kind of libeling, the Quraish demonstrated an incredible degree of tolerance and although being offended, never harmed Muhammad or any of his cohorts.

Compare this to the treatment of the Baha'is in Iran. Baha'is do not insult Muhammad or his Allah, nor do they reject the Imams or disagree with any part of the Quran. All they say is that their messenger is the Promised One of the Muslims. This is nothing compared to Muhammad's insults of the beliefs of the people of Quraish. Nevertheless, Muslims have not spared any act of atrocity against the Baha'is. They killed many of them, jailed them, tortured them, beat them, denied them of their human rights and treated them with utter inhumanity. None of that was done against Muhammad and his followers in Mecca even though he constantly confronted their gods with showers of taunts and would curse their sacred beliefs as if daring them to persecute."

In short, when Muhammad came to power in Medina, a city north of Mecca, he offered Islam and his hand of friendship to the Jews and expected their support in exchange. But later, when the war between the Muslims and the Quraish tribe in Mecca took place, Jews were not interested in going to war or to support

Muhammad in the way he was expecting. Therefore, they faced a harsh retaliation against their whole tribe.

By the way, it is recorded in the Quran that it was okay for Mohammad to attack the caravans and to take the booty to feed his people. It even says that 1/5 of the booty belonged to Allah's Prophet and his family. This action by Muhammad and his people is so ironic because we see that the God of the Bible fed the children of Israel for forty years while they were in the wilderness, and He never told them to attack anyone!

That is why to this day if you live in their territories, you either obey or you pay! This is not "free will" as God ordained. Even Jesus never forced anyone to follow Him. "But as many as received Him, to them He gave the right to become children of God, to those who believe in His name: who were born, not of blood, nor of the will of the flesh, nor of the will of man, but of God." (John 1:12-13)

False gods and false Prophets:

There have been many false gods and Prophets from the early times. We see them not only among the pagan Arabs, but as I previously cited, in the Holy Bible as well. Here is an example of one recorded in the Bible:

1st Samuel Chapter 5:1-8

1 *Then the Philistines took the ark of Yahweh and brought it from Ebenezer to Ashdod.*

2 *When the Philistines took the ark of Yahweh, they brought it into the **house of Dagon** and set it by **Dagon**.*

3 *And when the people of Ashdod arose early in the morning, there was **Dagon**, fallen on its face to the earth before the ark of the LORD. So they took **Dagon** and set it in its place again.*

313

4   *And when they arose early the next morning, there was* **Dagon***, fallen on its face to the ground before the ark of the LORD. The head of Dagon and both the palms of its hands were broken off on the threshold; only Dagon's torso was left of it.*

5   *Therefore neither the* **priests of Dagon** *nor any who come into* **Dagon's house** *tread on the threshold of Dagon in Ashdod to this day.*

6   *But the hand of the LORD was heavy on the people of Ashdod, and He ravaged them and struck them with* **tumors, both Ashdod and its territory.**

7   *And when the men of Ashdod saw how it was, they said, "***The ark of the God of Israel must not remain with us, for His hand is harsh toward us and Dagon our god.***"*

8   *Therefore they sent and gathered to themselves all the lords of the Philistines, and said, "What shall we do with the ark of the God of Israel?"*

There is another example in Exodus 4:2-3 and 7:8-12, for those who wish to read more about false Prophets.

We can see clearly from these short stories that false Prophets did exist long ago, imitating Jehovah God and misguided many. I am not saying that 'Allah' is a false God, since Arab Christians use that name as Jehovah God, but we need to examine if the writings, which appear in the Quran, are really from Jehovah God or someone else.

Listening to the Quran, Allah often assures Mohammad and his people that they will be victorious in their fights against the infidels, while I read in the Bible that God will deliver the enemies into the hands of Israel. Look at the war of 1948, one nation against many. Israel is surrounded by many nations who want to wipe them out of the map, but they are not able to do so since they are going against God's promises.

I have recorded a more meaningful comparison between Islam and Christianity in appendix 1, which is at the end of this book.

Now, Othman the forth Caliph, one of the righteously guided rulers, either himself or under his leadership, ordered to burn all false (not acceptable) Islamic scriptures. He compiled (the good ones) what he presumably used to make the Quran as it is today, which by the way, are not even in the chronological order of the alleged revelations to Muhammad. (Chapter 96 in the Quran is the first revelation). *See reference notes 1,2,3 at the end of this chapter.

Now, a few very serious questions arise here:

1. Why did Othman order the destruction of those so-called 'false' (not acceptable) scriptures, since according to hadith, they were accepted by Muhammad [3] and what was Othman's motive?
2. Why did they even have 'false' scriptures floating around since Allah was the protector of them, according to the Quran?
3. Was there anything changed or abrogated to benefit their way of governing people and other faiths?

After Mohammad died, the decision making fell in the hands of his companions. Many civil wars took place, not to mention their discord with Jewish tribes. Othman was encouraged to put the Quran together in written form before they lost the men who kept the scripture in memory, and so they could combine it with what was already written down[1,2].

Now, Muslim scholars claim that what was burned was nothing more than different Arabic dialects. I can not accept this for this reason: You may speak a different dialect even using the same exact words, and that is why, according to the Hadith, Muhammad himself accepted those so called dialects.[3]

Perhaps the Quran was intended only for the people of Arabia of the 6th century A.D. since there were so many untamed and violent people who lived among them. There was so much violence that they killed their own daughters after birth, just because the baby was not a boy!

Maybe they needed to be under the law first to appreciate grace! I really don't know why this religion surfaced. It certainly is not for the whole world.

I know that the Quran has some great verses within its pages that correspond with the Bible, as I have already described some of them in my previous chapters. Yet, at the same time, it contains many verses with different meanings from what the Bible teaches. Here are a couple of examples:

(Bible) Genesis 1:26-27 "Then God said: Let us make man in our image, to be like ourselves." Therefore, <u>God created man in His own image</u>; God patterned them after Himself; male and female He created them."

(Quran) Sura 2:30 "Behold, thy Lord said to the angels: I will create a <u>vicegerent</u> on earth. They (angels) said: Wilt thou place therein one who will make mischief and shed blood? while

we do celebrate thy praises and glorify thy holy name?   He (Allah)
said: Surely, I know that which ye know not."

(Bible) Gen 2:15-17 "The Lord God placed the man in the
Garden of Eden to tend and care for it. But the Lord God gave him
this warning: You may freely eat any fruit in the garden except
fruit from the tree of the knowledge of good and evil. If you eat of
its fruit, you will <u>surely die</u>."

(Quran) Sura 2:35 "We (Allah) said: O Adam! Dwell thou
and thy wife in the Garden, and eat ye freely (of the fruits) thereof
where ye will; but come not nigh this tree lest ye become
<u>wrongdoers</u>."

Notice in both instances what God is speaking is spiritual,
while what Allah is speaking is carnal!

That is why salvation in the Bible is a spiritual
transformation, while in Islam salvation is by works.

Here is a better clarification: Jesus is speaking, "It is the Spirit
who gives life; the flesh profits nothing. The words that I speak to
you are spirit, and they are life." (John 6:63)

"God is Spirit, and those who worship Him must worship in
spirit and truth." (John 4:24)

Pilate therefore said to Him, "Are You a king then?"
Jesus answered, "You say *rightly* that I am a king. For this cause I
was born, and for this cause I have come into the world, that I
should <u>bear witness to the truth</u>. Everyone who is of the truth hears
My voice." (John 18:37)

What is the Truth?

Jesus said: I am the way, <u>the truth</u>, and the life. (John 14:6)

In other words, when God said He patterned mankind after Himself, it is spiritual. And when he said to man, "you shall surely die", it is also means spiritual death or spiritual separation from God the Father. But, when Allah referred to man as vicegerent and wrongdoers, he was pointing to a physical person and carnal action. This is very important to understand since all of God's laws and commandments are spiritual. Our body will die and return to dust but our spirit will live eternally- either in heaven (if saved) or in hell (if Jesus is rejected).

When I spoke to one of my nephews who is studying Islamic Theology, he pointed out the scripture in Genesis when God created Adam and Eve, walking and talking with them. He said it did not make any sense to him about how God could walk and talk. He was right to say that it does not make sense. 1 <u>Corinthians 2:14</u> "But the natural man does not receive the things of the Spirit of God, for they are foolishness to him; nor can he know them, because they are spiritually discerned."

Now, to better understand the condition of Adam and Eve before their fall, and what the scripture meant by walking and talking with God, we can turn to the second Adam, (Jesus Christ). Jesus spent a great amount of time talking with the Father. He was so in tune with the Father that He knew His will without any hesitation. That is why He spoke with much authority and often said, "I and the Father are One!"

"The difference between believers who rested in Christ only, and those who trusted in the law, is explained by the history of Isaac and Ishmael. These things are an allegory, wherein, besides the literal and historical sense of the words, the Spirit of God points out something further. Hagar and Sarah were appropriate

318

symbols of the two different dispensations of the covenant. The true church from above, represented by Sarah, is in a state of freedom, and is the mother of all believers who are born of the Holy Spirit. They were by regeneration and true faith, made a part of the true seed of Abraham, according to the promise made to him.

The two covenants of works and grace are also called legal and evangelical figuratively. Works and fruits brought forth in a man's own strength are legal, but if arising from faith in Christ, they are evangelical. The first covenant spirit is of bondage unto sin and death. The second covenant spirit is of liberty and freedom; not liberty to sin, but in and unto duty. The first is a spirit of persecution; the second is a spirit of love." (Matthew Henry commentary)

Again, I have been taught from an early age that you do not question or argue with the Quran since it is the word of Allah. It has been claimed that the Quran is the greatest miracle of God, given to Mohammad, his last messenger. This seems to create a problem, to say that the Quran is a miracle from God, while other scriptures are not! It just does not make any sense at all since God the Father has always talked to mankind through his chosen messengers, and these last days through His Son. Besides, what could be greater than the "salvation of mankind" through Jesus Christ? Not to mention all the miracles that was done through Him. Miracles like healing the sick, feeding a multitude of over five thousand with a small boy's lunch, giving sight to the blind, raising the dead by His command. The storms obeyed Him, demons recognized the Son of God and were afraid of Him, death could not hold Him, the Tomb could not keep Him, and the list goes on… for He is alive forevermore!

Now, just to be fair, I would like to point out one very important thing in favor of my Muslim brothers and sisters. For that I would like to take you to the Book of Acts in our Christian Bible:

"The Apostle Paul was compelled by the Spirit and testified to the Jews that Jesus is the Christ, but when they opposed him and blasphemed, he shook his garments and said to them, "Your blood be upon your heads; I am clean! From now on I will go to the gentiles. And he departed from there and entered the house of a certain man named Justus, one who worshiped God" (Acts 18:6-7)

Again another passage: "…Men of Athens, I perceive that in all things you are very religious; … I even found an altar with this inscription: 'TO THE UNKNOWN GOD'… as some of your own poets have said, 'For we are also His (God's) offspring.' (Acts 17:22-23, 28)

And again, "There was a certain man called Cornelius, a devout man and one who feared God, with all his household, who gave alms generously to the people, and prayed to God always. About the ninth hour of the day he saw clearly in a vision an angel of God…" (Acts 10:1-3)

Here is the point. God-fearing Muslim brothers and sisters are worshippers of the same God as we are, however they are misguided about the scripture and the real reason why Christ came. A true Muslim will turn to Christ, just like Cornelius and other Gentiles mentioned in the preceding scripture from the Bible.

320

Those who reject Christ as Lord and Savior will have to stand judgment before the very person of Christ whom they reject!

Now, here is where the rubber meets the road!

The reason I changed my faith from Islam to Christianity is this: Aside from the uniqueness of Christ, Christianity and the Gospel teaches about peace, brotherhood and love. Jesus Christ himself always spoke about loving and praying for one another, even your enemies. Unfortunately, Islam and the Quran always talk about wars and killing others, especially non-believers, and that has been the way since Mohammad came to power in Medina. Those beliefs and teachings were passed on to me from an early age. I would like to invite you to visit the site below to see for yourself how an Imam, or the leader of a mosque, teaches his congregation how to hate Jews and Christians!

http://www.tangle.com/view_video.php?viewkey=d7d9bf74191e0 06d8e24&sp=1   *(Last time the URL was viewed and valid 6/11/09)*

Chapter or Sura 2:216 says: "Fighting is prescribed for you (like a doctor telling his patient!), and you dislike it. But it is possible that you dislike a thing which is good for you, and that you love a thing which is bad for you. But Allah knows and you know not."

(Sura 2:256) says, "There is no compulsion in Islam" and all Muslim scholars know about this verse. But, if you ask any of them, "Are Muslims **free** to change their faith to any other religion if they choose to do so?" the answer is absolutely not! If they find out about it, you must face an Islamic court for possible punishment. But that is not the case if someone from another religion wants to become a Muslim. So, shall we say that Islam is the fastest growing <u>forced</u> religion in the world today?

Since we are talking about Islam as a forced religion, I can not help but to briefly talk about the recent events in Iran regarding the presidential election of June 2009. What started as a simple people's right to vote, turned to conflict and uprising as their freedom, once again, was crushed and stolen by the supporters of Ahmadinejad, the current president of Iran.

I watched many news clips and pictures coming out of Iran via Television and internet. All were pointed to how the election was stolen and vote tampering took place by the people who supported the incumbent president Ahmadinejad. I saw thousands of people, young and old, men, women and students, demanding freedom from the <u>dictatorship of the Islamic Republic</u>. The leader of the country, instead of recognizing the will of the people by looking into the allegation of vote tampering, chose to do what they do best; to silence and punish those who were pro-reform with live bullets and police brutality.

The Islamic government stopped every source of communication between the demonstrators, put the opposition leadership on house arrest, forced all foreign media to stop broadcasting, or made them leave the country. And finally, the final word came down from Supreme leader Ayatollah khamenei that his support went to his puppet, Mr. Ahmadinejad. This was another slap to the face of Islam by the examples of this Islamic Republic!

This was the second wave of killing and severe punishment; the first being the revolution of 1979 by the same Islamic Republic with the followers of the Prophet Mohammad and the Quran as their guide!

Under Sharia law, (Islamic law) or this forced religion, leaving Islam for another religion is punishable by death. Polygamy is allowed for men. Marriage is nothing but a contract between a man and his women, which can be broken easily by men, but not by women. Divorce is allowed for men by a simple phrase, "I divorce you" three times, but not for women. Children traditionally belong to the father in a divorce. Male survivors inherit twice the inheritance since they are responsible for women.

I am reminded of a single woman in Syria who had a relationship with a man. Because she was a disgrace to the family, her own brother stabbed and killed her. Authorities knew about him killing her, yet they never arrested him because they agreed with what he had done, and that she received what she deserved!

Well, this is not for me, especially when I read a similar story in the Bible where Jesus responded in love and compassion, forgiving her sin:

"The scribes and Pharisees brought to Jesus a woman allegedly caught in an act of adultery. And they said to Him, "Teacher, this woman was caught in adultery, in the very act. Now Moses, in the law, commanded us that such should be stoned. But what do You say?"

He said to them, "He who is without sin among you, let him throw a stone at her first." Then those who heard it, being convicted by their conscience, went out one by one, beginning with the oldest even to the last. And Jesus was left alone, and the woman standing in the midst. When Jesus saw no one but the

323

woman, He said to her, "Woman, where are those accusers of yours?

Has no one condemned you?"
She said, "No one, Lord."

And Jesus said to her, "Neither do I condemn you; go and sin no more."
Then Jesus spoke to them again, saying, "I am the light of the world. He who follows Me shall not walk in darkness, but have the light of life." (John 8:2-12)

This is true religion where you find a safe haven, a place of rest, a place where there is **no fear**, where He is your hiding place, and not being condemned. Don't you just love Him!

Jesus is the only One who came to purge the sin of the world, presenting us righteous before the Holy Father. No other Prophet claimed or was able to bring mankind to the same righteous status before a Holy God. (Hebrews 1:3)

Often, Muslim scholars focus their attack on the free nations in the west, labeling them corrupt and full of filth, while boasting about their own country, 'with no filth' since it is an Islamic State. Listening to the Late Sheikh Ahmad Deedad in one of his speeches over the internet, I heard him claim that the majority of Christians in the west were alcoholics. He attributed this to when Jesus turned the water into wine!

I have personally witnessed the same filth in Iran under the Shah and the new Islamic Republic. Sin is not a matter of religion.

Sin is part of every human flesh. I would be lying if I were to say that I don't have any problems with it at all, and if you are honest with yourself, you would say the same. Jesus said in Matthew 5:28 "But I tell you that anyone who looks at a woman lustfully has already committed adultery with her in his heart." We may bring it under control but it is still part of us all.

Jesus Christ is the only Son of man who lived perfectly and without sin. Therefore:

1) *God is Holy and man is not. In order for a Holy God to have a relationship with sinful man, a mediator must be found. That mediator is no one except Christ Jesus.*

2) *Christianity is impossible in the power of the flesh, for it takes the Spirit of God to work in the Child of God, to do the will of God.*

In other words, we cannot do it with the power of our flesh. That is why I cannot be righteous on my own, unless I am deceiving myself; pretending by giving extra alms to the mosque, or to the poor, and thinking that I am 'buying my own salvation'. Salvation is not that cheap! You can not enter paradise on your own merits. Jesus is the answer, hope, and assurance. The invitation is given by Him, **{behold, I stand at the door and knock...Rev.3:20};** the action is ours to take. All we have to do is open the door.

In His Majestic name

Saiid Raiipour

SaiidR@Bellsouth.net

Notes:

1) The initial revelations were written on different sort of parchments, tablets of stone, branches of date trees, other wood, leaves, leather and even bones.

2) I asked Anas bin mali: "Who collected the Quran at the time of the Prophet?" He replied, "Four, all of whom were from the Ansa: Ubai bin Ka'b, Mu'adh bin Jabal, Zaid bin Thabit and Abu Zaid." Bukhari 6:61:525

Othman 644-656

Main article: Origin and development of the Quran

During the time of Othman, by which time Islam had spread far and wide, differences in reading the Quran in different dialects of Arabic language became obvious. A group of companions, headed by Hudhayfah ibn al-Yaman, who was then stationed in Iraq, came to Othman and urged him to *"save the Muslim ummah before they differ about the Quran"*. Othman obtained the manuscript of the Quran from Hafsah and again summoned the leading authority, **Zayd ibn Thabit**, and some other companions to make copies of it. Zayd was put in charge of the task. The style of Arabic dialect used was that of the Quraish tribe. Hence this style was emphasized over all others.

Zayd and other Companions copied many copies. One of these was sent to every Muslim province with the order that all other Quranic materials, whether fragmentary or complete copies, be burnt. When standard copies were made and were widely available to the Muslim community everywhere, then all other material was burnt voluntarily by Muslim community themselves. This was important in order to eliminate variations or differences in the dialect from the standard text of the Quran. The <u>Caliph</u> Othman kept a copy for himself and returned the original manuscript to <u>Hafsah</u>.

3) Therefore I suggest, you (Abu Bakr) order that the Qur'an be collected." I said to 'Umar, "How can you do something which Allah's Apostle did not do?" 'Umar said, "By Allah, that is a good project. "Umar kept on urging me to accept his proposal till Allah opened my chest for it and I began to realize the good in the idea which 'Umar had realized." Then Abu Bakr said (to me). 'You are a wise young man and we do not have any suspicion about you, and you used to write the Divine Inspiration for Allah's Apostle. So you should search for (the fragmentary scripts of) the Qur'an and collect it in one book." Hadith

Appendix I

Comparison of
Islam and Christianity

In order to help my dear readers even further, I have included an excerpt from another source that might help you to better understand the comparison of our Christian Bible and Islamic Quran. The source and credit goes to "The Way of Righteousness". They also have one hundred lessons online concerning the Bible, for those who wish to learn more about God and His "TRUTH".

THE WAY OF RIGHTEOUSNESS PRESENTS:

Muslims are My Friends

With so much media attention given to radical, violent Muslim groups, we need to remind ourselves that most Muslims are friendly, hospitable, peace-loving people. They are our neighbors and our friends. In general, I feel more comfortable speaking with Muslims than I do with secularized Americans. Unlike so many in the West, most Muslims fear God, sense His impending judgment, and are willing to talk about God and the Prophets. For those unfamiliar with a Muslim's basic beliefs and practices, the following observations may be helpful.

Islam, Muslims and Allah

Islam is the religion of Muslims. The Arabic word Islam means submission (to Allah). Muslim (or Moslem) means one who submits. Allah is the Arabic word for God. Islam's fundamental concept of God is that God is one. God is great, indescribable, almighty, and compassionate – especially to Muslims. Everything that happens in the world has been predetermined by God. Muslims believe that God has revealed His will, but not Himself, to humankind. Muslims view their relationship to God as a master-slave relationship, with no possibility of a more intimate father-son relationship.

Five Pillars

The roughly one billion Muslims around the world find themselves in widely differing socio-economic-cultural circumstances – ranging from the wealthy oil sheiks of the Persian Gulf to the rural farmers of West Africa. While local culture and perspectives affect Muslim beliefs considerably, all Muslims assent to Islam's "Five Pillars." Most Muslims believe that they must fulfill these five duties to atone for their sins and merit a place in paradise.

The Five Pillars of Islam are:

The Witness (Shahada): La illaha illa Allah, wa Mohammed Rasul Allah. "There is no god but God, and Muhammad is the Prophet of God."

Ritual Prayers (Salat): Five times daily at hours specified, in the Arabic language, facing toward Mecca, preceded by a ceremonial washing of face, hands and feet.

Alms (Zakat): Sharing 2.5% of one's wealth with those in need.

Annual Fast (Saum): An obligatory, dawn-to-dusk, month-long fast which takes place during Ramadan, the ninth month on the Islamic lunar calendar.

Pilgrimage to Mecca (Hajj): Required of all able-bodied Muslims who can afford it, at least once in a lifetime.

The Prophets and the Qur'an

Most Muslims profess belief in the Prophets of the Bible. The Qur'an names more than twenty Bible Prophets, including Abraham (Ibrahim), Moses (Musa), David (Dawud), John the Baptist (Yahya) and Jesus the Messiah (Isa al Masih). Muslims consider Muhammad (born in Mecca, Saudi Arabia, in 570 A.D. and buried in Medina in 632 A.D.) to be the last and greatest Prophet.

Muslims maintain that God revealed His will through four holy books: the Torah ("Taurat") of Moses, the Psalms ("Zabur") of David, the Gospel ("Injil") of Jesus, and the Qur'an (also spelled Koran) of Muhammad. Many Muslims assert that the Qur'anic revelation annuls the earlier revelations, but this assertion has no clear support from the Qur'an. They believe that Muhammad (who never learned to read or write) received the Qur'anic verses over many years from the angel Gabriel in a desert cave near Mecca. Muhammad recited the verses to his followers who wrote them down. Years after Muhammad's death, these verses were collected into a single book known as the Qur'an – which means "recitation."

The Qur'an has 114 chapters (suras) and is about two-thirds the length of the New Testament. Muslims venerate the Qur'an and are profoundly affected by its Arabic language and poetic style. Though most Muslims have never read the entire Qur'an, it is their point of reference for every area of life: religion, family, health, ethics, economics and politics. Like the Bible, the Qur'an affirms the reality of God and Satan, angels and evil spirits, a coming day of resurrection and judgment, a hell to shun and a paradise to gain. But the similarity ends there. The Qur'an's descriptions and definitions of these realities differ greatly from those recorded by the Prophets of the Bible.

God

The Qur'an presents God as a single entity. "Say not, 'Three.' Forbear, it will be better for you. God is only one God! Far be it from His glory that He should have a son!" (4:172) {Note: "4:172" means chapter 4 and verse 172 of the Qur'an. However, the verse may be as many as five verses away in different versions of the Qur'an.} This and other Quranic verses (5:116), combined with the Roman Catholic Church's unscriptural practice of praying to Mary, have caused many Muslims to think that Christians believe in three gods–God, Mary and Jesus. This is a tragic misunderstanding of what a true Christian believes. The Bible says: "There is one God and one Mediator between God and men, the Man Christ Jesus." (1 Timothy 2:5)

The Bible clearly condemns polytheism and idolatry, and consistently confirms the oneness of God, declaring: "You shall worship the LORD your God, and Him only you shall serve!... The LORD our God, the LORD is one!" (Matthew 4:10; Deuteronomy 6:4,13; Mark 12:29) Oneness, however, does not preclude depth and dimension. The Qur'an reveals God as unknowable and one-dimensional. The Bible reveals God as self-revealing and tri-dimensional – Eternal Father, Eternal Son and Eternal Holy Spirit.

Satan, Sin and Man

The Qur'an teaches that Satan became the Devil (Iblis) when he stubbornly refused to bow down to Adam at God's command. (7:11-18) Adam is said to have been in a heavenly Paradise before he ate the forbidden fruit. After Adam transgressed, God sent him down to earth. The Qur'an views Adam's disobedience as a minor slip rather than a major fall. According to many Quranic scholars, all Adam had to do to get back into God's favor was to learn and recite certain prayers. (7:18-30; 2:30-40)

While the Bible portrays God as absolutely holy and man as totally depraved, the Qur'an portrays man as weak and misguided. In the Muslim view, man does not need redemption; he only needs some guidance so that he might develop the inherently pure nature with which the Creator has endowed him. If he will be faithful in his prayers, almsgiving and fasting, God is likely to overlook his sins and usher him into Paradise, a garden of sensual delights.

Jesus

Every Muslim professes to believe in Isa (the Quranic name for Jesus). By this they mean that they believe that Jesus is one of 124,000 Prophets that he was sent uniquely to the Jews, that he denied the "Trinity", that he predicted the coming of Muhammad, that he was not the Son of God and that he was not crucified! The Bible calls such a Jesus "another Jesus." (2 Corinthians 11:4)

The Quranic profile of Jesus presents Muslims with a difficult paradox. While certain verses declare that Jesus was "no more than a Prophet" (4:171-173; 5:75; 2:136), others ascribe to him characteristics and titles attributed to God, but never attributed to any other Prophet. For example, the Qur'an affirms that Jesus was born of a virgin, that he was righteous and holy, and that he possessed the power to create life, open the eyes of the blind, cleanse the lepers and raise the dead. (3:45-51; 5:110-112; 19:19) Furthermore, the Qur'an calls him the Messiah (Al Masih), the Word of God (Kalimat Allah) and the Spirit [Soul] of God (Ruh Allah), (4:171,172). These supernatural descriptions and titles have caused many Muslims to seek the truth about who Jesus really is.

One day, a devout Muslim man said to me, "The Qur'an calls Jesus Ruh Allah. If Jesus is the Soul of God, then He must be

God!" This Muslim was beginning to grasp one of the most basic truths of Holy Scripture – not that a man became a god – but that God became a Man in order to reveal Himself to the children of Adam and save them from their sins. Sometime later, at the cost of being cast out by his family, this same Muslim boldly acknowledged Jesus as his Savior and Lord.

The Son of God

The ultimate sin in Islam is "shirk" (Arabic for association). Shirk is the sin of regarding anything or anyone as equal to God. The Qur'an rejects Jesus' title as the Son of God. "They say: 'Allah has begotten a son. God forbid!" (2:110) "Say: 'If the Lord of Mercy had a son, I would be the first to worship him.'" (43:81; 4:172; 5:72.73) Unfortunately, many Muslims interpret "Son of God" in a carnal sense. They understand the term to mean that God took a wife and had a son by her! In several Way of Righteousness lessons, we explain from the Bible why the Prophets, the angels, and God Himself call Jesus the Son of God. These simple explanations have helped many Muslims so that they no longer say, "Astaghferullah!" ("God forgive you for this blasphemy!") when they hear Jesus being called by His rightful title as 'The Son of God'.

The Bible gives three main reasons why Jesus is called the Son of God. Interestingly, the Qur'an contains verses that appear to affirm all three of these reasons.

1. The Bible calls Jesus the Son of God because He came from God. (Isaiah 7:14; Luke 1:34,35) Similarly, the Qur'an teaches that Jesus came directly from God that He was born of a virgin, that He had no earthly father. (3:47; 19:20) Also, the Qur'an sets Jesus apart from all other Prophets by calling Him the Messiah (the Anointed One). (4:157,171,172) Unlike Adam, who was formed from dust, the Messiah came from heaven.

2. The Bible calls Jesus the Son of God because He is like God. He has God's holy and sinless character and all of God's mighty attributes. Like Father, like Son. (Hebrews 1:1-9; Matthew 17:5) The Qur'an calls Jesus "a holy son." (19:19; 3:46). While the Qur'an speaks of the other Prophets' need of forgiveness (38:24; 48:1), it never attributes a single sin to Jesus. Also, it ascribes to Jesus supernatural powers that God alone possesses. (3:45-51; 5:110-112)

3. The Bible calls Jesus the Son of God because He is One with God. He is the Eternal Word who has always been One with God. (John 1:1-18; Philippians 2:5-11) Similarly, the Qur'an calls Jesus the Word of God and the Soul/Spirit of God (4:171,172). Just as, in some mysterious way, a person is forever one with his words, spirit, and soul – so God and Jesus Christ are eternally One.

The Cross

All the Prophets of the Bible, in one way or another foretold the Messiah's sacrificial death. But the Qur'an says: "They denied the truth and uttered a monstrous falsehood against Mary. They declared: 'We have put to death the Messiah, Jesus the son of Mary, the apostle of Allah.' They did not kill him, nor did they crucify him, but it appeared so to them." (4:157) While Quranic scholars interpret this verse in a variety of ways, most Muslims fervently deny the historical and Scriptural records concerning Jesus' death on the cross. They believe it inappropriate that a great Prophet like Jesus should die such a shameful death. Thus, Muslims dismiss the central message of the Prophets of the Bible – that Jesus the Messiah willingly offered Himself as the final sacrifice to pay the sin-debt of the world "that the Scriptures of the Prophets might be fulfilled." (Matthew 26:56)

The Qur'an omits the Good News of atonement through Jesus' shed blood by which God "might be just and the justifier of the one

334

who has faith in Jesus." (Romans 3:26) The Muslim sees no need for the sin-bearing death of the sinless Messiah. The Qur'an says, "No soul shall bear another's burden" (6:164; 17:14-16; 39:7). Islam teaches that God excuses sin based on man's repentance and good works. (42:26,31; 39:54,55) The Qur'an bases salvation on what man can do for God. The Bible bases salvation on what God has done for man, saying, "not by works of righteousness which we have done, but according to His mercy He saved us..." (Titus 3:4)

Islam's Sacrifice

While Islam denies the Messiah's death on the cross – it faithfully commemorates an Old Testament sacrifice which prefigured the Messiah's sacrificial death. Every year, on the tenth day of the last month of the Islamic calendar, Muslims celebrate the Feast of Sacrifice (Id al-Adha). On this day Muslims around the world slay carefully selected rams (or lambs, male goats, cows or camels) in commemoration of the ram that God provided on the mountain to die in the place of Abraham's son. Tragically however, they overlook the fact that, about two thousand years after God provided the ram for Abraham, God fulfilled the symbolism of Abraham's sacrifice. For on the same mountain (not far from where the Dome of the Rock is located today), Jesus the Messiah willingly shed His righteous blood as God's sufficient and final payment for sin. And three days later God raised Jesus from the dead – the triumphant Savior and Lord of all who believe.

Through Jesus' voluntary substitutionary sacrifice, God has revealed His great love and mercy to humankind. The Messiah's death and resurrection perfectly fulfilled God's plan of salvation about which the Prophets wrote – thus eliminating the need for continued animal sacrifices. Yet millions persist in sacrificing animals while ignoring the purpose, meaning and fulfillment of the animal sacrifice.

The Qur'an says...

Many are surprised to learn that the Qur'an commands Muslims to believe the Torah, the Psalms and the Gospel. The Qur'an says: "If you are in doubt concerning what we revealed to you, then question those who read the Scripture that was before you." (10:94) "We sent down the Torah in which there is guidance and light." (5:44) "We have revealed to you as we revealed to Noah and the Prophets after him, and as we revealed to Abraham, Ishmael, Isaac, Jacob, and the tribes; to Jesus, Job, Jonah, Aaron, Solomon and David, to whom we gave the Psalms." (4:163) "We sent forth Jesus, the son of Mary, to follow in the footsteps of the Prophets, confirming the Torah which was before him, and we gave him the Gospel with its guidance and light, confirmatory of the preceding Torah; a guidance and warning to those who fear God. Therefore let the people of the Gospel judge according to what God has sent down therein. Evildoers are those that do not judge according to God's revelations." (5:46) "Those who treat the Book, and the message we have sent through our apostles, as a lie, will know the truth hereafter: when, with chains and collars around their necks, they shall be dragged through scalding water and burned in the fire of hell." (40:71). The Qur'an contains dozens of similar verses.

The Dilemma

Such Quranic verses confront sincere Muslims with a serious dilemma: How can one accept both the Bible and the Qur'an when they clearly contradict each other? Furthermore the Qur'an emphasizes the high risk involved: to treat any of the Writings of the Prophets as a lie is to be "burned in the fire of hell." Many attempt to resolve their dilemma by contending that the original

Bible has been lost or falsified and is no longer reliable. Yet this explanation does not satisfy those who know their Qur'an which says: "The Word of God shall never change. That is the supreme triumph." (10:64) "None can change the decrees of God." (6:34). The Qur'an claims that it was given to confirm and guard the preceding Scriptures. Muslims must ask themselves, "Would the Qur'an confirm a corrupted, unreliable book?"

Some suggest that Christians and Jews falsified the Bible after the time of Muhammad. This argument is disproved by the fact that today's Bibles are based on hundreds of ancient manuscripts which date to a time long before Muhammad. The Bible we are reading today is in harmony with the Bible of Muhammad's time. "Allahu Akbar!" God is great – great enough to preserve His eternal Word for every generation.

The bottom line is that those who read the Bible with a desire to understand it will discover that it defends itself. The best defense is a good offense. "The Word of God which lives and abides forever" presents an awesome offense.

"All men are like grass, and all their glory is like the flowers of the field: the grass withers and the flowers fall, but the Word of the Lord stands forever!" (1 Peter 1:23-25)

The Way of Righteousness

Wolofs say, "Truth is a hot pepper" and "Whoever wants honey must brave the bees." Similarly, the penetrating power of God's Truth and everlasting sweetness of God's way of righteousness makes going after it worth every possible risk – even ostracism, persecution, and physical death.

The Prophet Solomon wrote: "In the way of righteousness is life (a relationship with God), and in its pathway there is no death (separation from God)!" (Proverbs 12:28) Does this claim sound too good to be true? Friends, with God – nothing is "too good to be true." Allahu Akbar! God is great!

To all who submit to God's way of righteousness, He promises to give freely that which religion can never provide: Salvation from the penalty and power of sin, a credited-righteousness, assurance of sins forgiven, a cleansed conscience, a deep peace, an untouchable joy, a new nature, a personal relationship with God, an eternal home with Him in Paradise, and infinitely more!

To all who have read or heard these one hundred lessons – we commend you to God, the Compassionate, the Merciful, the Righteous – who extends this life-giving and life-transforming promise to all who will claim it:

You will seek Me and find Me,
when you search for Me
with all your heart."
(Jeremiah 29:13)

Appendix II

The Gospel for Muslims
Plain and simple

Assalamu alaikum

The Gospel of Jesus is Good News. That is what "gospel" means in Greek. It is the good news because Jesus has removed the requirements of keeping the Law in order to obtain salvation and that through Jesus, we can obtain eternal life. Jesus made it possible for people to receive the free and complete gift of salvation by faith.

Our father Abraham believed God and it was counted to him as righteousness (Gen. 15:6). It was his faith in God that made Abraham righteous before God, not keeping the law, not keeping the commandments.

The Law of God is perfect because God is perfect. The Law is a reflection of the character of God. It is wrong to lie because lying is against God's character. It is wrong to steal because stealing is against God's character. That is why the Law tells us what is wrong. God is not arbitrary and neither is His Law.

Though the Law is good and perfect, no man can keep it perfectly. No person can keep the Law.

Jesus taught us that to even look on a woman with lust in your heart is to commit adultery with her (<u>Matt. 5:27-28</u>). You see, the Law of God is not simply to govern actions. It is for our hearts and attitudes. Purity of heart is what God wants from us. Purity of heart down to the deepest part of our being. Why? Because God's heart is the Purest and Most Holy of all. And since the Law was spoken by Him and came from Him, the Law is Perfect and Holy. **That** is the level of perfection you must have when trying to keep the Law.

However, we are not able to keep the Law. We sin. We fail. The Law says do not lie, but shows us where we lie -- in our very hearts. It says do not commit adultery, but shows us where we commit adultery -- in our hearts. The Law of God is perfect. We are not. God is perfect and Holy. We are not. We are not able to keep the Law of God because we are finite, limited, and affected by sin. How can anyone ever hope to please God through keeping the Law? How can anyone ever hope to please God and attain heaven by doing good deeds? It is not ourselves that we must please, but a Holy and Pure God.

The Good News

The Good News is that you do not have to try and keep the Law of God to please Him. You do not have to try and raise yourself to the level of God's Perfection by trying to keep His Holy and Perfect Law. You cannot do that. If you thought you could, then your heart is full of pride. What you can not do, Jesus did do. He kept all the Law perfectly (<u>1 Pet. 2:22</u>).

Jesus said that *"Greater love has no man than this, that he lay his life down for his friend,"* (John 15:13). Jesus laid his life down for his friends. Jesus performed the greatest act of love in the universe. He died for our sins. He paid the penalty of breaking the Law, which is death. If this were not so, there would be no damnation. Jesus took our sins and died on the cross in our place (1 Pet. 2:24). This great act of love is unsurpassed in all the world. It means that you can, like Abraham (Gen. 15:6), be righteous by faith. All you need is faith in Jesus.

Are you tired of trying to keep all the Laws in Islam as you strive to do more good deeds than bad deeds in the hope that on the Day of Judgment your good deeds will outweigh your bad? Because you earn in large part your salvation, you cannot know whether or not you will be saved. If you are tired of trying to be perfect, of trying to obtain Paradise through your works, then you need Jesus. Jesus said, *"If any of you are heavy laden, come to me, and I will give you rest,"* (Matt. 11:28).

Jesus forgave sins in Luke 5:20 and 7:48-49. He walked on water (Matt. 14:25). He rose from the dead (Matt. 28:6). Have you done more than He in keeping the Law or performing miracles? Has even the Prophet Muhammad done more than Jesus? The Good News is that you, like Abraham, can be made righteous by faith. Do you want the righteousness that is by faith? Or, do you want to earn Paradise through your deeds? Can you earn it? Have you done it so far? Have you been doing enough?

Jesus said:
- that He gives eternal life, (John 10:28-30).
- that He received all authority in heaven and earth, (Matt. 28:18).

- that He was the Way the Truth and The Life, (John 14:6).
- that He will resurrect people on the Last Day, (John 6:40, 44, 54).
- that the Holy Spirit bears witness of Him, (John 15:26).

Do you want to try and please God through keeping the Law of Allah or by the grace of Christ? Is the greatest act of love to ask you to earn heaven through good deeds or is it to be a sacrifice in order to give to you what you cannot attain yourself? In which is the greatest act of love?

If you want the eternal life that Jesus can give you, then trust what He did on the cross and do not rely on your own works to please God. Trust Jesus by faith.

It is not Muhammad who forgives sins. Jesus does that (Luke 5:20; 7:48-49). Jesus said, *"Believe in God. Believe also in me,"* (John14:1).

Like Abraham, be righteous in God's eyes . . by faith.

CHRISTIAN APOLOGETICS & RESEARCH MINISTRY

Special Thanks:

I want to thank all those who contributed and helped to make this book possible. This is done for the glory of the Father and the Son and the Holy Spirit.